IMAGES
of America

LINCOLNTON
Photographs from the Clyde C. Cornwell Collection

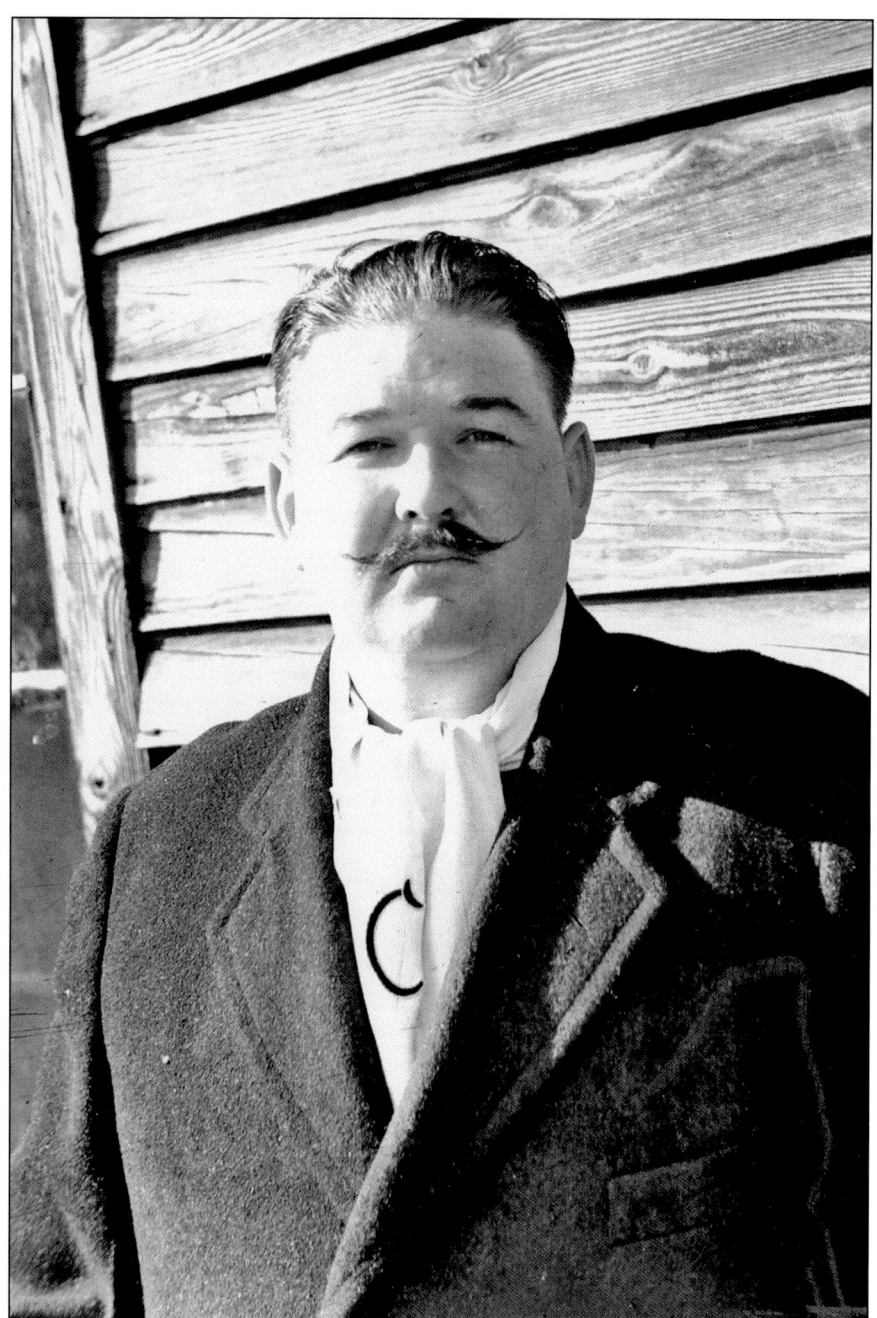

CLYDE C. "BABY RAY" CORNWELL. From the collection at the Lincoln County Museum of History, this is one of two photographs of Clyde "Baby Ray" Cornwell. This moment, captured by an unidentified photographer, shows a dapper and rotund Cornwell. As a freelance photographer, Baby Ray Cornwell's images filled The Lincoln County News for 30 years, and his small section called the "Rovin' Photographer" showcased some of Lincoln County's citizens as well as their opinions of local, state, and national issues. Cornwell is remembered as a "Johnny on the Spot," who seemed to find his way to every major car accident, wedding reception, birthday party, and civic function in the county.

IMAGES of America

LINCOLNTON
PHOTOGRAPHS FROM THE CLYDE C. CORNWELL COLLECTION

Jason L. Harpe
Lincoln County Historical Association

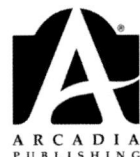

ARCADIA
PUBLISHING

Copyright © 2011 by Jason L. Harpe
ISBN 978-0-7385-1640-0

Published by Arcadia Publishing
Charleston, South Carolina

Printed in the United States of America

Library of Congress Control Number: 2004101125

For all general information, please contact Arcadia Publishing:
Telephone 843-853-2070
Fax 843-853-0044
E-mail sales@arcadiapublishing.com
For customer service and orders:
Toll-Free 1-888-313-2665

Visit us on the Internet at www.arcadiapublishing.com

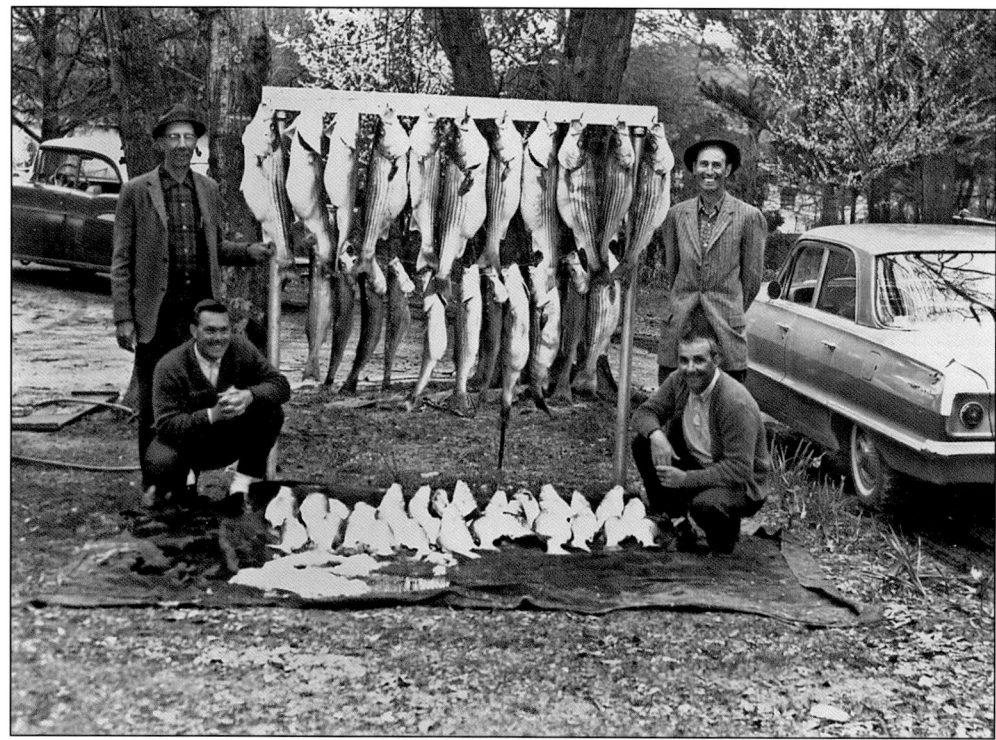

THE CATCH OF THE DAY. This group of fishermen, on a fishing "safari" to Santee Cooper, South Carolina, during the late 1960s, displays 53 striped bass with a combined weight of 510 pounds. Pictured from left to right are as follows: (front row) Eurey Lawing and Bobby Turner; (back row) Dick Turner and J.D. Turner. The photographer, Baby Ray Cornwell, found the proud fishermen at the home of Dick Turner beyond Hilltop on Highway 150 in Lincolnton.

Contents

Acknowledgments		6
Introduction		7
1.	Claimin' Kin	9
2.	Books and Brawn	35
3.	Sun Up to Sun Down	53
4.	Floats, Debutantes, and Cotton Candy	79
5.	Service to God and Community	91
6.	Salt of the Earth	107

Acknowledgments

As the Lincoln County Historical Association's third publication from Arcadia's *Images of America* series, this book furthers our mission of presenting the history of Lincolnton and Lincoln County through the medium of photography. The two previous titles on Lincoln County covered a 200-year period, from the time of the county's founding to the present, and included images from all of Lincoln County's townships. We procured these images from nearly 100 generous lenders and utilized their memories to write short, succinct captions. This publication is very different in many ways from the two previous books, but it does require us to acknowledge a number of individuals and families for the information they supplied to help compile this work.

First, I would like to acknowledge the foresight and commitment of Paul Dellinger and Elsie Keever for keeping these images in Lincoln County. We are forever indebted to them for purchasing these images and donating them to the Lincoln County Museum of History. They have ensured the existence of Clyde "Baby Ray" Cornwell's collection for years to come. Paul has retained a few of the images for his collection, and I have noted them throughout the book with a credit line that reads: Courtesy of Paul Dellinger.

Extra special thanks to Bill Beam, Lincoln County Historical Association president, for his ever-present support, encouragement, and unfailing dedication to the collection and preservation of Lincoln County history. Without his uncanny ability to locate and procure photographs, artifacts, objects, and information, these and other publications would not be possible.

Thanks to Scott W. Smith for purchasing and donating a small collection of Baby Ray Cornwell's negatives that he found on eBay to the museum. Thanks also to many people for spending time identifying people and places in the images and providing recollections about Baby Ray Cornwell, including the following: John Anderson, Donna Axum (Miss America 1964), Cindy Cagle, Taffy Cagle, Robert Cantwell, David Choate, Jerry Cochrane, Ralph Cochrane Jr., Ronnie Cornwell, Bobbi Jean Crowell, Milton Crowell, Jack L. Dellinger, Paul Dellinger, John Digh, Shelly R. Early, Wayne Finger, Joe Ford, Sally Fox, Carolyn Gilbert, Darrell Harkey, Ause and Julia Harvey, Mack Harvey, Paul Haynes, David Heavner, Mary H. Heavner, Bill Hoffman, Fred Houser, Herman "Humpy" Howard, Tom Howard, John Hoyle, Bo King, Jack Lassiter, Carolyn R. Lee, Robert Lineberger, John Lockman, Ken and Betty Mace, Leroy Magness, Barbara McNeill, Barbara Miller, Helen Peeler, Joe and Kay Polhill, Bob Ramseur, Jerry Robinson, Betty G. Ross, Joanne Shelton, Randolph Shives, Brat Stroupe, Bobby Turner, Bud Warlick, J.J. Wyckoff, Rudolph Young, and Vicki T. Yount.

Introduction

The Clyde "Baby Ray" Cornwell Photograph Collection includes over 20,000 acetate negatives and black-and-white and color images, spanning from the late 1930s to the late 1970s. Contained in the collection are images of weddings, parades, public officials, churches, civic organizations, religious organizations and activities, family reunions, tent revivals, business openings, construction, catastrophes, houses, county and city buildings, birthday parties, sports groups, school groups, library bulletin boards, and even corpses. In comparison to the number of images and subjects covered in this large collection, this book barely scratches the surface. We have attempted to provide a representative portion of the collection based on subject matter, image quality, rarity, and families not represented in the two earlier *Images of America* books.

Most, if not all, of the developed images carry the ink from the block stamp that bears the advertising label: CLYDE C. CORNWELL, PHOTOGRAPHER/"SPECIALIZING ON PHOTOS IN YOUR HOME." The yellowed, discolored, and tattered sleeves that Baby Ray Cornwell used to hold his negatives are a testament to the many years of handling. Indecipherable scribble on the front or back of the negative sleeves is the only source of identification for the event or events he captured. Some of the names, events, and dates on the negative sleeves have not matched the actual negative, so we have attempted to identify the image to the best of our abilities, utilizing newspaper articles, wedding announcements, and the collective memory of the community.

Found in these images are the lives of prominent politicians, mill workers, small businessmen, ministers, Boy and Girl Scouts, farmers, city and county workers, men and women of the military, "4-H-ers," and even Miss America 1964. The time and places that they occupy make up a 40-year period that saw Works Progress Administration (WPA) projects, soldiers leaving for World War II, construction of new buildings and housing developments, the baby boomer generation, the early waters of Lake Norman, six Presidents, integration, and the advent of rock 'n roll. Clyde "Baby Ray" Cornwell, always in his station wagon, along with Frazier's Studio of Lincolnton, captured this time period and supplied the local newspapers, individuals, families, and businesses with candid, posed, and artistic photographs of Lincolnton's citizens. Cornwell, known to everyone as Baby Ray, received his nickname from his mother. She began calling him this after discovering a likeness between Clyde and the character Baby Ray that was featured in early school primers. Though very little is known about the background, aspirations, and workings of Baby Ray Cornwell, most locals remember him as a robust man with camera ready to capture another slice of Lincolnton's happenings.

Thanks to the foresight and commitment to history of two Lincoln County Historical Association members, Paul Dellinger and Elsie Keever, the citizens of Lincolnton and Lincoln County can enjoy Baby Ray Cornwell's works for years to come. Their procurement of this collection and donation to the Lincoln County Museum of History will enable current and future generations to recognize, identify, and request copies of these photographs. Photographs from this collection adorn the walls of Aunt Bessie's Restaurant and Fatz Café in Lincolnton.

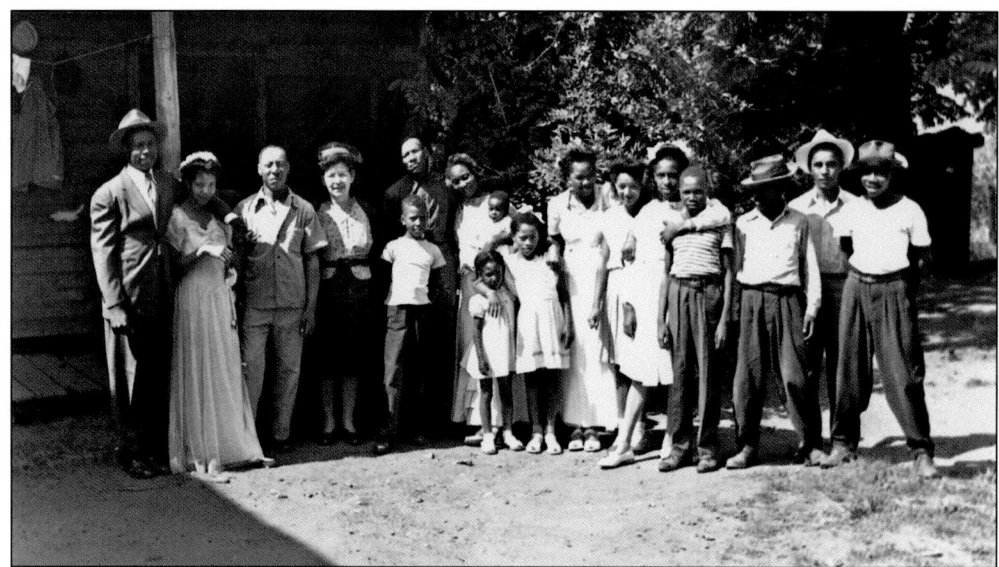

ALL IN THE FAMILY. The Nixon and Barnes families gather together near their home in Lincolnton during the 1940s. On this day, the family celebrated the wedding of Kemp and Dot Nixon. Members of the Nixon and Barnes families in attendance at the wedding celebration include Kemp Nixon, Dot Nixon, Roosevelt Barnes, Ella Barnes, Joe Nixon, Paul Nixon, Berlin Barnes, Sue Barnes, Libb Barnes, Suzy Nixon, Fred Nixon, Butch Nixon, Berlin Barnes Jr., Charley Barnes, Billy "Babe" Johnson, Evelyn Nixon Johnson, and Robert Nixon.

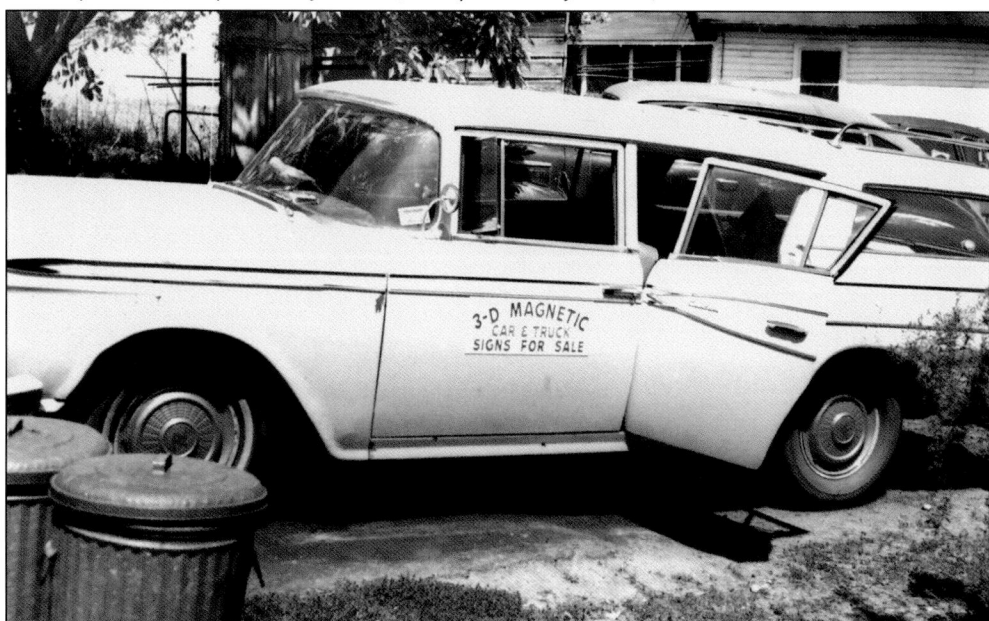

BABY RAY CORNWELL'S STATION WAGON. Baby Ray Cornwell makes a stop and forgets to close his door before photographing his car during the early 1950s. Cornwell is well known by most in Lincolnton as the "Rovin' Photographer" who drove his station wagon with the three-dimensional magnetic advertisement on the door and another car with his photography advertisement on top. Almost all of Lincolnton's residents over the age of 60 have fond memories of Baby Ray's photographs.

One
CLAIMIN' KIN

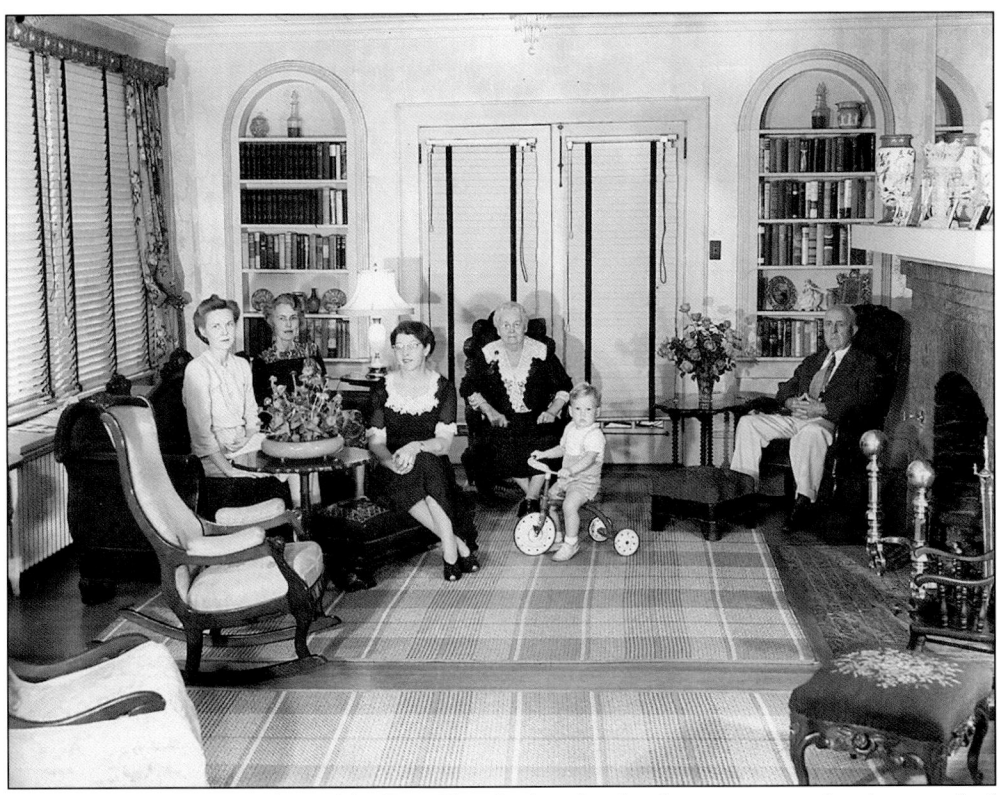

THE LIVING ROOM. Members of the F.H. Chamberlain family take a moment to be photographed in the living room of their home at the intersection of North Cedar Street and Sumner Street. Members of the family are, from left to right, as follows: Rosebud Blanton, Catherine Chamberlain, unidentified, Mrs. F.H. Chamberlain, unidentified, and Mr. Frank H. Chamberlain.

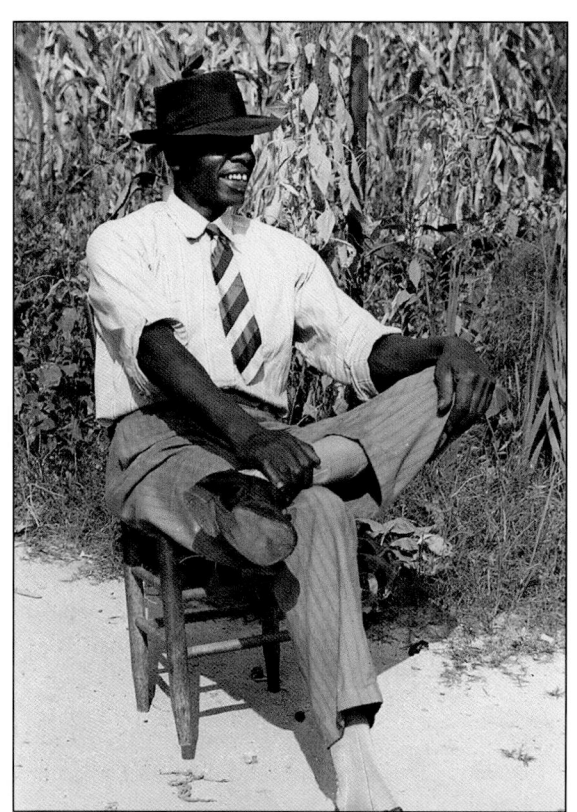

COOLIN'. Donning a splendid suit and hat, and taking it easy in a ladder-back chair near a corn field, John Henry Metts cracks a big smile for Baby Ray Cornwell's camera. Metts was a carpenter by trade from the Freedom Community in Lincolnton and a member of Providence Missionary Baptist Church. Sometime during the same photograph session, John Metts's three children—Willie P., Josephine, and Rufus—also stepped in front of the camera.

POSING ON PINE STREET. The Carpenter family is the proud new owner of a batch of puppies. Standing near the basement of their home on West Pine Street in Lincolnton, Claude Carpenter looks on as the sole member of the family not holding a puppy. Claude's wife, Minnie Bell, and two children, Shirley and Ralph, seem to be fairly happy with the new additions to their family.

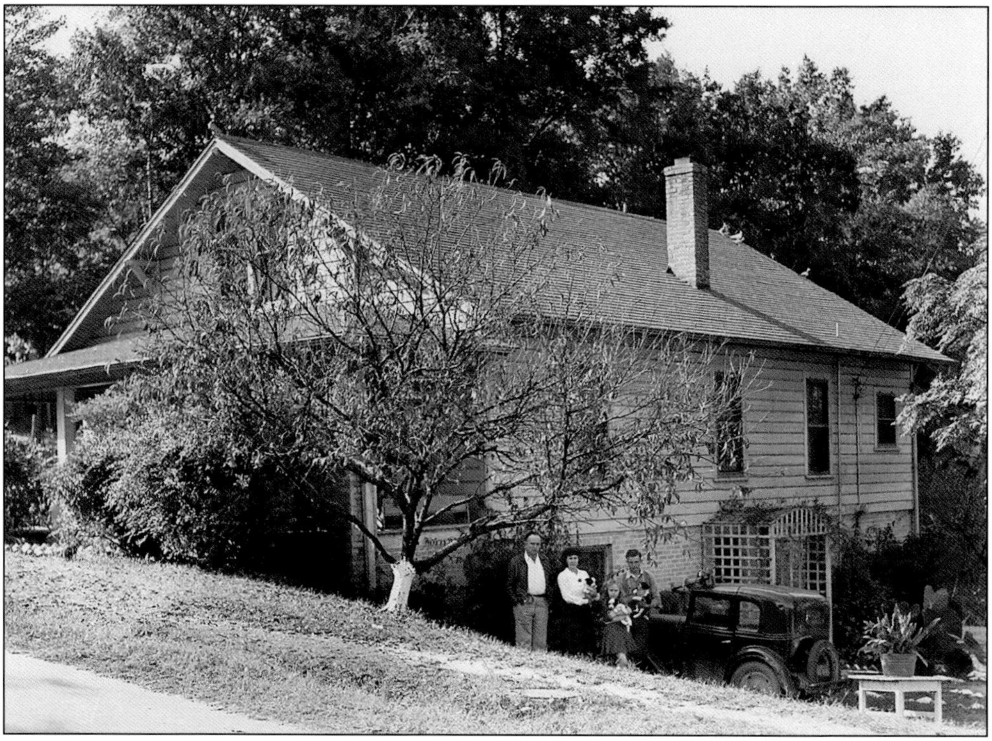

DAVIS-TUTHEROW WEDDING, SEPTEMBER 11, 1948. Mary Sue Tutherow holds the arm of her new husband, Sammie Stowe Davis, for this wedding photograph. The couple wed at the Methodist Church parsonage in Crouse. Mary and Sammie, both graduates of Union High School, took their honeymoon in the mountains of Western North Carolina and Washington, D.C.

RAMSAUR-DITMARS WEDDING RECEPTION, JUNE 3, 1944. The wedding party attends the reception for Earl Edward Ditmars and Margaret Euielia Ramsaur in the home of Mr. and Mrs. John Charles Ramsaur (parents of the bride) on Aspen Street. They were married at Lincolnton's First Presbyterian Church on Saturday, June 3, 1944. The members of the wedding party include the following: Mrs. Charles M. Ramsaur, matron of honor; Nancy Thompson, junior bridesmaid; Virginia Elliott, bridesmaid; Mary M. Nixon, bridesmaid; Frances Templeton, bridesmaid; Guy H. Thompson, best man; David Holmes, groomsman; Jack H. Ramseur, groomsman; Johnny Ramsaur, groomsman; and Charles M. Ramseur, groomsman.

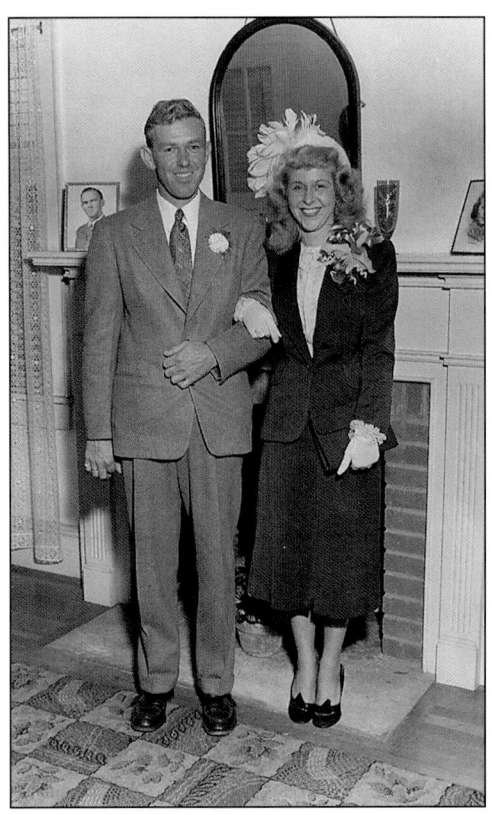

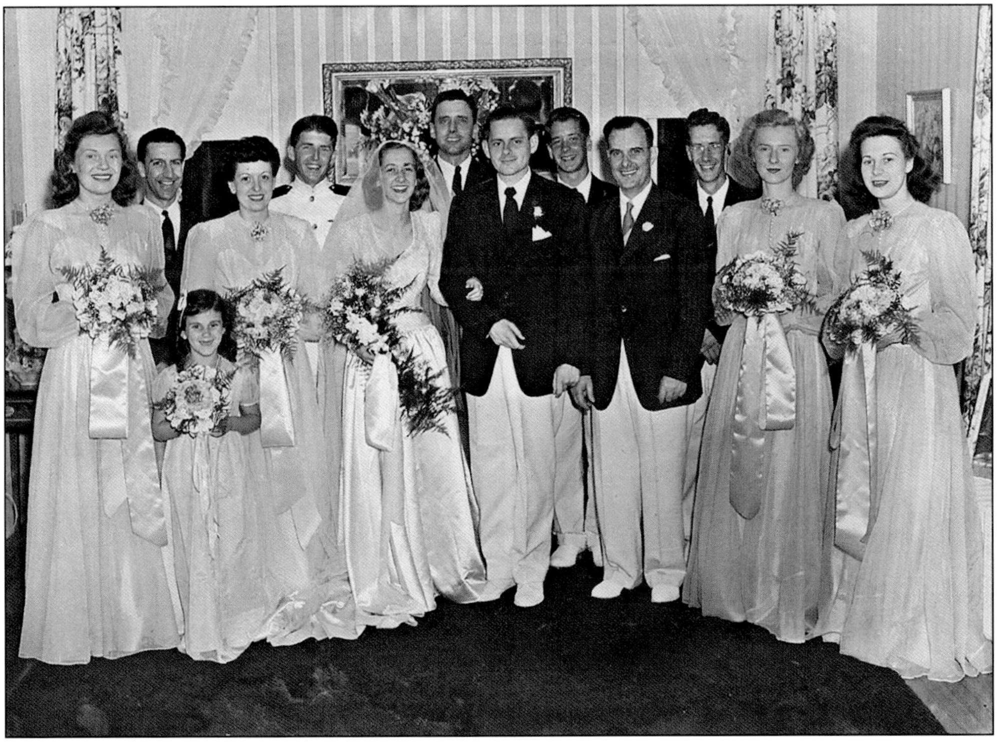

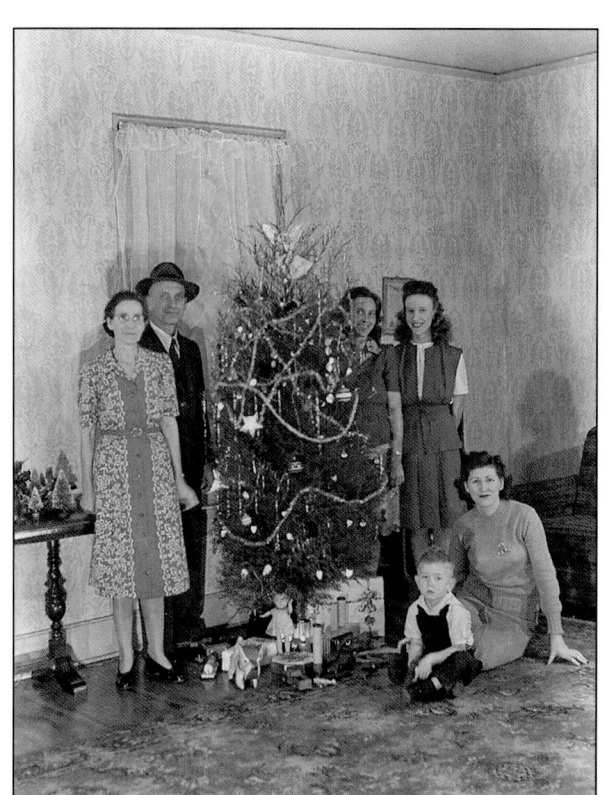

THE CENTER OF ATTENTION. Many families in Lincolnton invited Baby Ray Cornwell to be part of their family's holiday celebration by having him take their photographs. This Lincolnton family chose to pose around their Christmas tree and also to include a small table with miniature Christmas trees and seasonal arrangements. Throughout Cornwell's career as a small town photographer, he spent the majority of his life celebrating the holidays, reunions, and other festive events with other families.

CHILDS WEDDING. In this 1940s photograph, Miss Margaret Jane Childs stands beside her new husband, Rev. Harold Lindsey. Her wedding party looks toward the camera at the family home in Lincolnton.

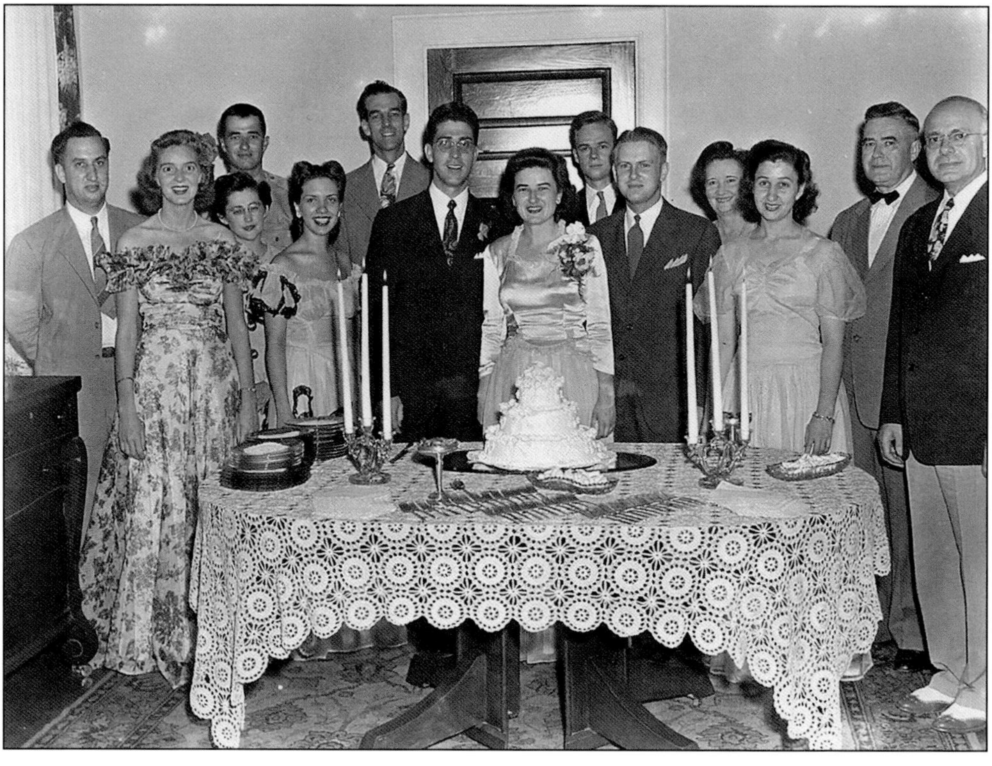

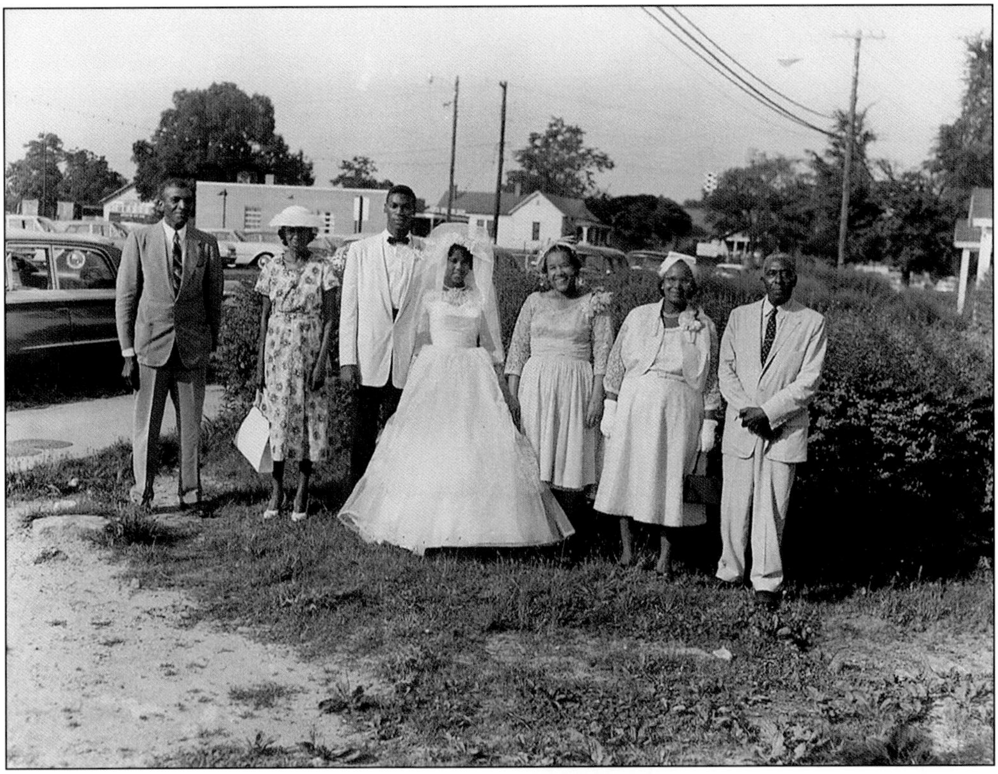

NEELY-ANDERSON WEDDING, JUNE 21, 1961. Members of the Neely and Anderson families pose for this post-wedding photograph on East Main Street in Lincolnton. The family members are, from left to right, as follows: Rev. Jake Neely, Mary Hazel Neely, Raymond Neely, Ruby Anderson Neely, Mary Anderson, Hattie Adams, and Morris Adams.

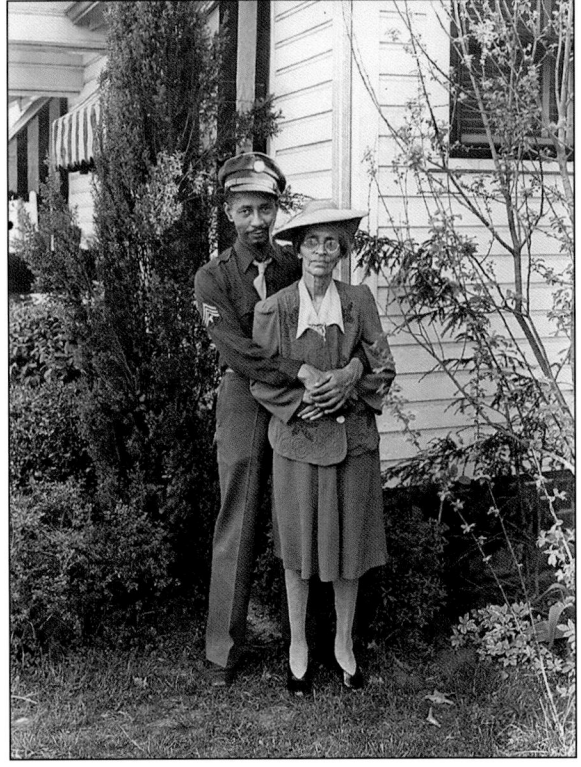

SHERWOOD REINHARDT AND MARY ANGEL REINHARDT, C. 1940S. Sherwood Reinhardt embraces his mother as they stand beside the home of Emory and Annie Loritts, located off of South Aspen Street in Lincolnton's Georgetown community.

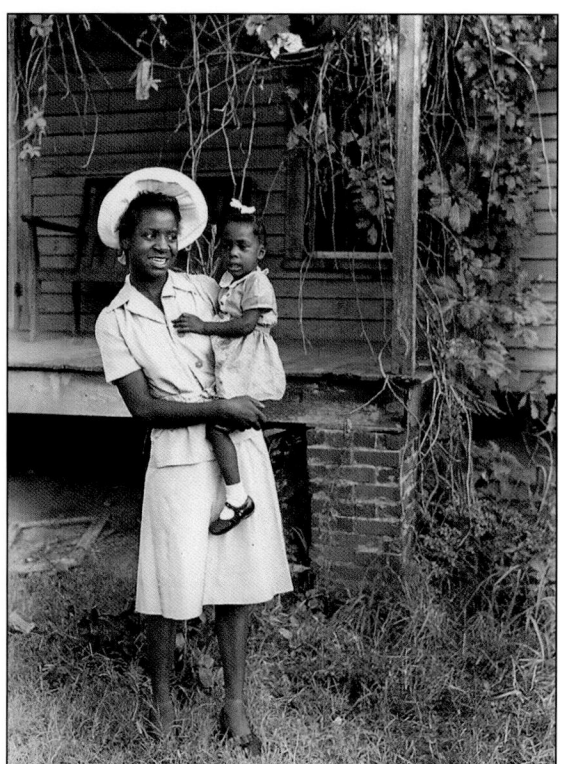

REDLINE NEIGHBORHOOD. Willie Mae Moore holds her daughter Joyce Ann Moore in front of their house on McBee Street in Lincolnton's Redline neighborhood.

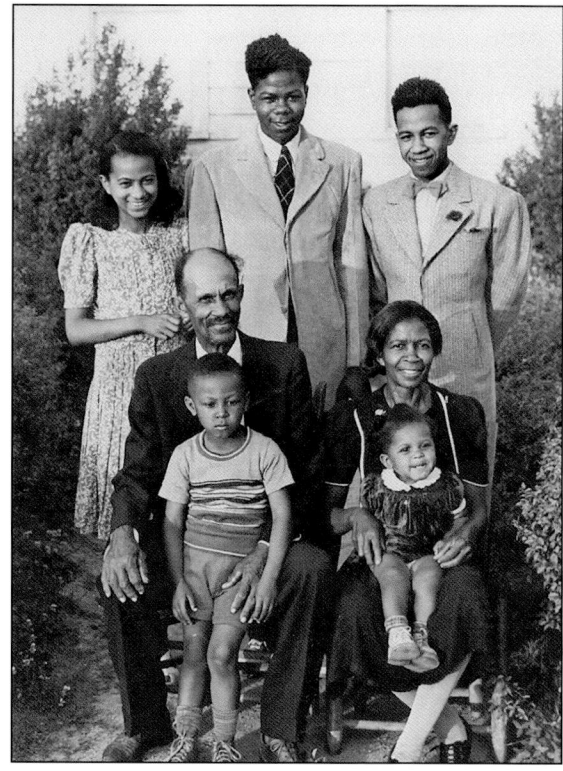

MARK LANDER FAMILY, C. 1940S. Near their home on Pine Street in Lincolnton, the Mark Lander family poses in their Sunday best. Members of the Lander family are, from left to right, as follows: (seated) Mark and Ophelia; (standing) Mary Frances "Biddy," Griffin, and Teuck. The two small children are unidentified.

RINGDOM COMMUNITY, LINCOLNTON. Sid Johnson fails to keep his eyes open for Baby Ray Cornwell's camera. Sisters Lula Bell "Dib" Sowell (left) and Viney Sowell (right) make sure that Sid does not lose his balance.

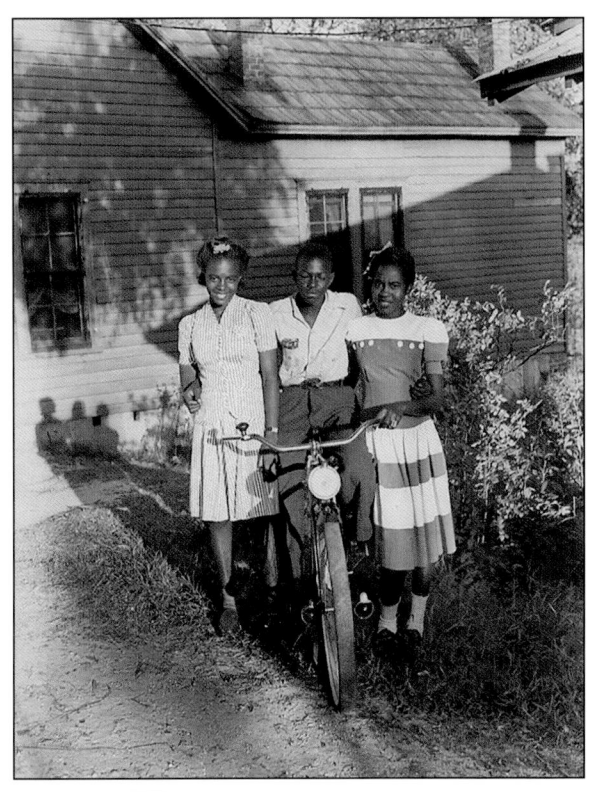

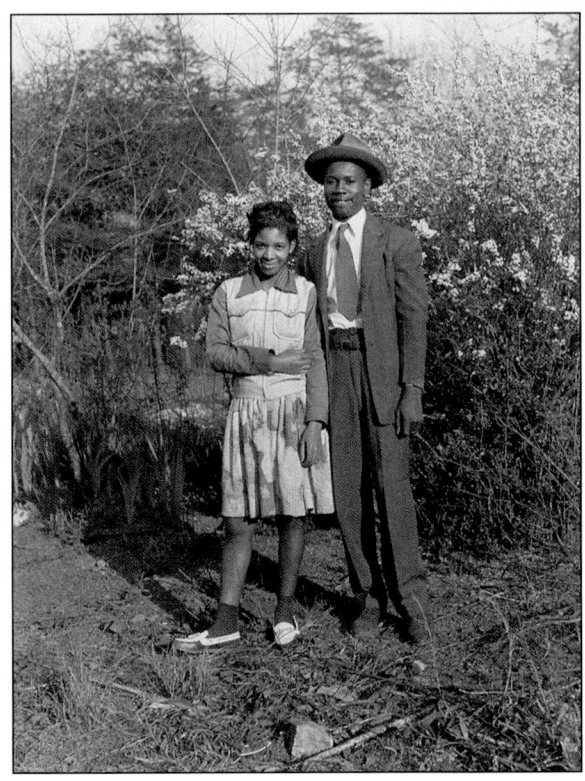

KEMP AND DOROTHY NIXON. Kemp and Dorothy Nixon show their affection in this 1940s image.

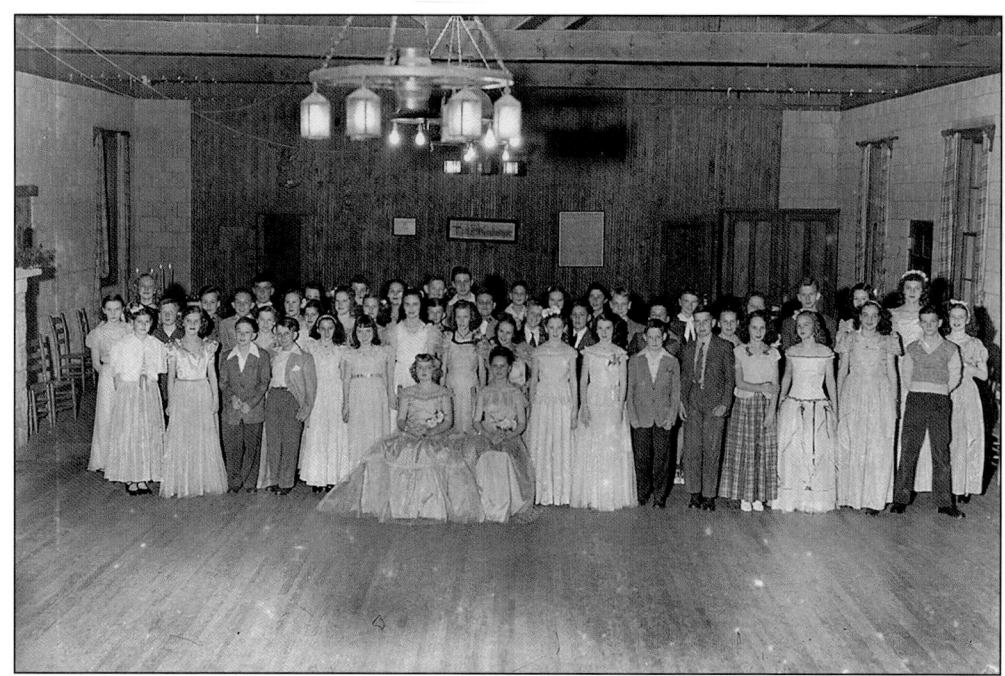

DRESSED TO IMPRESS. In this 1940s photograph, Doris Ann Lineberger and Libby Huggins are dressed to the "tee" for this party at the American Legion Hut in Lincolnton. The party, planned by Mrs. B.C. Lineberger, was just one of many that local mothers would hold during the summer months for their children. Baby Ray Cornwell was invited to take part in the festivities and captured the action in this photograph.

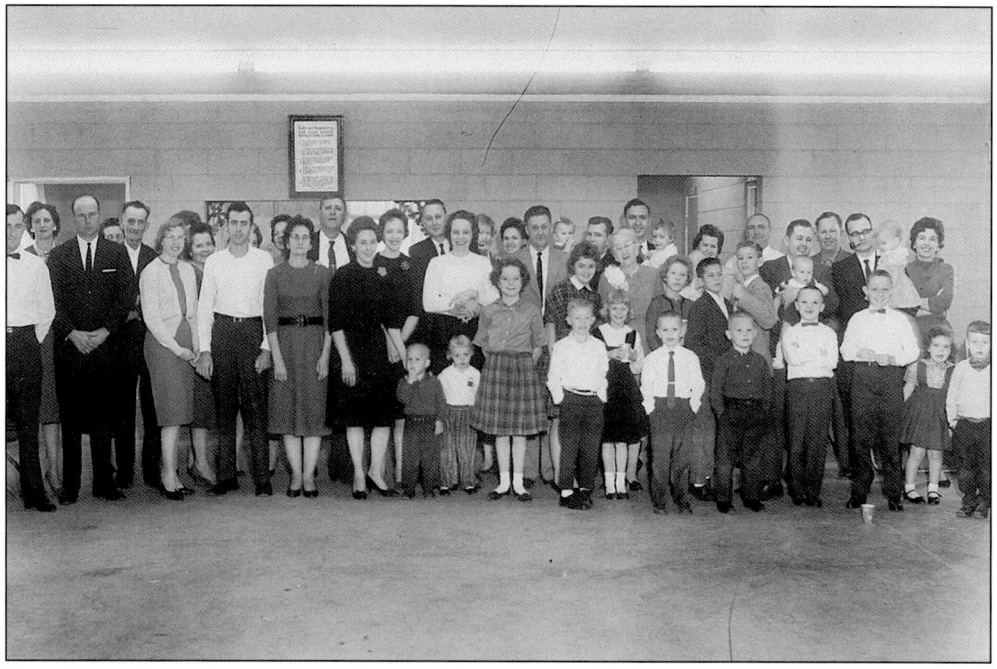

MRS. DAISY EUREY'S BIRTHDAY PARTY, MARCH 4, 1962. A large group of family and friends help celebrate Mrs. Daisy Eurey's birthday at the Buffalo Shoals Clubhouse in Lincolnton.

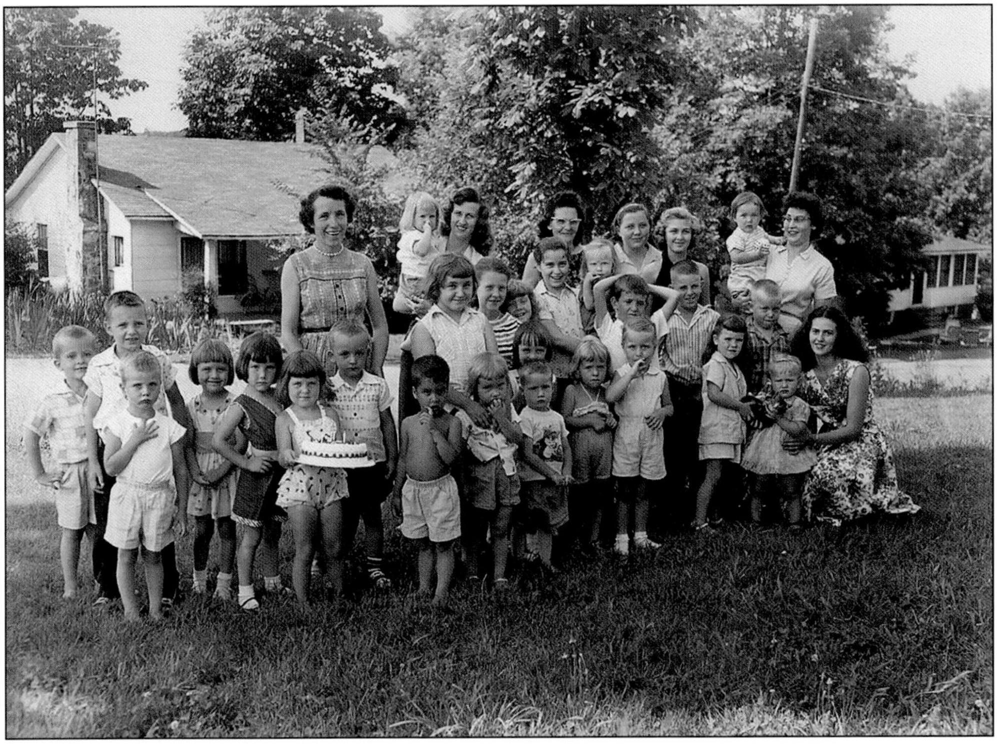

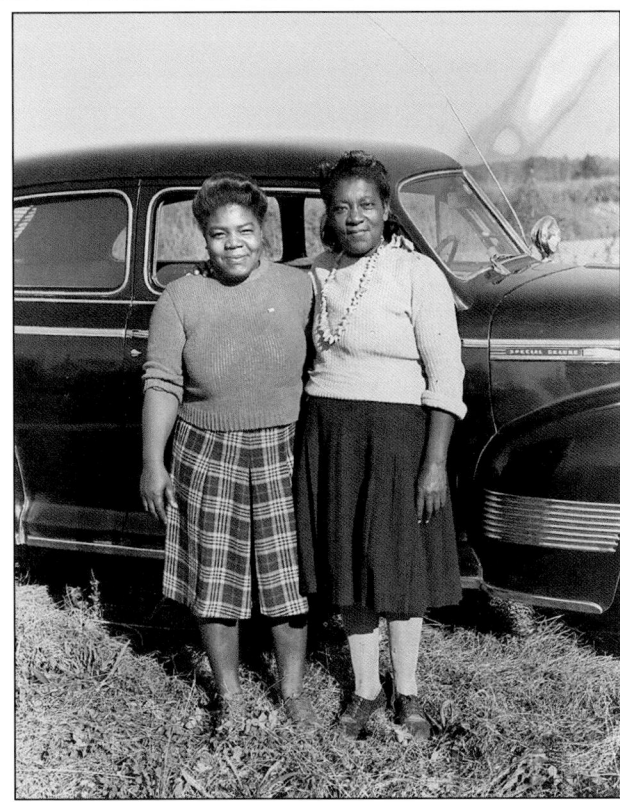

CINDY STAMEY BIRTHDAY PARTY, JUNE 1, 1958. On Grier Street behind Boger City Baptist Church in Lincolnton, the friends and family of Cindy Stamey gather to celebrate her birthday. Some of Cindy's young friends in attendance are Elaine Waters, Cindy Cagle, Joey Raby, Joseph Jordan, Taffy Cagle, Nancy Jordan Riley, Barbara Jean Stamey, and Teresa Stamey.

TWO OF A KIND. The "Special Deluxe" serves as a fitting background image for this Baby Ray Cornwell photograph. Captured in the Georgetown community, this image shows two African-American women dressed and ready for anything that comes their way. Helen Moore (left) shows her pretty smile as she puts an arm around an unidentified woman from the community.

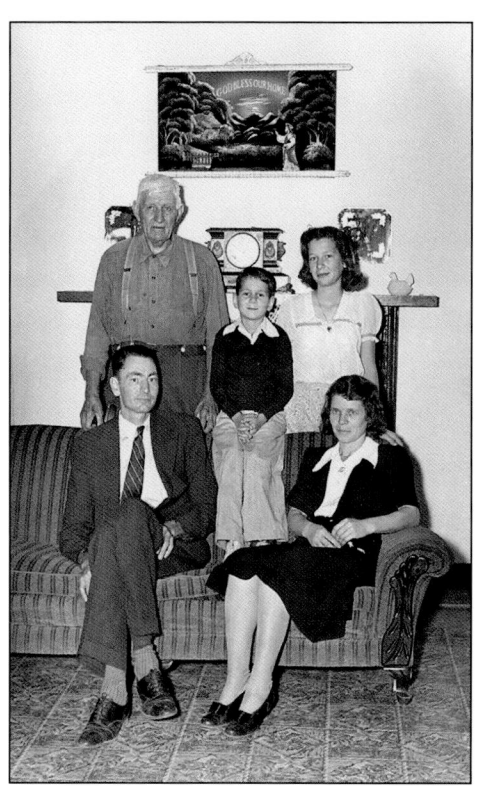

LITTLE MAN IN THE MIDDLE. The blessings of this home can be understood from the wall hanging that rests above the fireplace and mantel—"God Bless This House." This family lived in the Wampum Mill village and, like many others in this mill village, were part of the growth of the textile industry in Lincolnton. The Wampum Mill grew out of the textile industry's growth during the latter portion of the 19th century and the first quarter of the 20th century. During this period, mill owners built one- and two-story frame homes for their operatives, and Lincolnton witnessed the proliferation of the mill villages that included Wampum, Elm Grove, Long Shoals, Laboratory, Massapoag, and others.

SALLY MULLEN (FOX) BIRTHDAY PARTY, MAY 1950. In the company of a large of group of young friends, Sally Mullen (Fox) celebrates her birthday on Oak Street in Lincolnton. Warlick Funeral Home supplied the tent under which the group played with the Sherwood Forest bow and arrow sets that Sally received as a birthday gift.

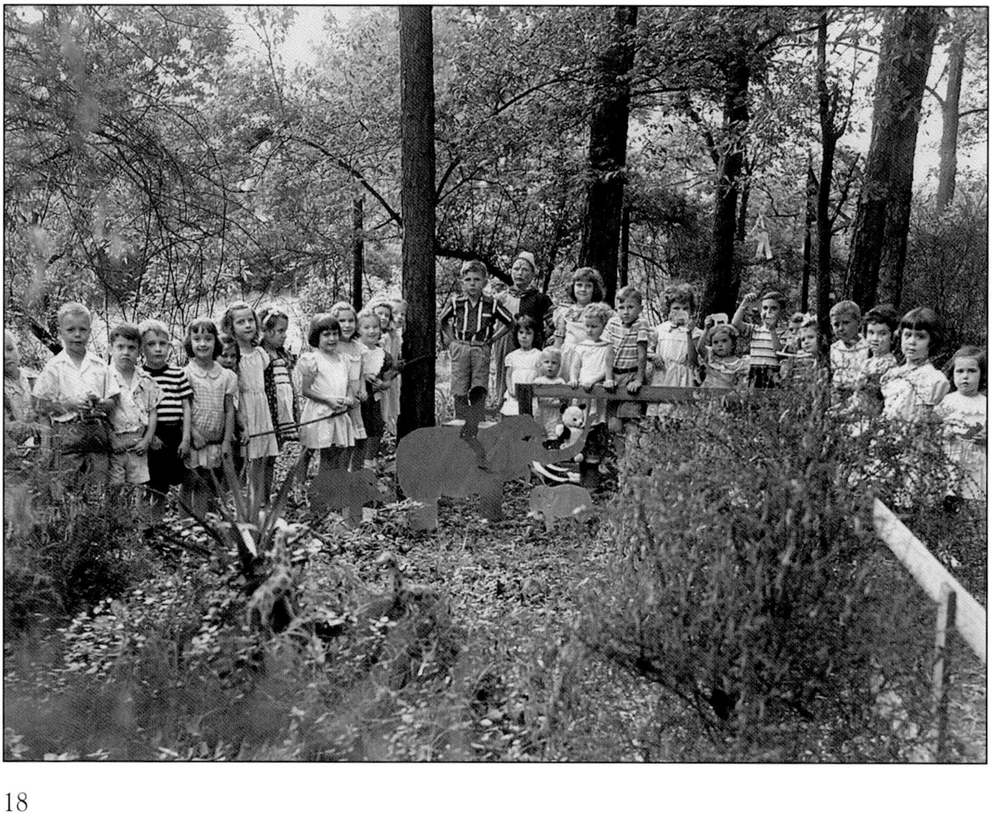

18

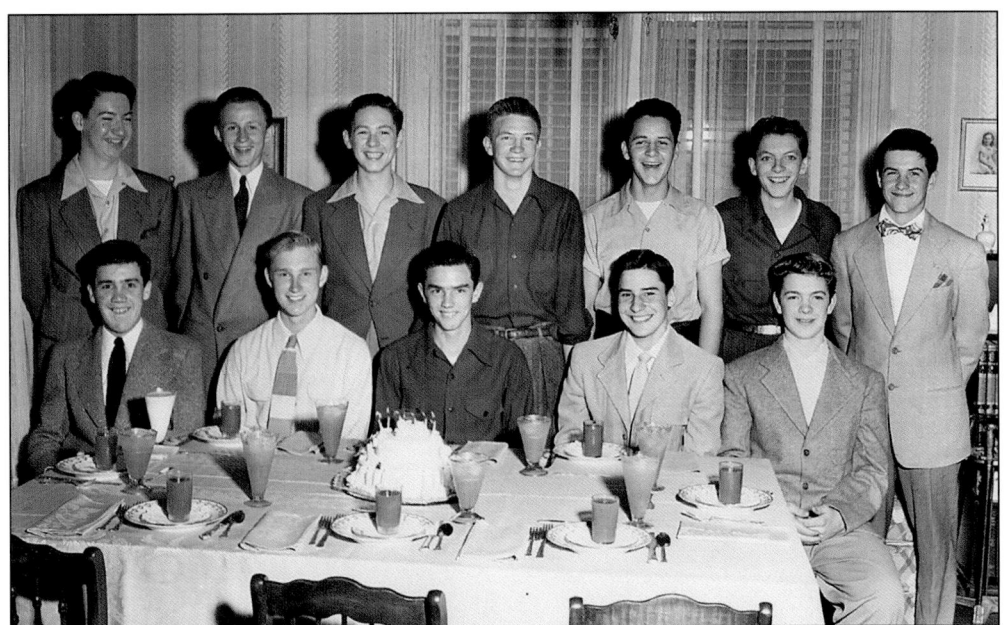

WHAT'S SHAKIN'? A group of young friends sit and stand in single file lines behind a table filled with milkshakes and a birthday cake for this special occasion in March 1948. The young men are identified, from left to right, as follows: (front row) Bill Huggins, Charles Lippard, Bill Rhyne, John Lowder, and Max Quinton; (back row) Rodney Robinson, John Shuford, Harry Lerner, Shirley Gabriel, Harry Hoyle, Max Craig, and Randolph Shives.

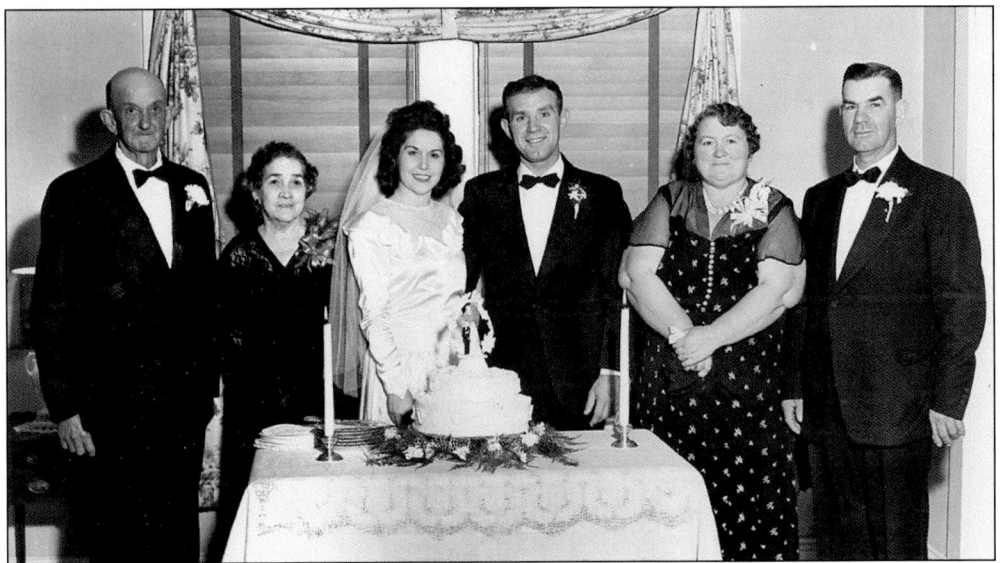

HOLY MATRIMONY. On a very special day in 1946, a newlywed couple and their parents hire Baby Ray Cornwell to capture and preserve a family memory for future generations. Paul Haynes and Alma Walls Haynes stand behind their wedding cake at the home of Mr. and Mrs. Harbin Haynes. The bride's parents, Mr. and Mrs. Tom Walls, stand on the left, and the groom's parents, Mr. and Mrs. Harbin Haynes, are on the right. Harbin Haynes started Haynes Dairy in Lincolnton in 1914. Currently, Haynes Dairy and Paul's Distributing are in their fourth generation of operation.

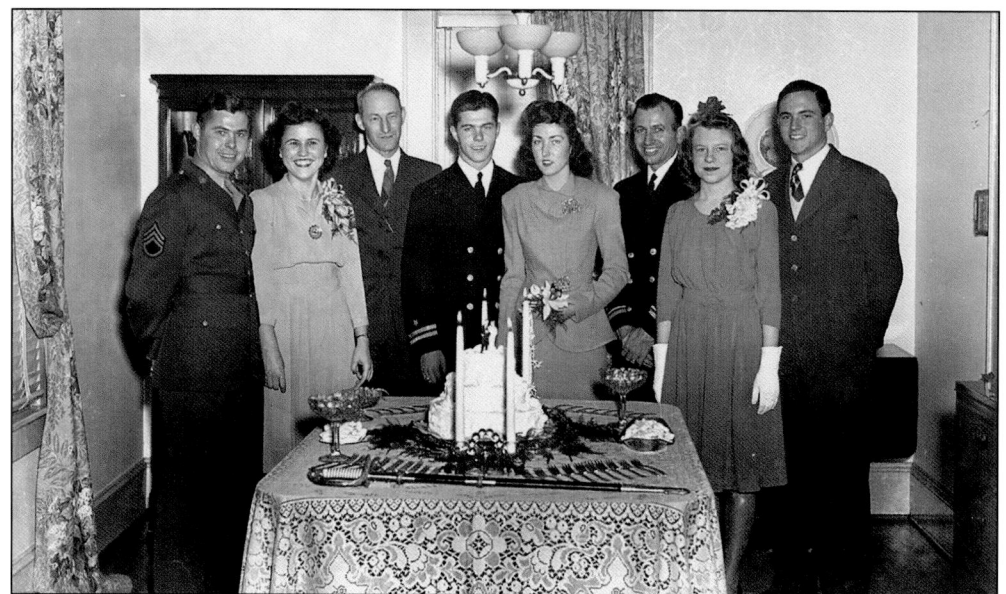

HOWARD-RATLIFF WEDDING, FEBRUARY 14, 1944. Lt. Thomas Herman Howard, Frances Chaulot, and their wedding party take a moment away from their reception for this photograph. The reception was held at the home of Mr. and Mrs. Gordon L. "Shine" Goodson, and members of the wedding party are, from left to right, as follows: Preston Asbury Howard, Helen McConnell Combs, Reverend Smith, Lt. Herman "Humpy" Howard, Frances Helen "Frankie" Ratliff Howard, Gordon L. "Shine" Goodson, Janet Howard Knox, and Newton Smith.

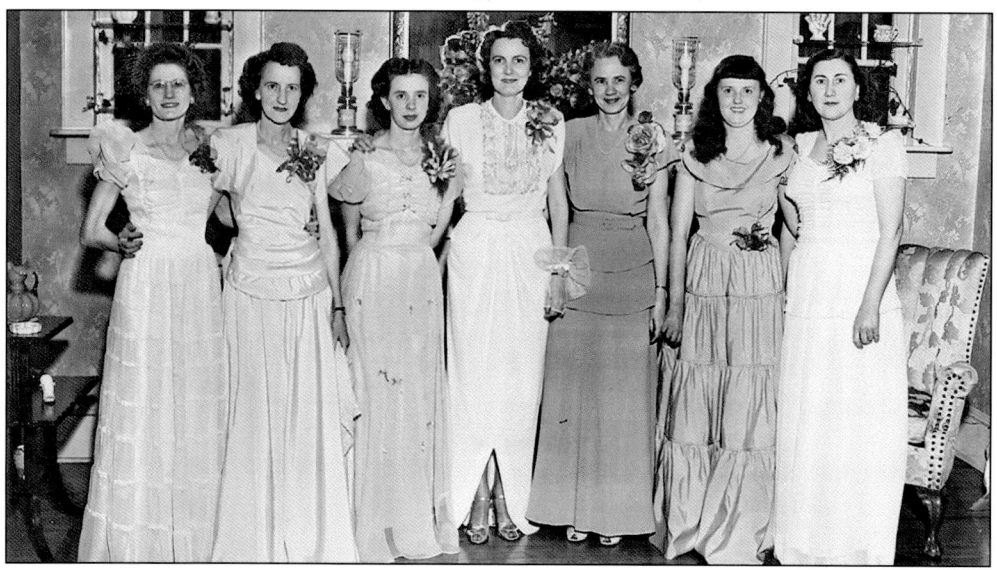

TWENTY-FIFTH WEDDING ANNIVERSARY. On April 1, 1948, Odell and Alda Harvey celebrated their 25th wedding anniversary at their home on Love Memorial School Road. Alda Harvey stands in the middle of a finely dressed group of ladies who are identified, from left to right, as follows: Zettie Huss Crawley, Lucille Hartman, Willie Bell Harvey Baker, Alda, Nell Harvey Allen, unidentified, and Mabel Crouse. Other family members who helped celebrate the special event were Ause Harvey, son of Odell and Alda Harvey, Miller and Ella Harvey (Odell's parents), and Ted and Etta Ramsey (Alda's parents).

MADE IN THE SHADE. In this 1940s photograph two girls from the Ringdom community are shown basking in the sun near a bus garage in Lincolnton.

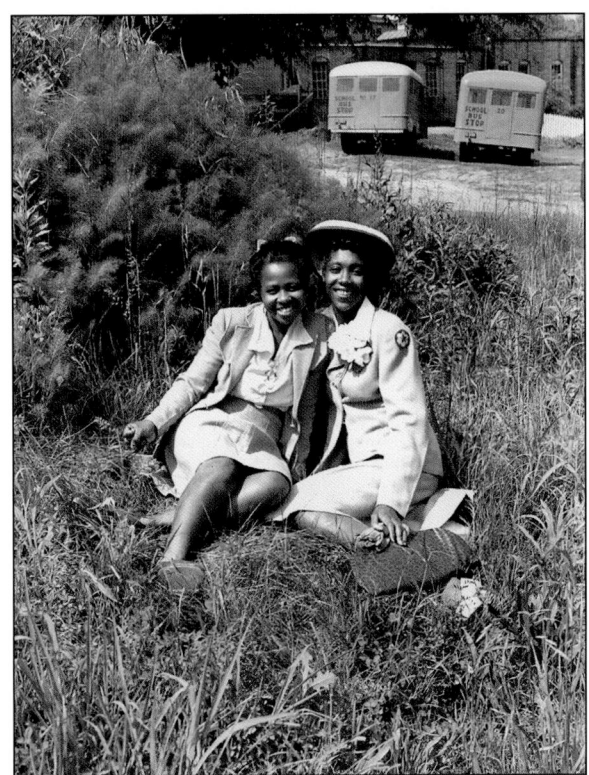

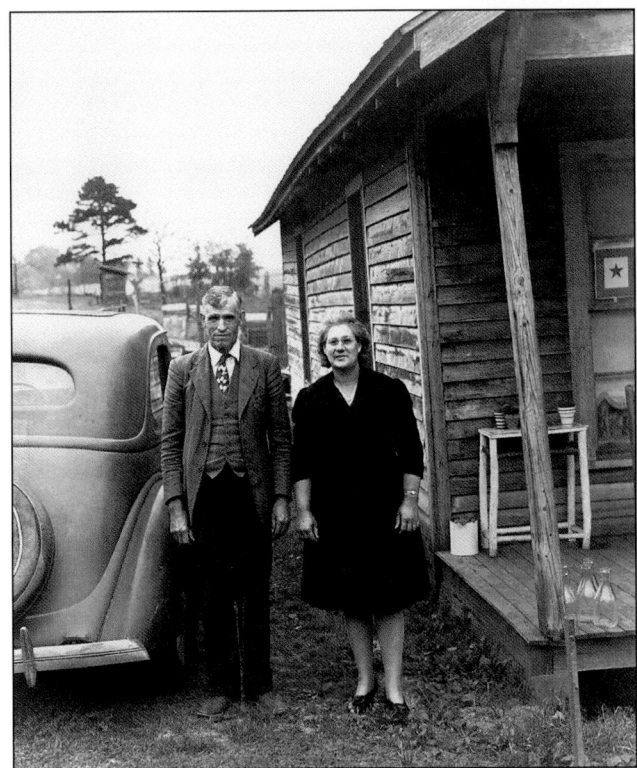

SINGLE STAR. This older couple from Lincoln County typifies many of the subjects seen through the lenses of Clyde "Baby Ray" Cornwell in this undated, unidentified photograph. The subjects of Baby Ray's photographs were not only Lincoln County's most prominent individuals and families, but also the county's most rural areas and citizens. The compositional qualities of his photographs display an artistic appeal and unique aestheticism.

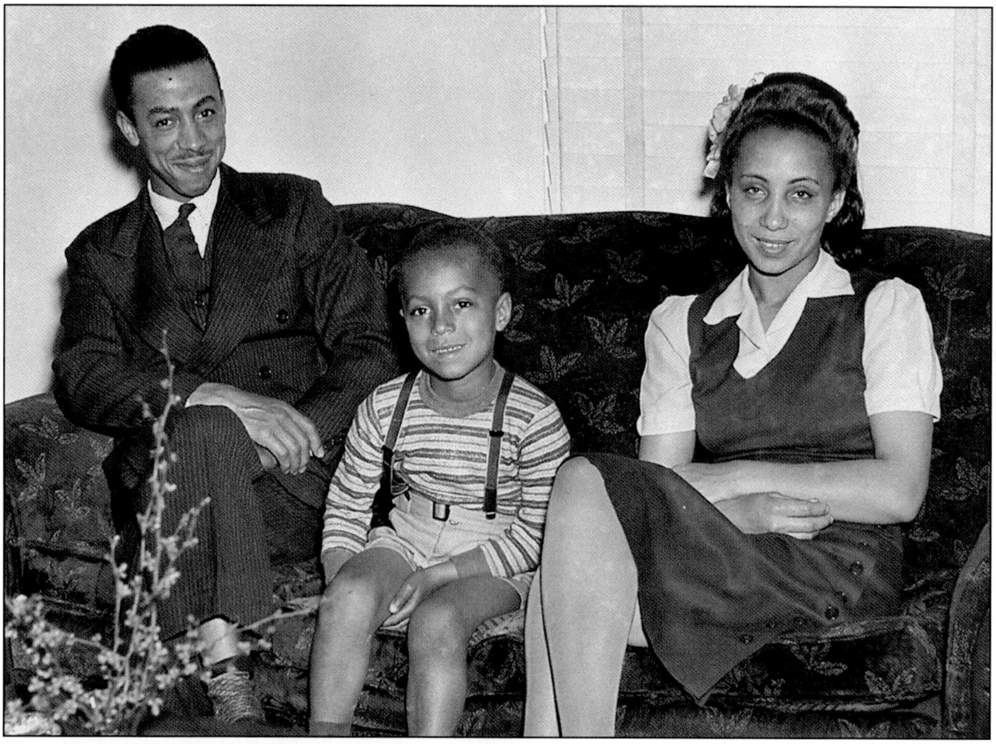

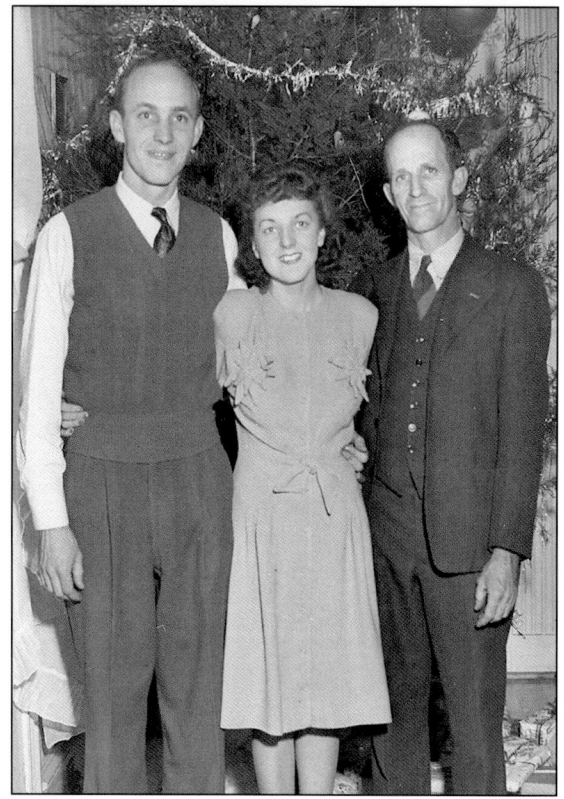

LEROY MAGNESS FAMILY. In this 1940s photograph the Leroy Magness family showcases big smiles in the living room of their Lincolnton home. Leroy married Dorothy Prue Nixon on June 2, 1938, and they had one son, John Knox Magness, who poses with them here. Leroy is well known in Lincoln County for his poetry and has published one book titled *Thoughts to Remember*.

IN THE HOLIDAY SPIRIT. Jacob J. "Jake" Wyckoff Jr. (left), Gladys Boyd Wyckoff, and Jacob J. Wyckoff Sr. stand in front of their Christmas tree for this 1946 photograph. Jacob Wyckoff Sr.'s home on North Aspen Street in Lincolnton served as the studio for this session with Baby Ray Cornwell. Cornwell took numerous photographs of the Wyckoff family during his career. Gladys Boyd Wyckoff was a G.I. bride from Northern Ireland who came to the states with Jake Wyckoff Jr.

SANTA CAME LATE IN 1945.
Clarence Edward "Butch" Lawing and Margaret Warlick Lawing sit with their son Michael Edward "Eddie" Lawing for this holiday photograph. Santa Claus left Eddie a note on his chalkboard wishing him a Merry Christmas. Butch Lawing, a career military man, had just arrived in Lincolnton on Christmas Eve 1945, but bad weather kept the couple and their son at Margaret's grandmother's house on Highway 150, where this photograph was taken.

MADE IN THE SHADE. The Hoyle family enjoys a nice summer afternoon at their home on North Laurel Street in Lincolnton. Harry Hoyle sits atop his trusty pony with his brother Hal Hoyle Jr. holding the reigns. Their parents, Hal Hoyle Sr. and Marie Hoyle, look on with smiling faces, and "Mack" stands behind the pony. Hal Sr. and his three sons—Hal Jr., Bill, and Harry—owned and operated Hoyle Motor Company of Lincolnton.

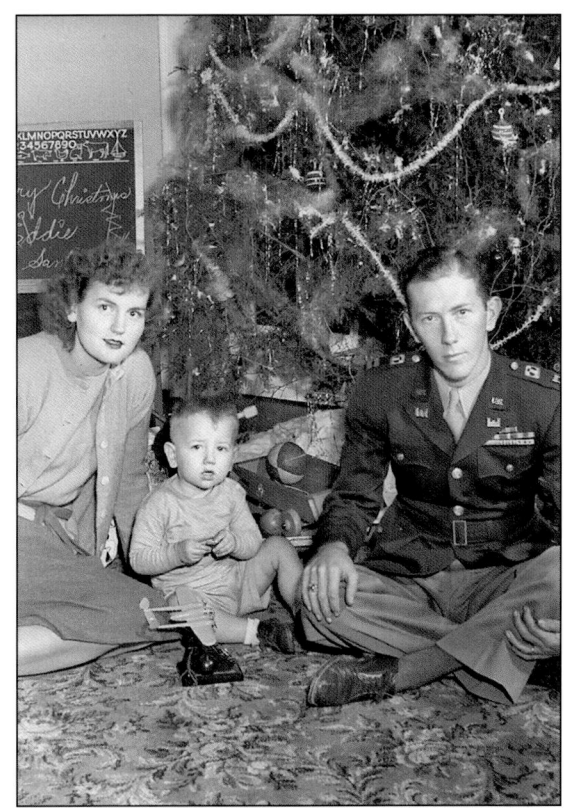

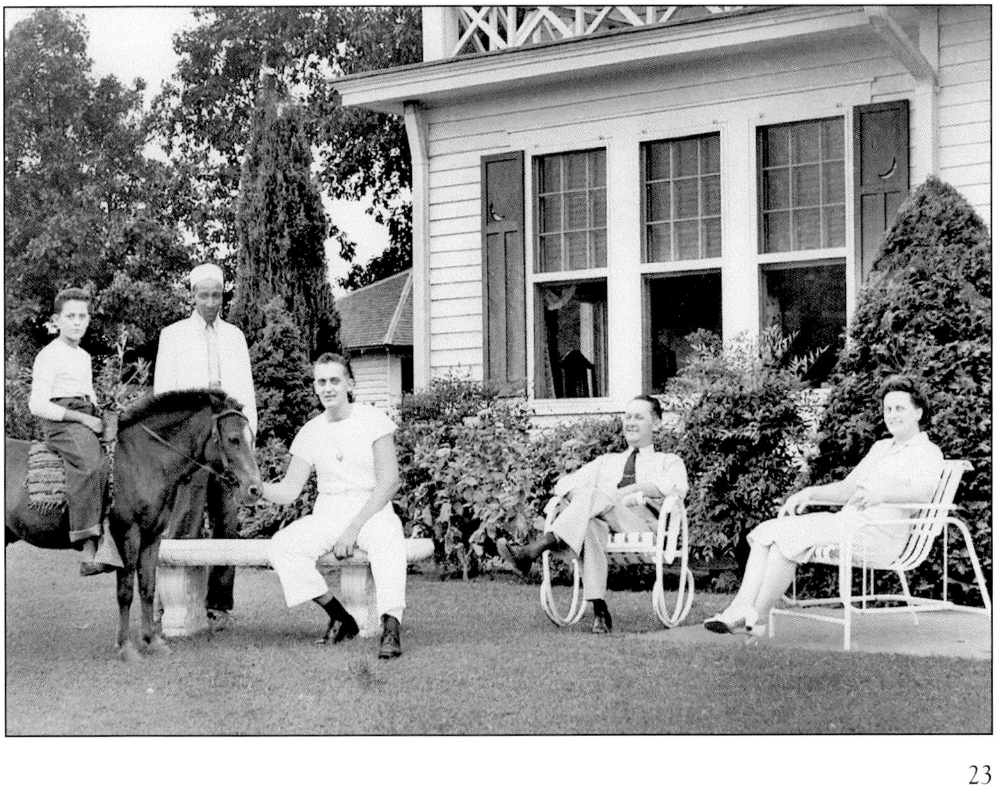

23

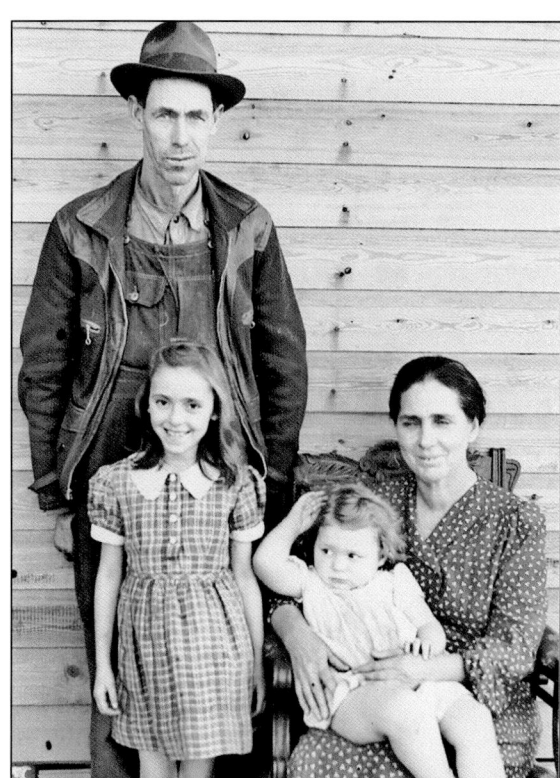

ALL IN THE FAMILY. As Lincoln County began to emerge with other areas in the South from Reconstruction, the textile industry stepped forward as the major economic force behind the area's growth and development. With the county's growth in population and the textile industry, Lincoln County ranked 29th in the state in the value of manufactured products. Elm Grove, one of Lincoln County's earliest cotton mills, was part of Lincolnton and Lincoln County's textile heritage for many years. This family, from the Elm Grove Mill village, poses beside their frame house for a Baby Ray Cornwell photograph.

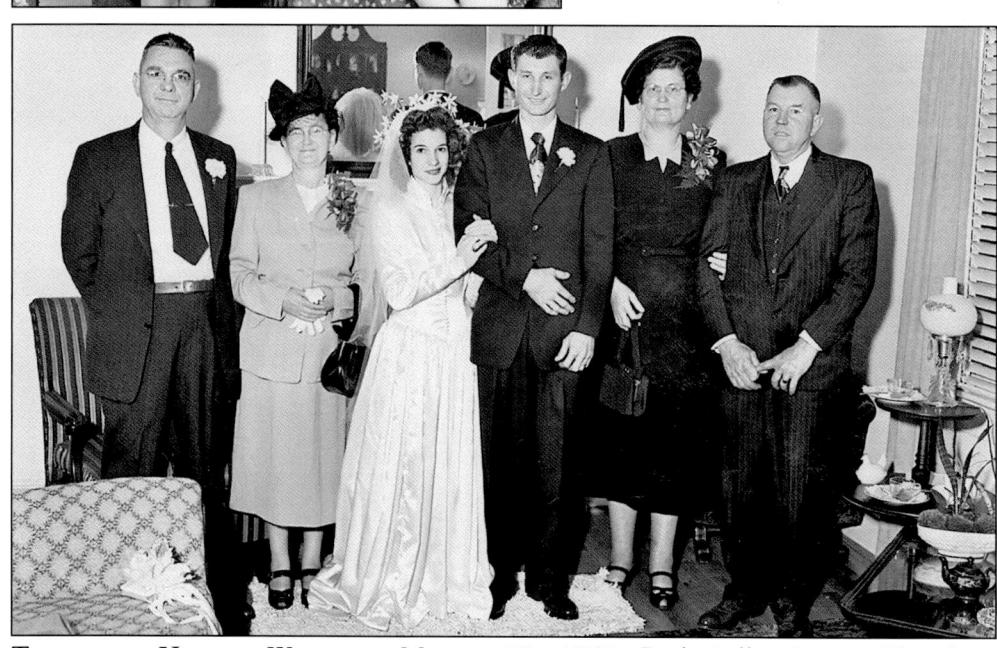

THORNBURG-HOUSER WEDDING, MARCH 18, 1950. Bride Lillie Juanita Thornburg (1930–2003) holds the arm of her new husband, Everette Ward Houser, for this photograph on March 18, 1950. Other members of the family in the living room are, from left to right, as follows: Dorus C. Thornburg, Ollie Kiser Thornburg, Catherine Mae Reep Houser (1903–1992), and Edney Monroe Houser (1901–1977).

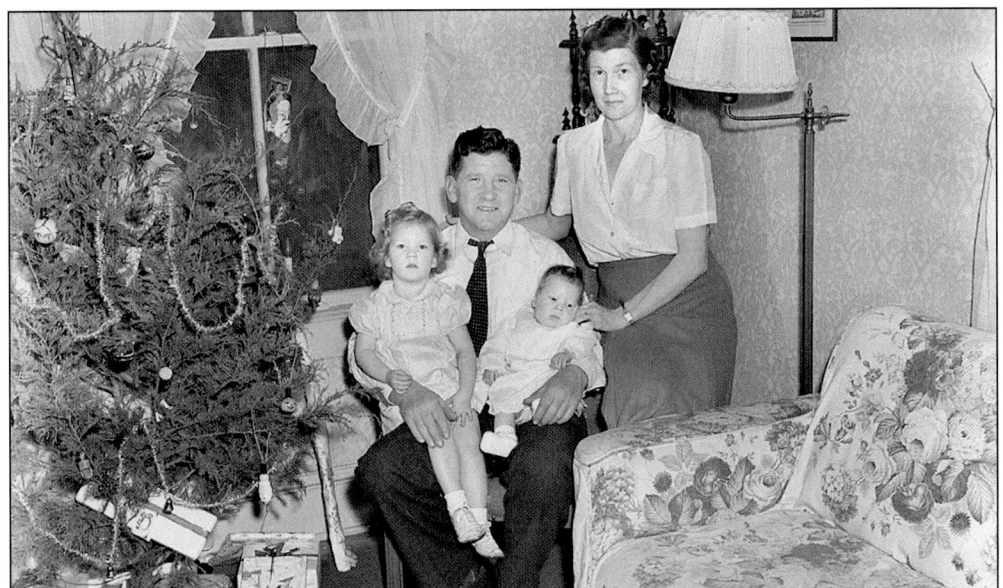

'TIS THE SEASON. In this 1940s photograph from the Cornwell Collection, gifts spill from under the family Christmas tree of the George and Vassey Page family. The Page family made their home on South Poplar Street in Lincolnton. George "Bud" Page is remembered as having an inventive mind and the creative ability to build beautiful pieces of furniture out of various types of wood. In addition to being a practicing cabinetmaker, Bud Page also worked for Eureka Iron Foundry on East Water Street in Lincolnton. Vassey Page rests on the arm of a straight chair as her husband holds their young children, Jane Page and George Page.

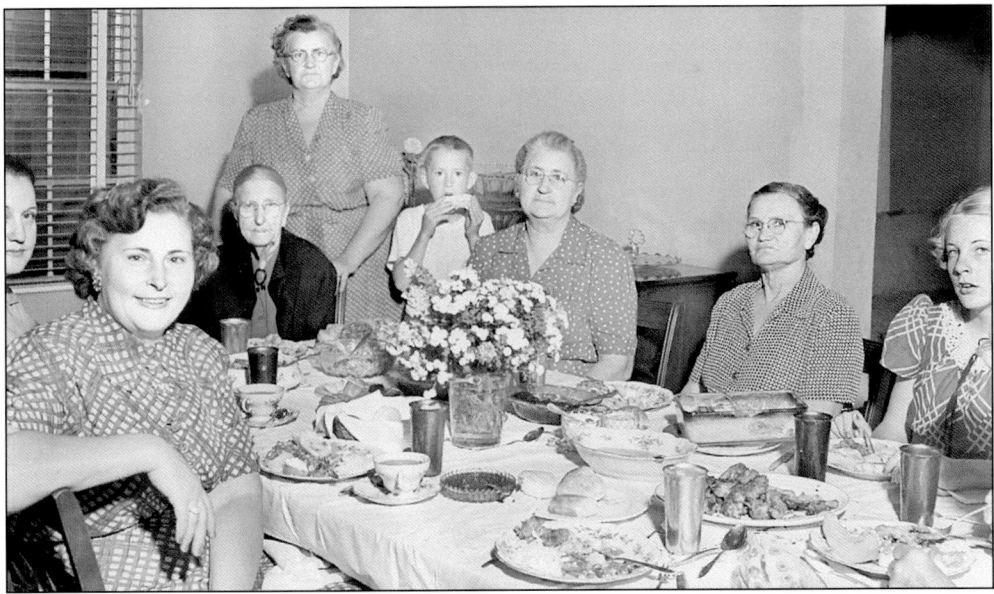

CAUGHT BY THE CAMERA. Baby Ray Cornwell catches a single young man as he takes a bite of food. This image was captured at the home of Mrs. O.A. Costner in Lincolnton during the 1940s. The ladies in attendance either finished their meal or decided to take a break for the Cornwell shot. Olive August Hoover (1877–1961) was married to Oscar Ambrose Costner on December 9, 1896, at Salem Lutheran Church, where they both were members.

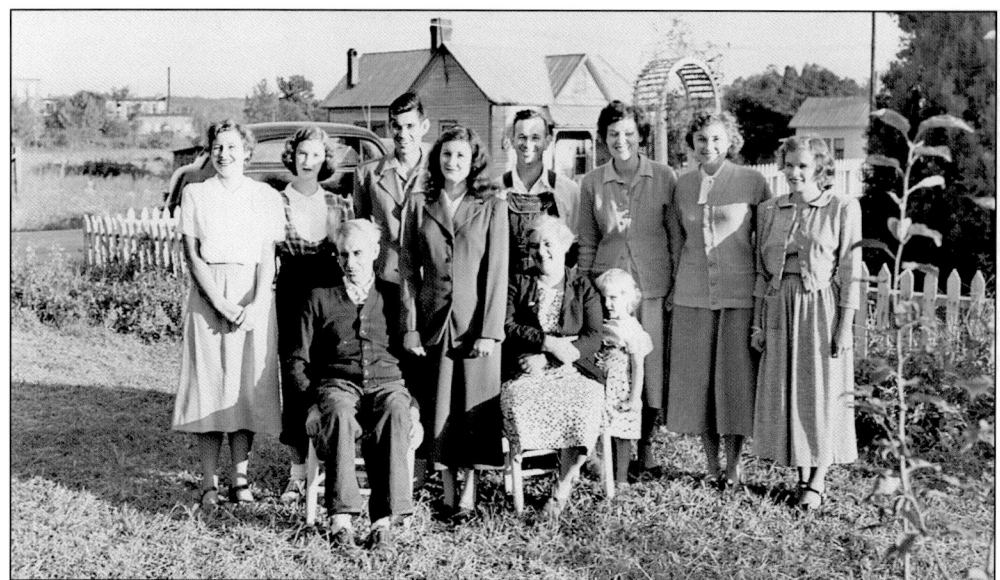

BYERS FAMILY, RHYNE HEIGHTS NEIGHBORHOOD, LINCOLNTON, SEPTEMBER 1949. The Byers family awaits the flash from the camera as the unassuming and modest homes of the neighborhood provide a well-suited background. Members of the family are, from left to right, as follows: (front row) Tate Byers, Idella Byers, and Sharon Jordon; (back row) Elaine Houser, Barbara Drum, Alton Byers, Phyllis Hovis, Windel Byers, Janet Schronce, Carolyn Gilbert, and Conette Heavner.

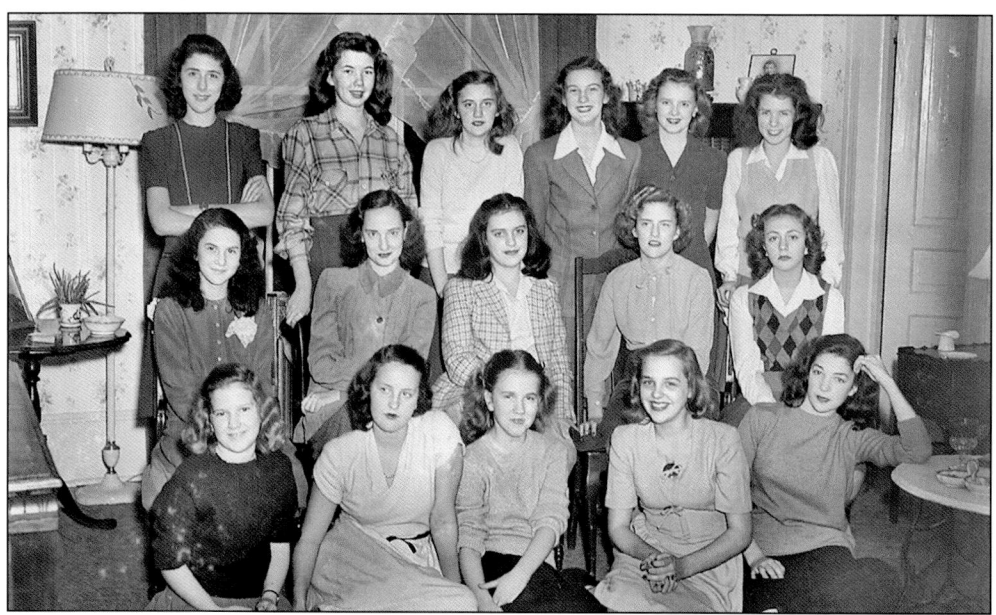

GIRLS' PARTY AT THE HOFFMANS'. Baby Ray Cornwell visited the home of William (Bill) and Inez Hoffman on South Aspen Street in Lincolnton for this photograph in the 1940s. The girls are identified, from left to right, as follows: (front row) Mary Hoffman, Mary Jo Whitener, Laura Hoffman, Ann Goode, and Doris Crowell; (middle row) Judith Boyles, Nancy Steelman, Margie Perry, Nancy Kessler, and Phyllis Costner; (back row) Mary Lohr, Susan Pickens, Bobbie Jo Belch, Betty Kincaid, Polly Dellinger, and Mary Miller.

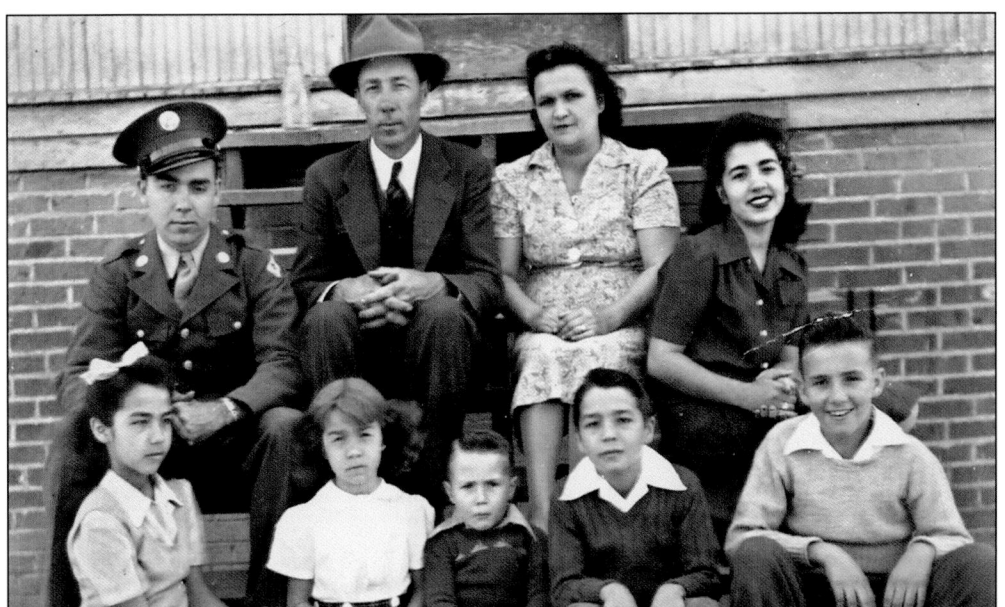

WARTIME. The Turner family of Lincolnton sits on the steps of their home in the Saxony Mill community for this 1943 photograph. Dick Turner hired Baby Ray Cornwell to capture this moment before his son Eloy left to fight for his country in World War II. Members of the Turner family are identified, from left to right, as follows: (front row) Shirley Turner, Norma Turner, Larry Turner, Edgar Turner, and Bobby Turner; (back row) Eloy Turner, Dick Turner, Myrte Turner, and Evelyn Turner.

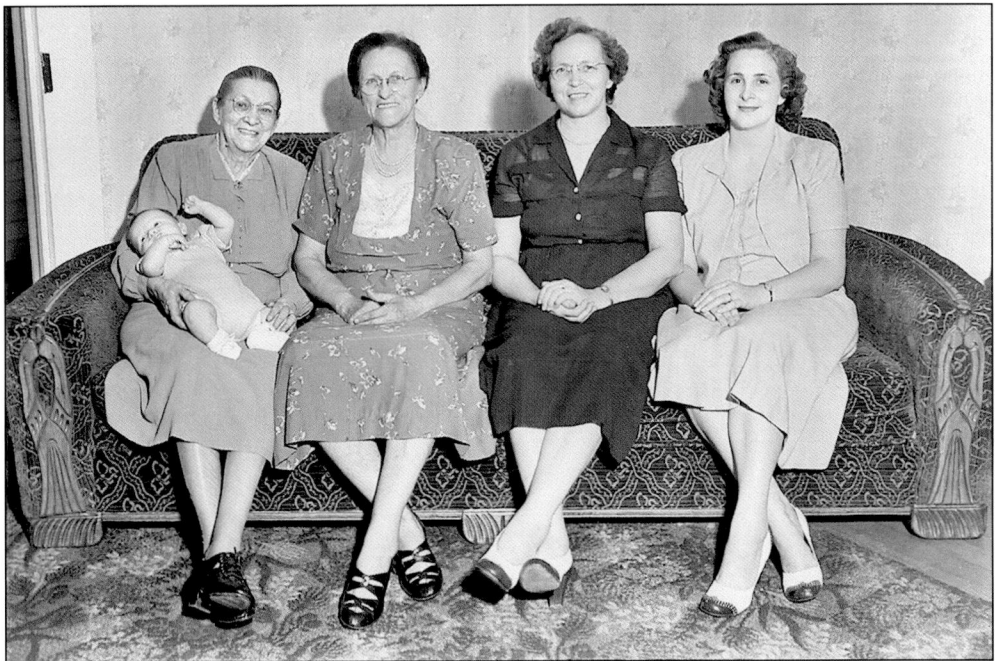

FIVE GENERATIONS. Labeling the negative sleeve "Boyce Cornwell 5 generations," Baby Ray Cornwell tells the brief story of this group of ladies and their family's evolution. Fittingly, the oldest female member of the Cornwell family holds the newest member.

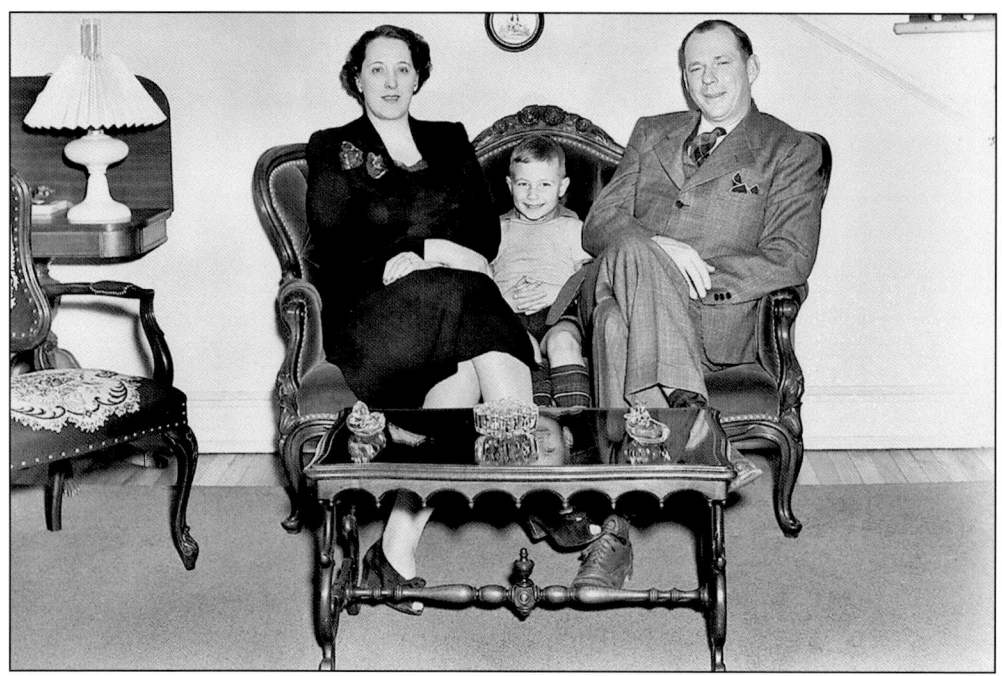

RALPH "SNAKE" COCHRANE FAMILY. The Ralph "Snake" Cochrane family rests on their formal sofa and smiles for this photograph during the 1940s. Ralph Cochrane, the son of Mr. and Mrs. J.E. Cochrane, was born on December 3, 1906, in Charlotte, North Carolina. His family moved to Lincolnton in 1911, and his father assumed a management position at Jones Fixture Company, now known as Cochrane Furniture Company, Inc. Upon graduation, Ralph began work in the furniture business with his brothers, A.B. and T.E. Cochrane. On August 31, 1932, Ralph married Ann Elmore of Vale. The couple had one son, Ralph Jr., who is included in the photograph above.

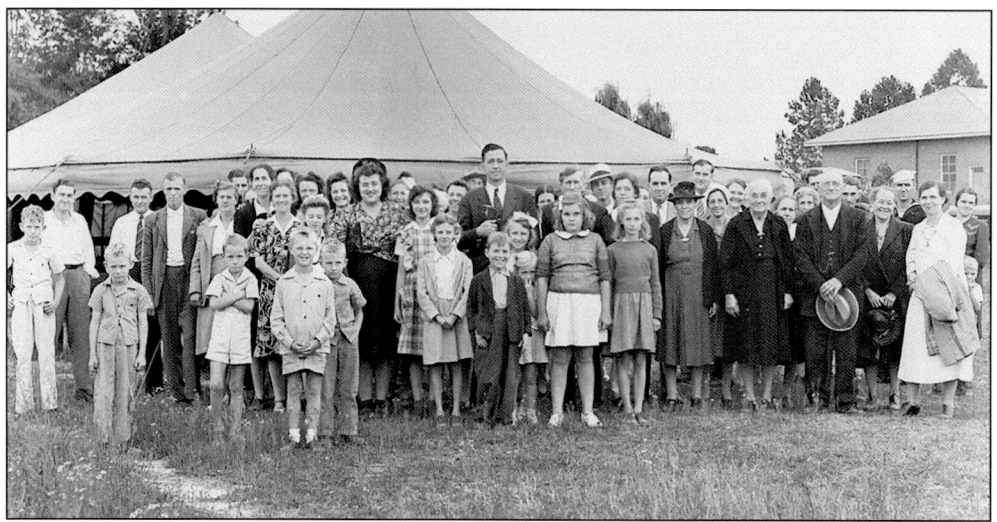

A GOOD DAY FOR A GATHERING. Assumed to be of a tent revival, this late 1940s photograph documents a small piece of the religious activities in Lincolnton. Though the location of the photograph is undetermined and those shown are unidentified, this photograph is witness to the welcome all citizens received at this spiritual enrichment.

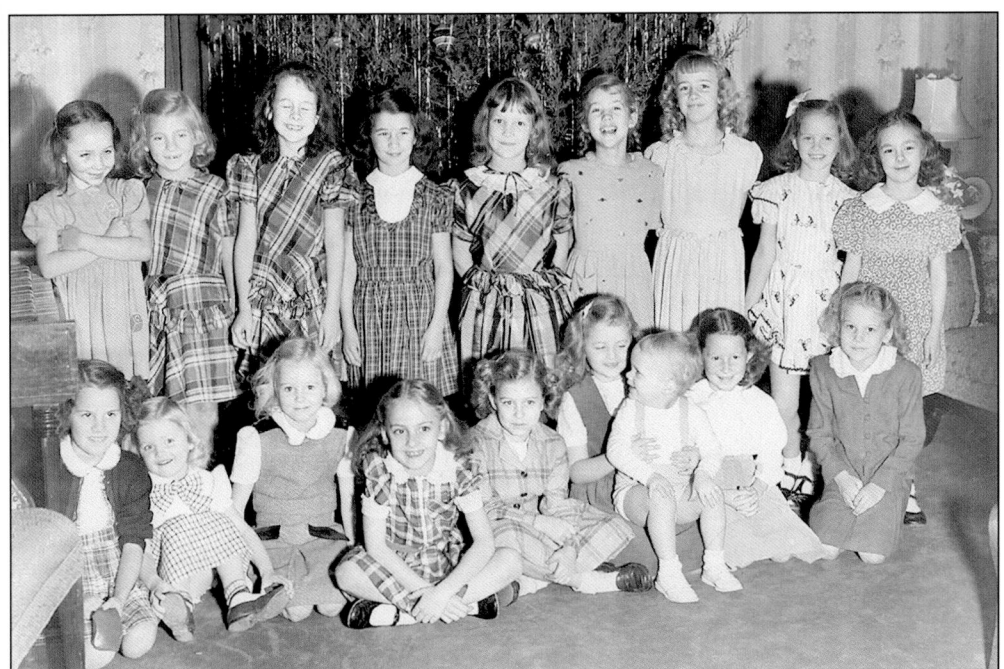

NINE YEARS AND COUNTING. Nancy Crowell celebrates her ninth birthday party on December 24, 1948, at the home of her parents, Mr. and Mrs. C.C. Crowell. The Crowell family lived on North Aspen Street. Nancy's friends and family who joined her to celebrate her birthday are, from left to right, as follows: (front row) Joy Johnson, Ann Willis, Shirley Polhill, Peggy Costner, Elaine Yoder, Pat Dellinger, Charles C. "Todd" Crowell III (on Pat's lap), Priscilla Ingle, and Linda Lou Brown; (back row) Susanne Beal, Gayle Burris, Judy Morris, Nancy Shidal, Nancy Jane Crowell (honoree), Crissy Crowell, Mary Emma Thompson, Judy Reinhardt, and Mary Jane Crowell.

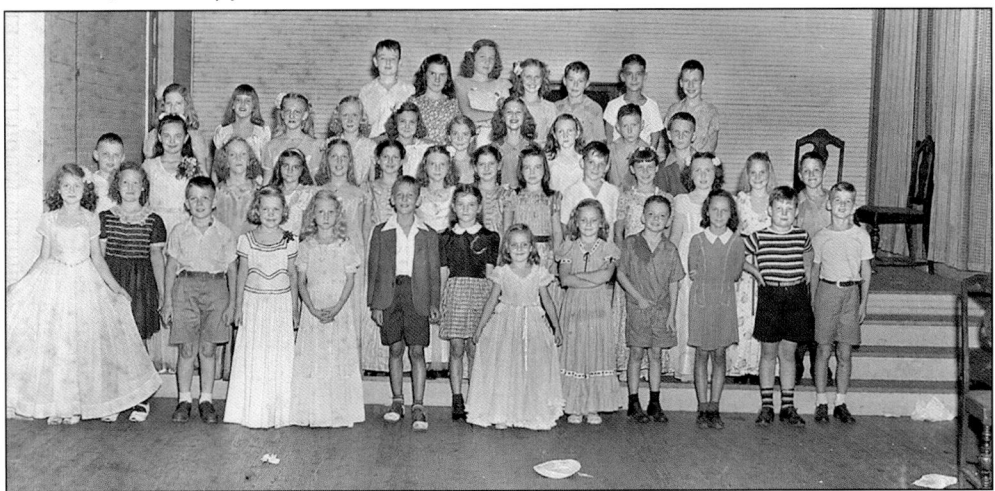

IF THESE WALLS COULD TALK. If the walls of this Lincolnton building could talk, they would tell the story of this 1940s party hosted by Mr. and Mrs. Alton Claytor. Alton Claytor, editor of *The Lincoln County News*, was very familiar with Baby Ray Cornwell's work, as he featured many of Cornwell's images from Lincolnton and Lincoln County in his newspaper from the 1940s to the 1970s. The Claytors held this party for their daughter Nancy.

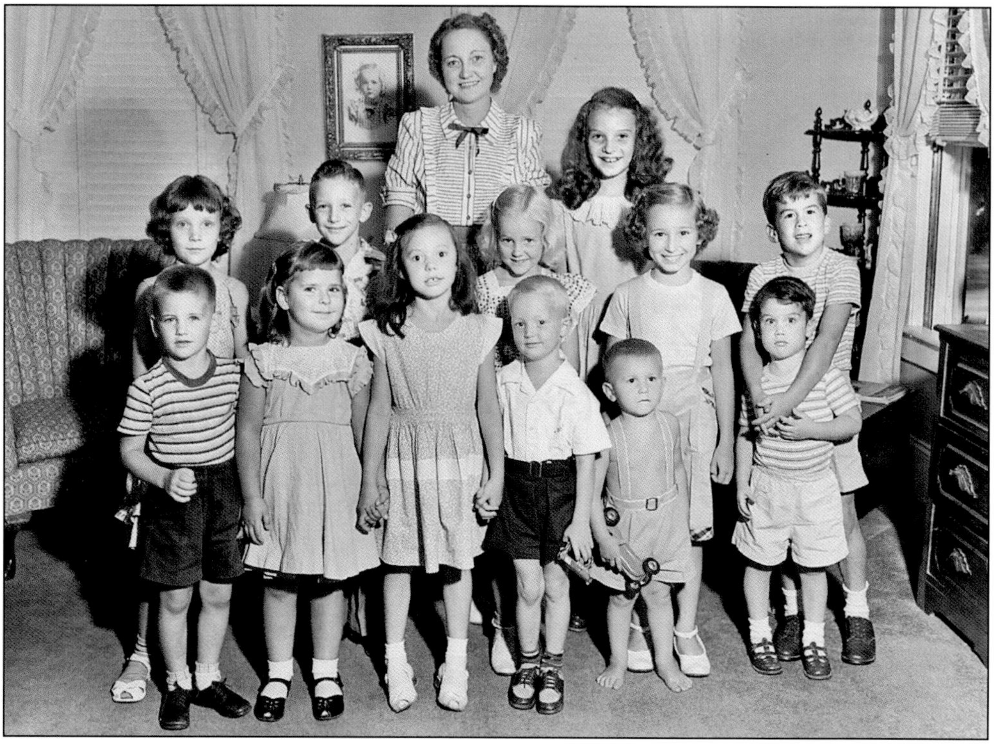

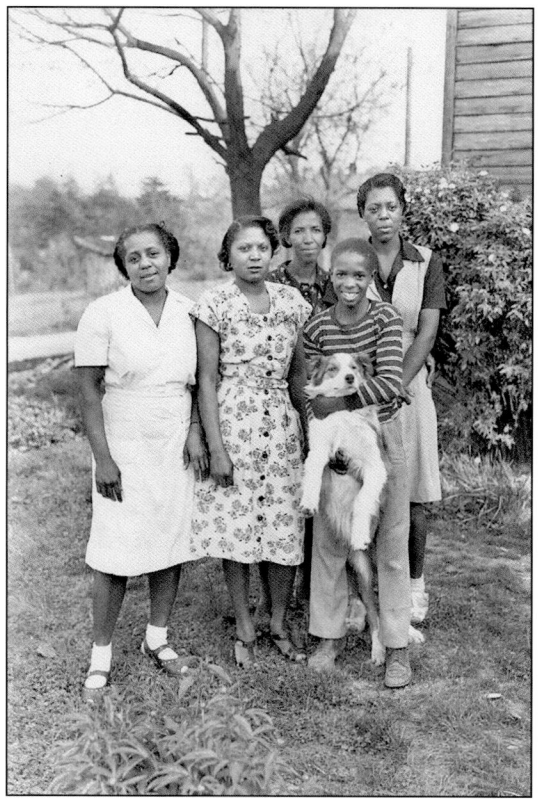

POLHILL PARTY. A portrait of Shirley Polhill hangs in the background of this photograph taken at the home of Joe and Martha Polhill in August 1948. The Polhill family lived at 728 North Oak Street in Lincolnton, and in their living room a small group of children lined up for the camera in front of Martha Polhill. The children are identified, from left to right, as follows: (front row) Danny Leonard, unidentified, Linda Lowe, Jack Polhill, unidentified, and unidentified; (back row) Martha Robinson, Bud Warlick, Martha Polhill, Shirley Polhill, unidentified, Delia Ford, and Bill Henderson.

FAMILY'S BEST FRIEND. A group of folks from one of Lincoln County's African-American communities poses for another Baby Ray Cornwell photograph. Pictured, from left to right, are Frost Robinson, Alene Ramseur, Lily Swan, unidentified (holding the dog), and Annie Davis.

LINK FAMILY, GEORGETOWN COMMUNITY, LINCOLNTON. Seated in a field near their home in Lincolnton's Georgetown community, from left to right, are Girtrude Link, Son Link, Son Link Jr., and Mary Link.

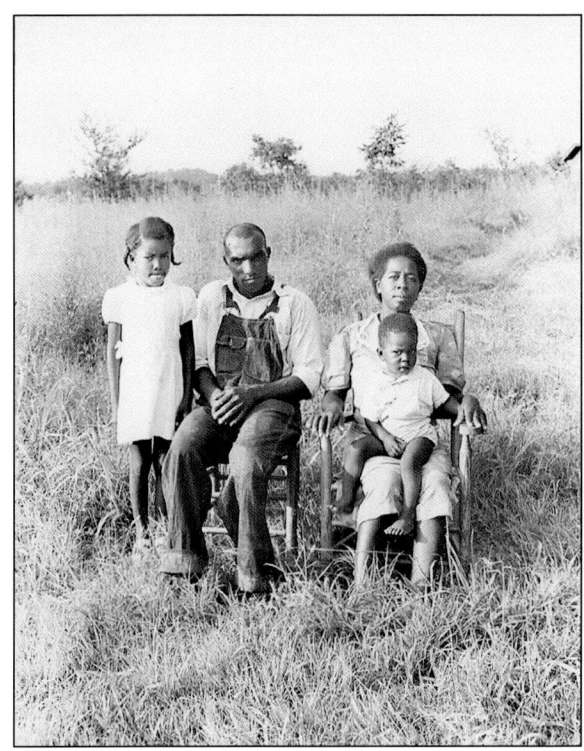

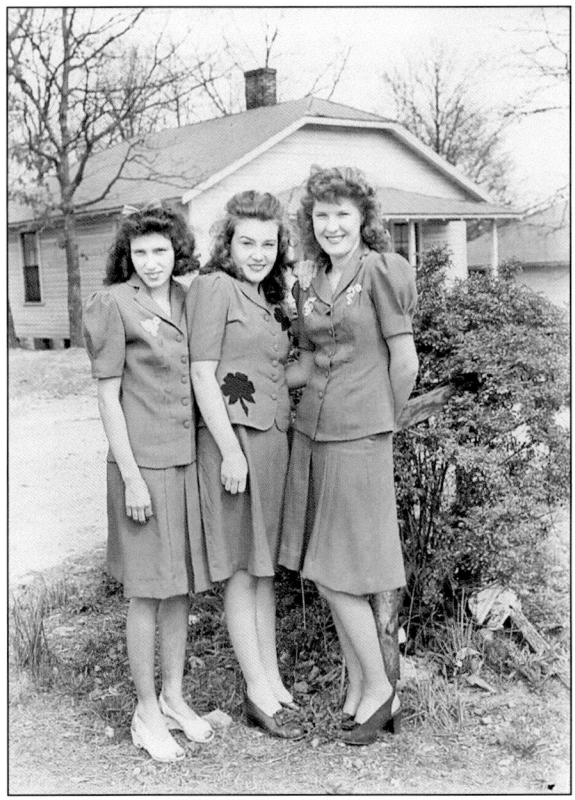

THREE OF A KIND. Ruby Harkey, Dean Canipe, and Virginia Peeler show their glamour and flare for this 1940s image. Standing in front of a mill house in Lincolnton's Saxony Mill community, the three could pass for a Hollywood trio from the day.

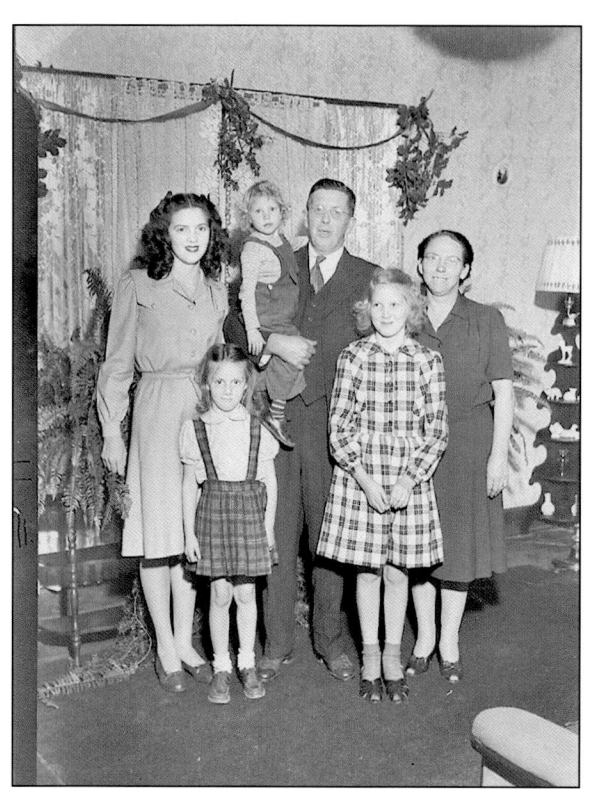

A Saine Family Christmas. The yuletide spirit can be seen in the festive visages of the Frank Saine family of Lincolnton for another of Cornwell's holiday images. Taken during Christmas of 1946, the Saine family stands in the living room of their Lee Street home with one family member absent. Madeline Saine married Lee Elmore on Christmas Day 1946 and missed the family photograph. The members of the Saine family are, from left to right, as follows: (front row) Carolyn and Betty; (back row) Marie, Phyllis, Frank, and Elizabeth. Frank Saine first owned and operated a leather, harness, and shoe shop on E. Water Street in Lincolnton. The shop later moved to South Academy Street.

Jesse Robinson Family. The Jesse Robinson family sits in an easy chair at their home on North Cedar Street for this 1940s photograph. Jesse R. "Hunky" Robinson first worked as a mechanic in 1932 with Heath Motor Company in Charlotte where he served as an apprentice. He later worked with Polhill Chevrolet Company in Lincolnton until he opened his own business on Lincolnton's Courtsquare in 1943. He married his high school sweetheart, Buna Keener, on August 2, 1932, and they had one son, Jerry Glenn Robinson.

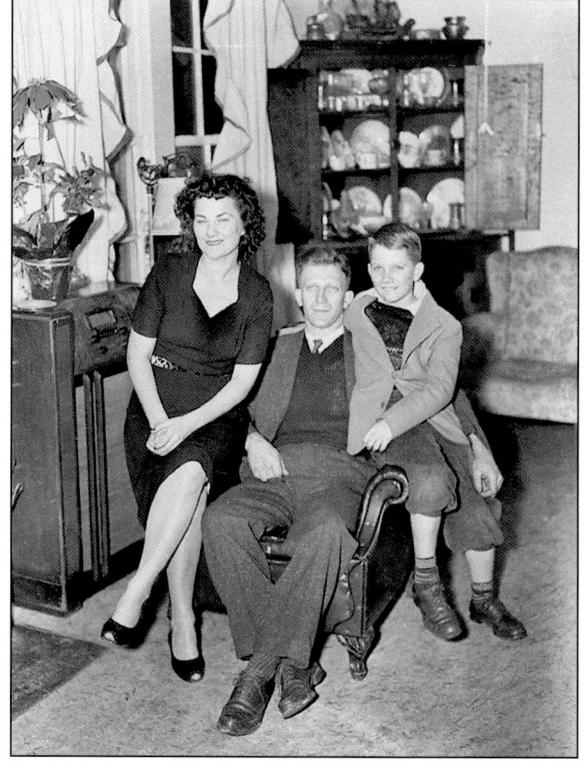

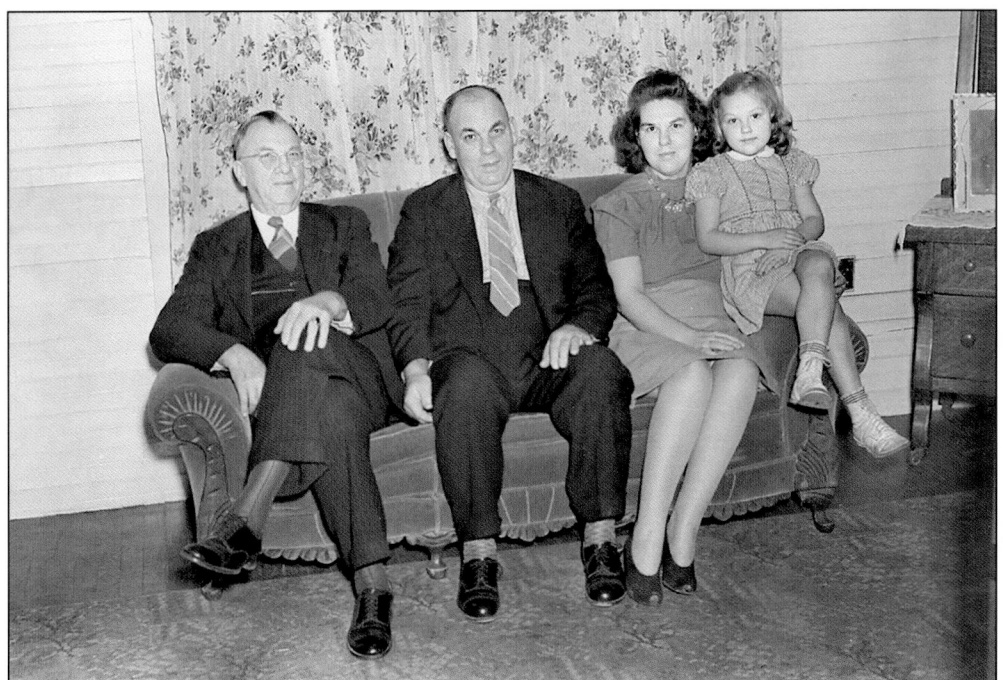

FOUR GENERATIONS. Four generations of the Smith family pose in Herman Smith's Lincolnton home. This picture was intended to document the lineage of the family. Though simple in design, the house boasts a single oak dresser with a runner and photograph.

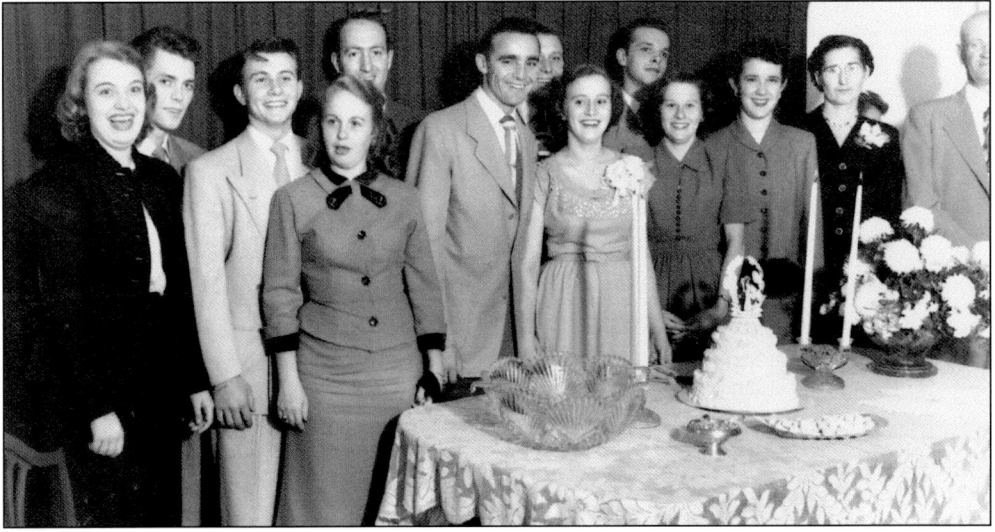

THE BIG DAY. This photograph shows the cake-cutting ceremony held at the home of Mr. and Mrs. Wes Turner on Highway 150 East. Married in October 1950, Jack Dellinger and Carolyn Turner celebrated the special event with many close friends and families. The members of the wedding party are identified, from left to right, as follows: (front row) Jean Heafner Harnack, Mary Carpenter Ramseur, Jack L. Dellinger, Carolyn Turner Dellinger, Betty Turner Hoffman, Queeta Ballard Ramseur, Kathleen Turner, and Rev. H.B. Jones; (back row) Bob Ramseur, Martin Turner, Bob Lineberger, Jim Moore, and Bryan "Jack" Dellinger. (Courtesy of Jack L. and Carolyn Dellinger.)

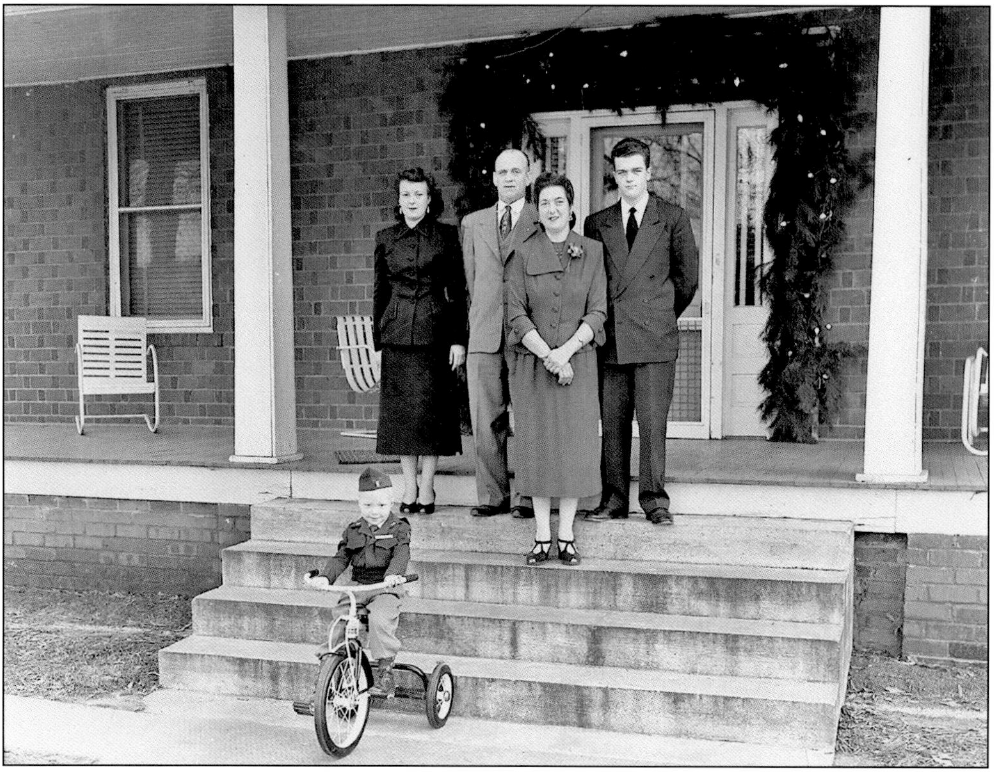

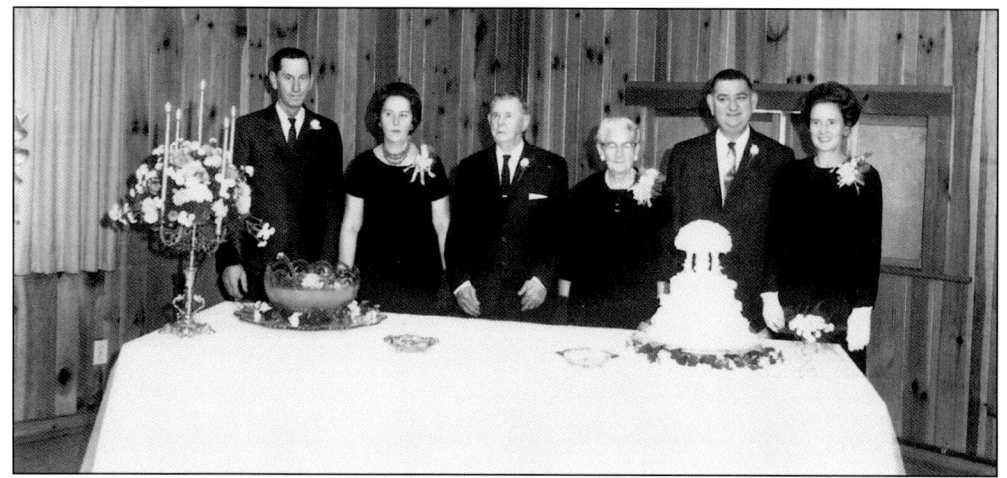

TYKE ON A BIKE. The Hoyle family stands outside of their home on North Aspen Street in Lincolnton. The youngest member of the family is shown in his military outfit sitting on the new bike Santa left for him.

GOLDEN WEDDING ANNIVERSARY. Claude Monroe Houser and Nannie Alice Coon Houser stand behind the decorated table as they celebrate their 50th wedding anniversary on November 8, 1964. Baby Ray Cornwell was able to help celebrate this landmark occasion with Mr. and Mrs. Houser and their family. Members of the family in attendance are identified, from left to right, as follows: Frank Monroe Houser (Riverdale, Georgia), Pauline Houser Scronce, Claude, Nannie, James Adolphus Houser, and Mary Lelia Houser Abernethy. (Courtesy of Helen Peeler.)

Two
Books and Brawn

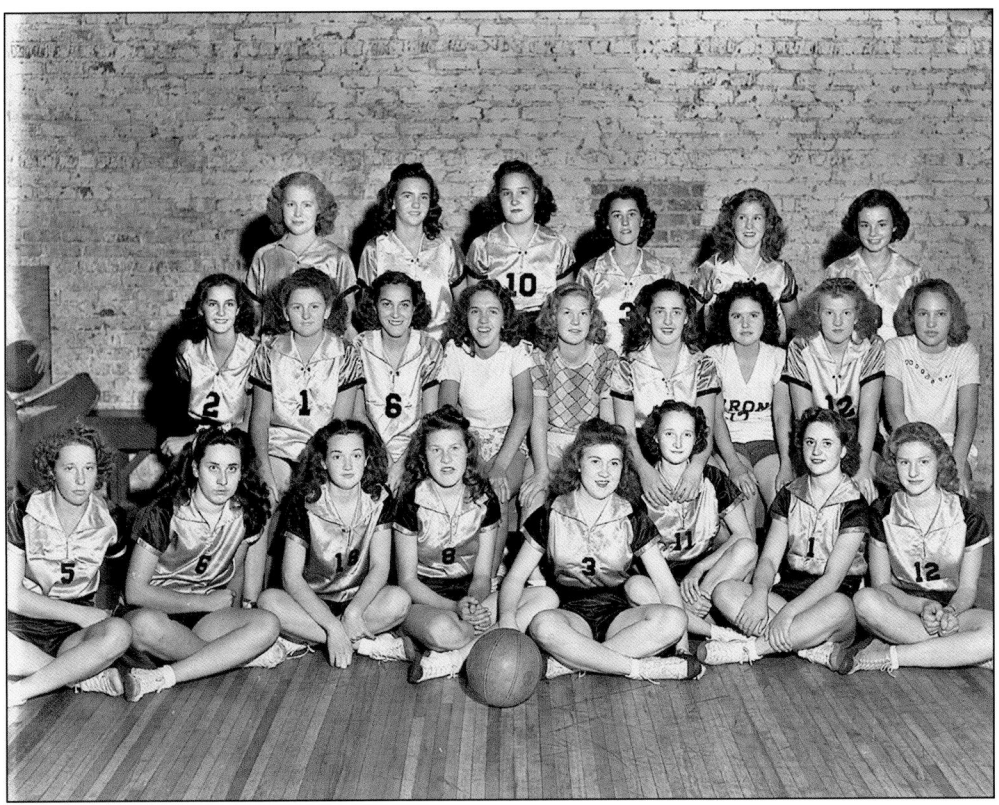

SUITED FOR THE TOURNAMENT. The ladies of the Lincolnton High School girls' basketball team take a time-out for this photograph at their 1940s tournament. The ladies are identified, from left to right, as follows: (front row) Betty Sue Ellis, unidentified, Bobbi Lockman, Rachel Coffey, Nancy Kiser, Romona Heavner, Betty Heavner, and Betty Reynolds; (middle row) Gloria Hallman, two unidentified persons, Gloria Hovis, Winnon Lineberger, three unidentified persons, and Barbara Carter; (back row) Betty Cornwell, unidentified, Faye Bost, two unidentified persons, and Beth Cornwell.

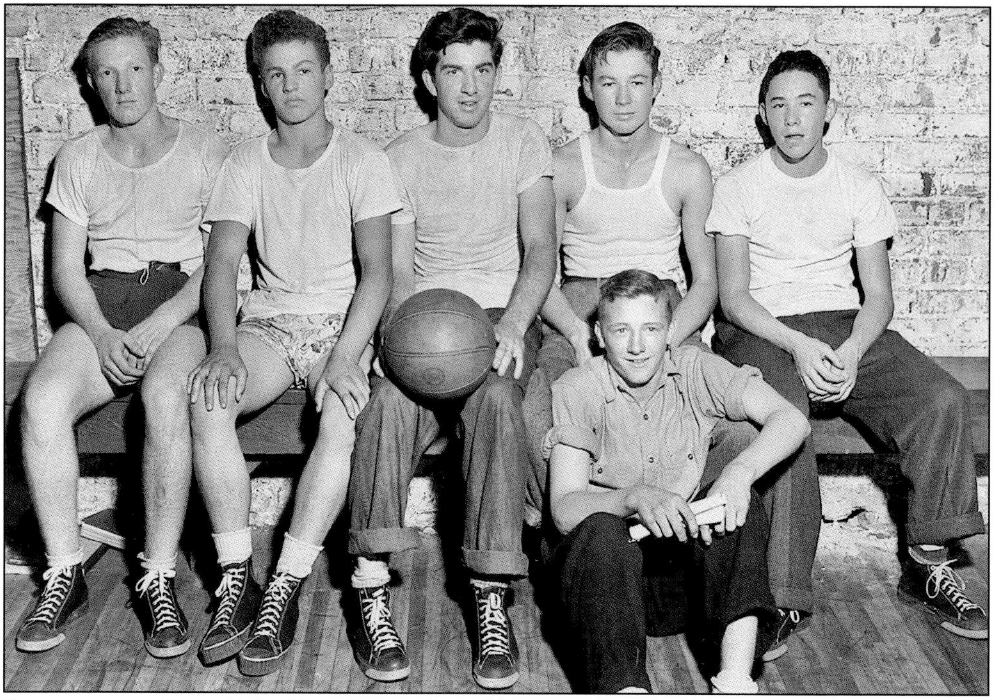

BOYS ON THE SIDE. Baby Ray Cornwell is able to catch a few members of the Lincolnton High School boys' basketball team for this 1940s shot. Members of the team are, from left to right, as follows: Jim Babb, unidentified, Jennings Benfield, Gene Ross, ? Cohen, and Steve Gabriel (seated).

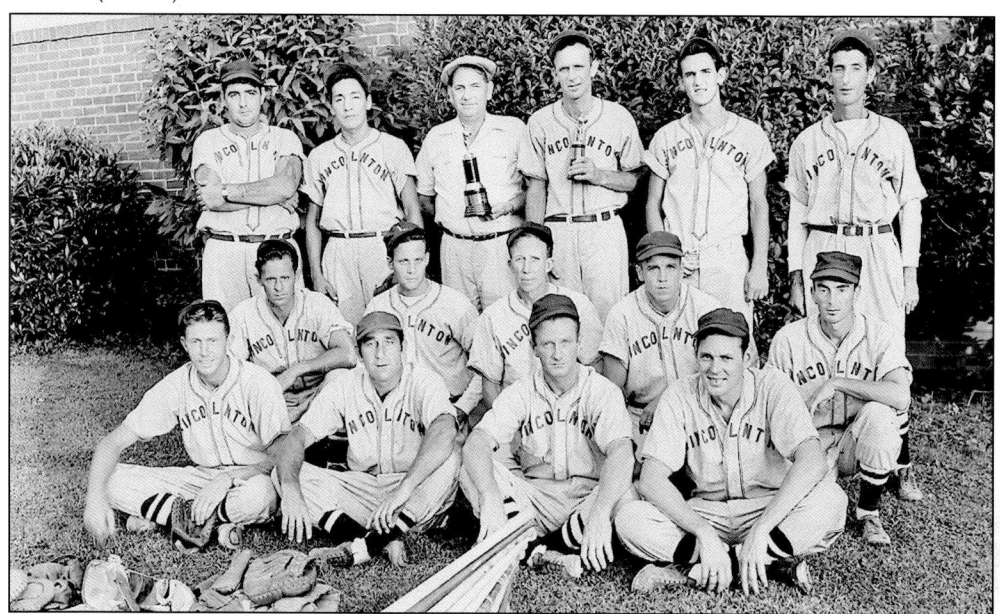

PRISON CAMP BALL TEAM. Baby Ray Cornwell visited the Prison Camp in Lincolnton to photograph their ball team on August 8, 1953. Though the formation of the team and the identification of these team members are uncertain, it can be assumed that the team was organized in the 1950s.

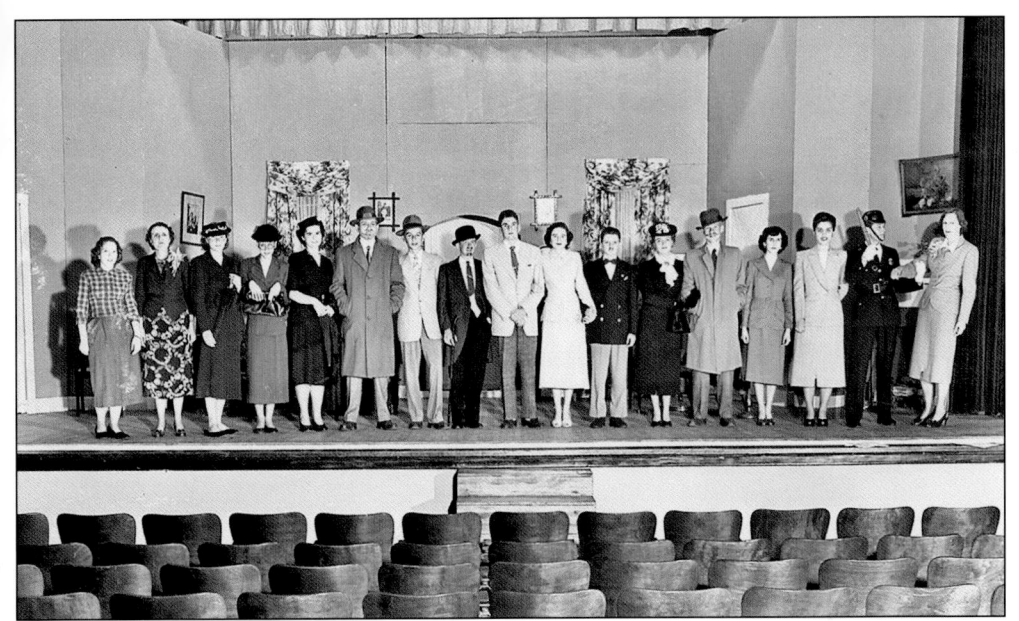

LINCOLNTON HIGH SCHOOL SENIOR PLAY, *UNCLE FRED FLITS BY*, APRIL 20, 1950. Lincolnton High School's senior class presented P.C. Wodehouse's play *Uncle Fred Flits By*, dramatized by Perry Clark at the Lincolnton High School Auditorium. Bill Elliott was cast as Pongo Twistleton, Sammy Lerner played the Crumpet, and Dale Adams played Uncle Fred. Other actors included Daisy Leatherman, Pat Drum, John Wise, Gordon Crowell, Jean Heafner, Norris Bost, Pat Shuford, Nancy Payseur, Joannah Burgin, Nancy Stamey, and Robert Seagle.

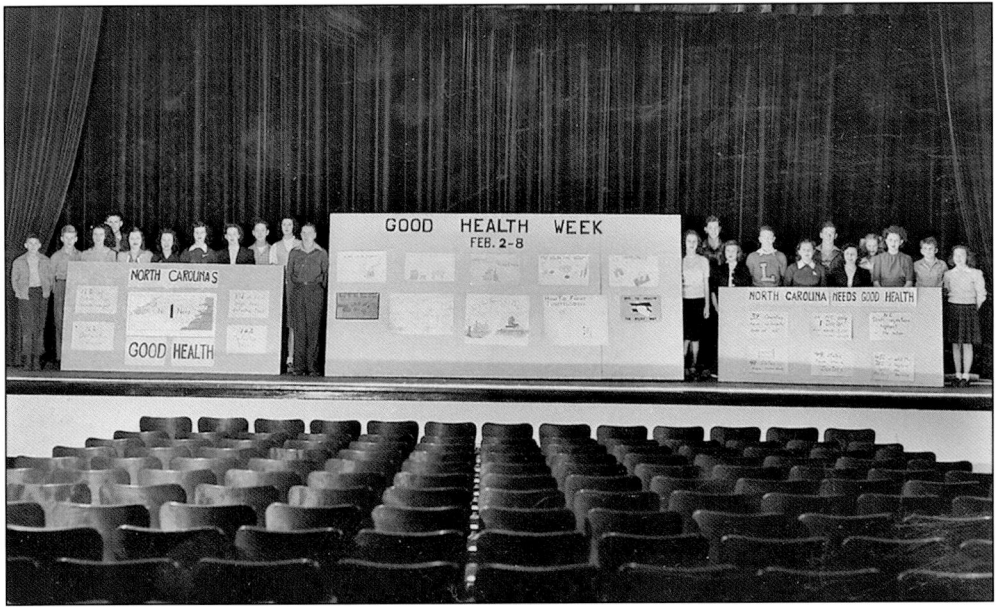

CLEANLINESS IS NEXT TO GODLINESS. On the stage of Lincolnton High School's auditorium, students hold up their Good Health Week billboards. Held from February 2 to February 8, Good Health Week was observed by various schools in the county, but Baby Ray Cornwell opted to photograph the students from Lincolnton High School.

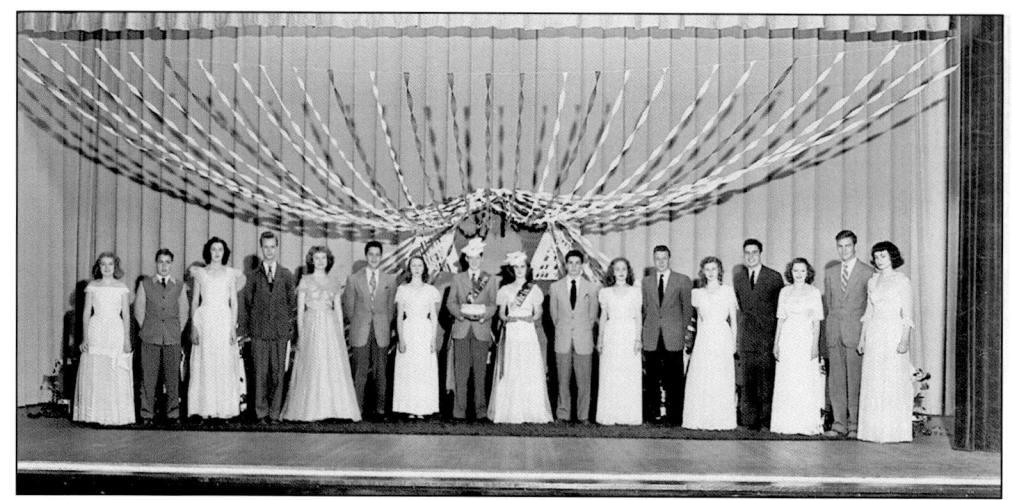

LINCOLNTON HIGH SCHOOL'S ST. PATRICK'S DAY PROGRAM, MARCH 17, 1948. In a special chapel program, the students of Lincolnton High School (LHS) crowned Libby Huggins and Jack Garrison as Saint Patricia and Saint Patrick. LHS's Student Government Council sponsored the St. Patrick and St. Patricia contest and sold votes for 1¢ each. All of the proceeds from the sale went to the student government fund. The contest was held in the high school auditorium with Student Government Council president Jimmy Babb acting as master of ceremonies.

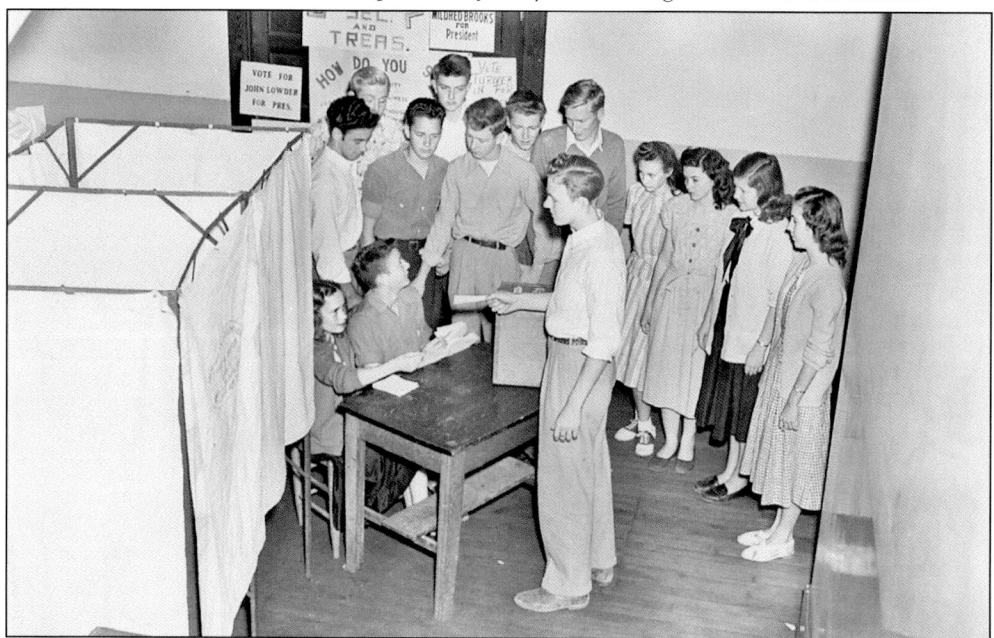

LINCOLNTON HIGH SCHOOL STUDENT GOVERNMENT ELECTION, MAY 1948. On May 10, 1948, Lincolnton High School's student body elected rising senior Mildred Brooks president of student government. Other officers included Betty Wise, vice president, and Beth Cornwell, secretary-treasurer. The student body nominated these students at a meeting on April 21. Each nominee had a campaign manager who distributed posters and handled all other publicity for their candidate, and each candidate was required to deliver a speech to the student body on April 30 in the auditorium. Outgoing student government officers included Jimmy Babb, president; Steve Gabriel, vice-president; and Elsie Hoffman, secretary-treasurer.

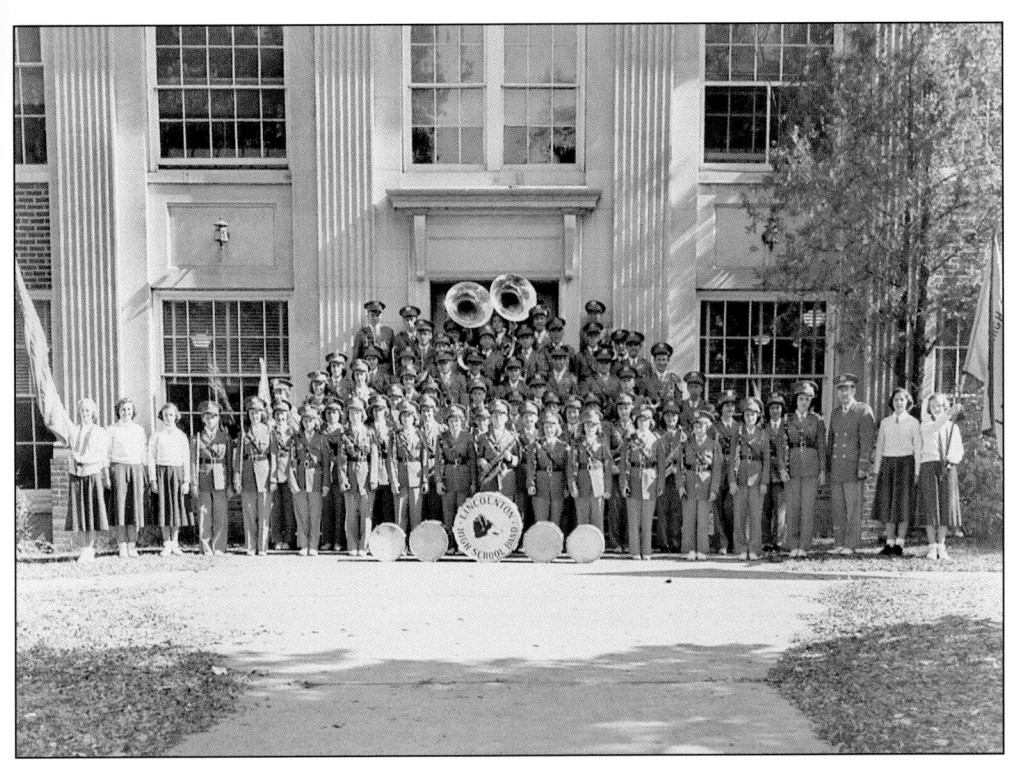

STRIKE UP THE BAND. Members of the Lincolnton High School Band line up behind their drums for this yearbook photograph in 1952. Officers of the 1952 Lincolnton High School band were the following: John Mauney, president; Eddie House, vice president; Elizabeth Love, secretary; Kay Johnson, librarian; Kay Frances Smith, librarian; Donald Buckley, publicity manager; David McCullough, property manager; Johnny Ingle, property manager; Sydney Robinson, historian; and Jim Mauney, student director.

DAPPER JACK. Dressed in a dapper suit and among many friends, Jack Dellinger looks over as Baby Ray Cornwell takes his photograph at the Lincolnton High School graduation of 1946. Jack returned to Lincolnton after serving in the Army Air Corps during World War II, and he graduated with the 1946 class. (Courtesy of Jack L. and Carolyn Dellinger.)

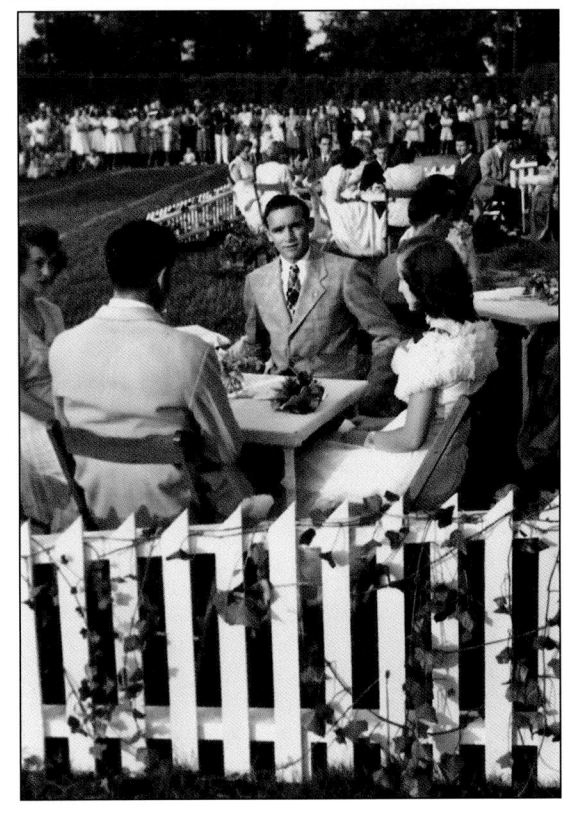

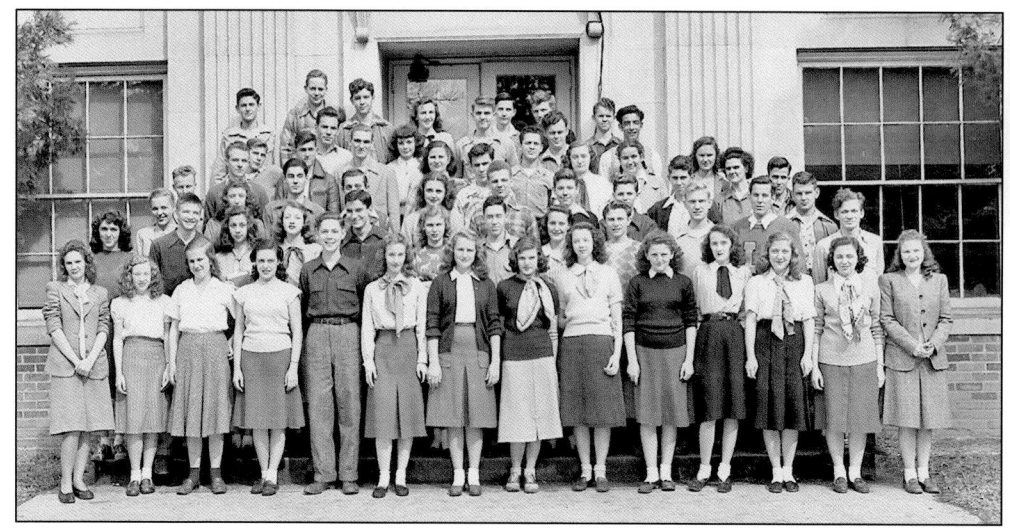

LINCOLNTON HIGH SCHOOL FRENCH CLUB, 1948. Lincolnton High School's French Club stands poised for the yearbook superlative photograph on February 25, 1948. Officers of the 1948 French Club were the following: John Lowder, president; Fred Harrill, vice-president; Anne Goode, secretary; Harry Hoyle, treasurer; and Miss Margaret McKinney, faculty advisor.

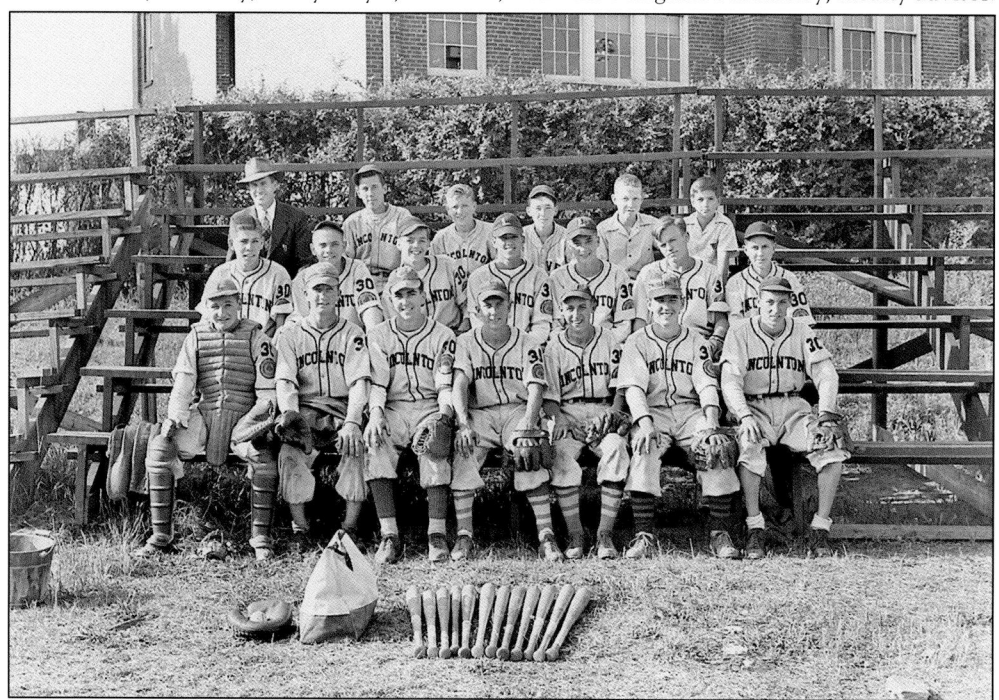

TOOLS OF THE TRADE. Bats, balls, and a single mitt occupy the foreground of this photograph of a Lincolnton High School baseball team from the 1940s. Members of the team are identified, from left to right, as follows: (front row) Vernon Schrum, John Stamey, Glenn Reynolds, Garland Hedspeth, Jack Harwell, John Hugh Weaver, and Frank Rudisill; (middle row) Doyle Bynum, Joe Bill Cornwell, Benny Cochrane, Jack Heavner, unidentified, Ralph Carpenter, and Davy Kiser; (back row) Coach Jack Kiser, Bill Beatty, Steve Gabriel, ? Cohen, and managers William Ingle and Randolph Shives.

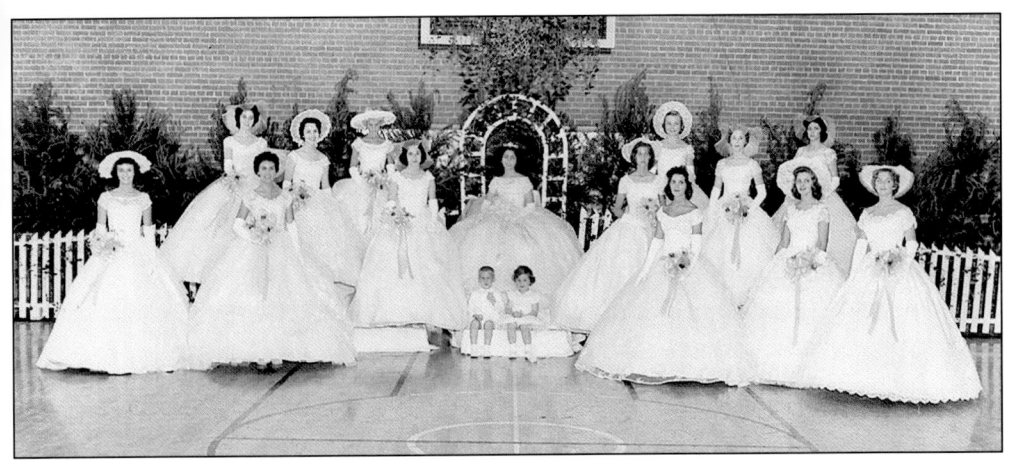

THE QUEEN AND HER COURT. Two mascots are seated in front of the Lincolnton High School May Day Queen and her court for this Baby Ray Cornwell photograph on May 29, 1959. May Day celebrations date back to ancient Rome and have been celebrated by many cultures for centuries. The May Day celebration culminates in dancing around a Maypole wrapped with colorful streamers, as children, queens, and others perform old dances. Children also pick May flowers and place them in handmade baskets to leave on the front porches of neighbors and friends.

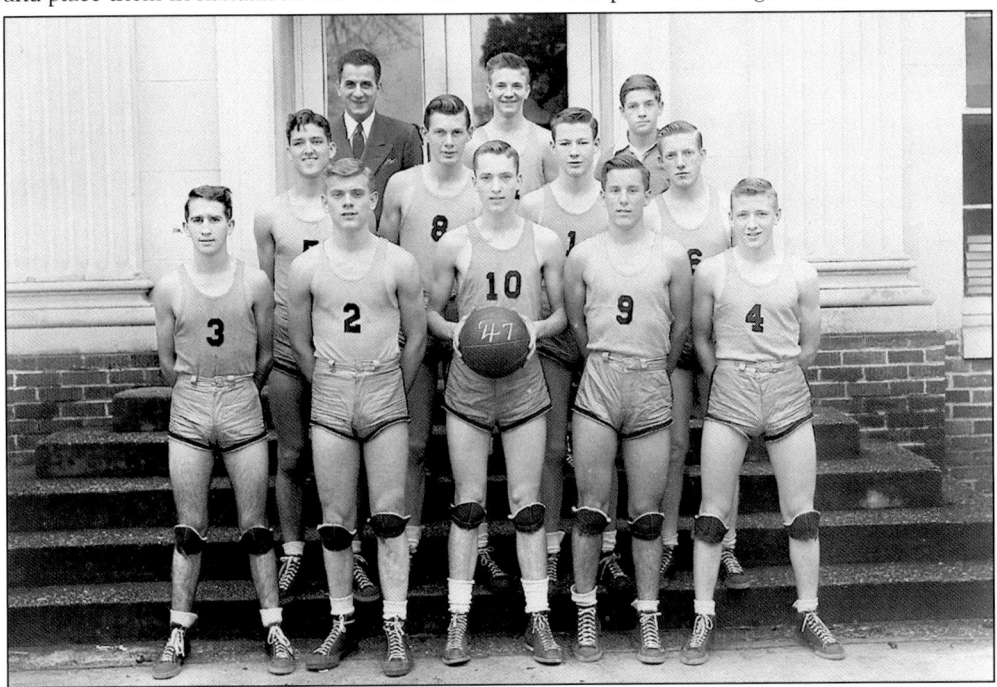

LINCOLNTON HIGH SCHOOL BOYS' BASKETBALL TEAM, 1947. In the uniforms of the 1940s, complete with protective kneepads, the Lincolnton High School boys' basketball team poses for a 1947 yearbook photograph. Members of the team and their positions are the following: Steve Gabriel, forward; Bill Beattie, forward; Gene Ross, forward; Jack Heavner, center; Junior Roach, center; Paul Baker, center; Neil Finger, guard; William Byers, guard; Leslie Elmore, guard; Charles Auten, guard; Shirley Gabriel, guard; Max Robinson, guard; Joe Billy Cornwell, guard; and Jim Babb, guard. A.M. Troianio was the team's coach, and Randolph Shives served as the team's manager.

41

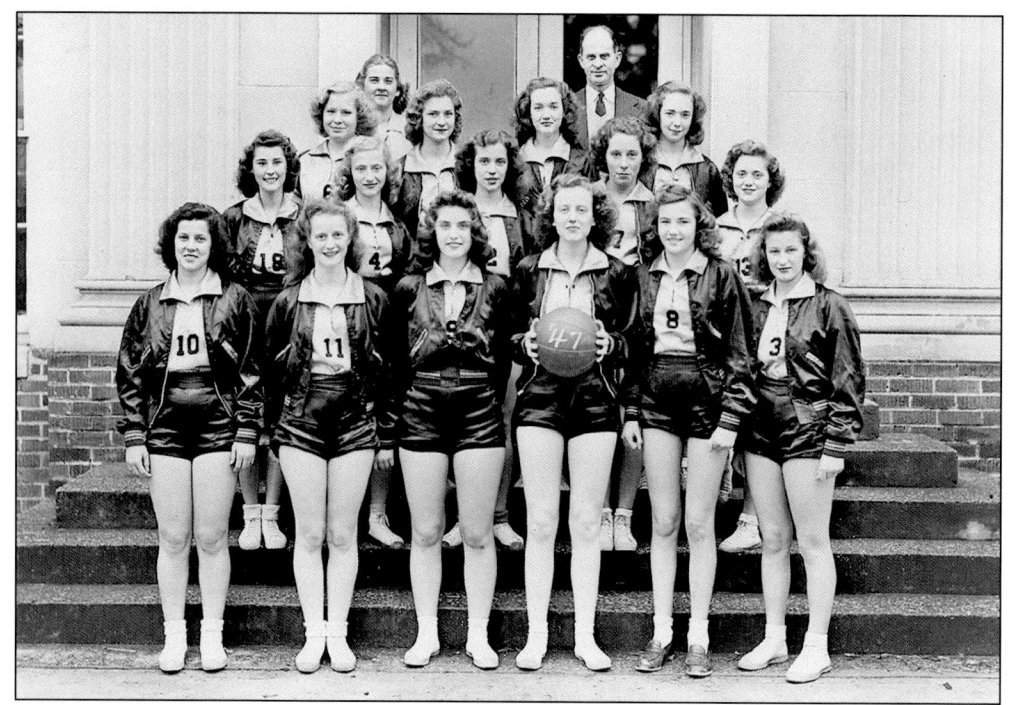

LINCOLNTON HIGH SCHOOL GIRLS' BASKETBALL TEAM, 1947. Coach Jack Kiser stands on the top stair above his team for this 1947 yearbook photo. Members of the team and their positions are the following: Betty Beattie, forward; Bernice McCurry, forward; Dean Smith, forward; Betty Reynolds, forward; Betty Laney, forward; Pat Cagle, forward; Daphine Johnson, forward; Betty Cornwell, guard; Betty Dellinger, guard; Betty Heavner, guard; Pat Shuford, guard; Betty Sue Beal, guard; Bobbie Jean Lockman, guard, and Betty Jean Ellis, guard. Elizabeth Ferguson served as the team's assistant coach.

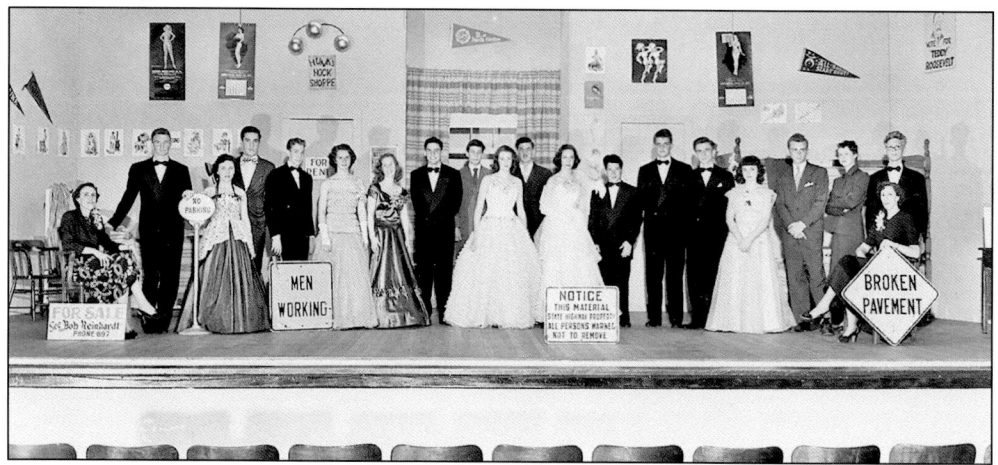

LINCOLNTON HIGH SCHOOL PLAY BEST FOOT FORWARD, APRIL 22, 1949. The cast of Lincolnton High School's play *Best Foot Forward* stand in their casting attire following Friday evening's performance on April 22, 1949. The played is centered around the boys' dormitory at Winsocki Prep School, where the students prepare to receive the girls who are visiting for the school's annual dance. Mary Whisonant and Sarah Yoder produced the play, with assistance from Sue Rhodes, Ann Fuller, Miller Nantz, Mrs. M.S. Beam, and Carrie Roseman.

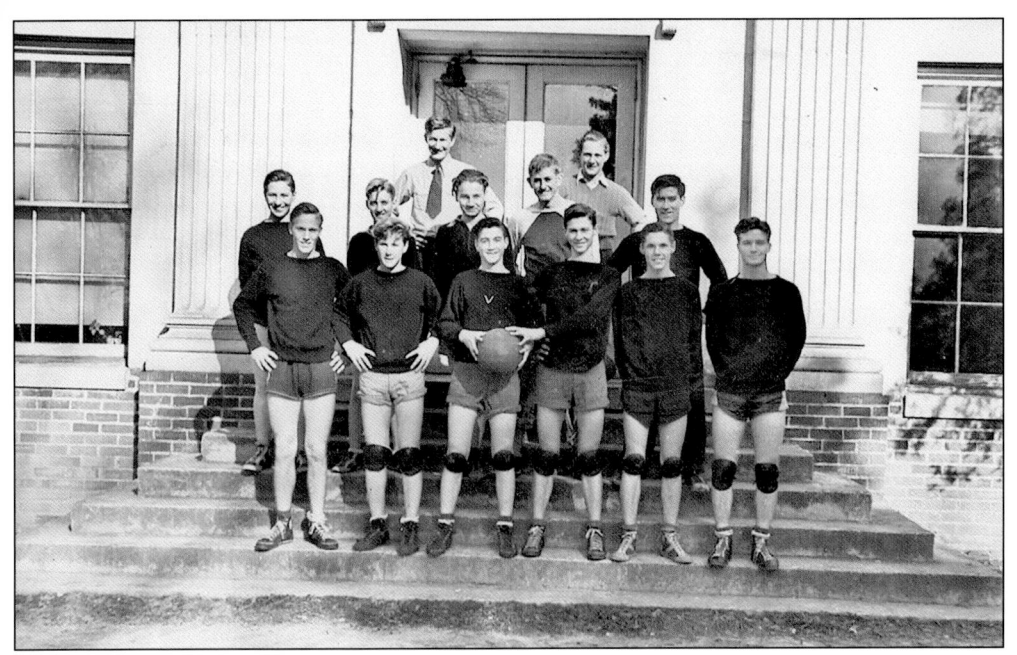

GAME TIME. The Lincolnton High School boys' basketball team stands poised and smiling for this Baby Ray Cornwell yearbook photograph, c. 1942. Team members are identified, from left to right, as follows: (front row) Bill Chapman, Ray Reinhardt, Charles Gabriel, Jack Yoder, Wade Dodgin, and Paul Gabriel; (middle row) Donald Clanton, Bill Yoder, Garmon Schrum, Buster Knight, and Oscar Elmore; (back row) Managers Junior Seagle and Cecil "Brat" Stroupe.

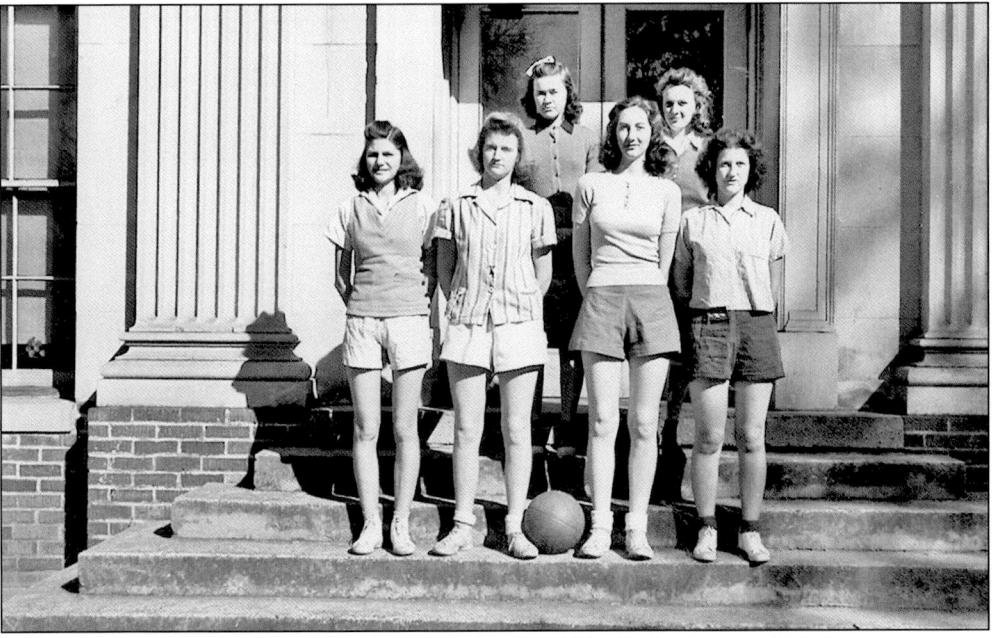

ALL IN THE WRIST. The Lincolnton High School girls' basketball team of 1942 chooses not to hold the ball for the team's photograph. The ladies of the basketball team are identified, from left to right, as follows: (front row) Helen Hallman, Betty Gabriel, Louise Devine, and Sue Baity; (back row) Helen Ross and Betty Biggerstaff.

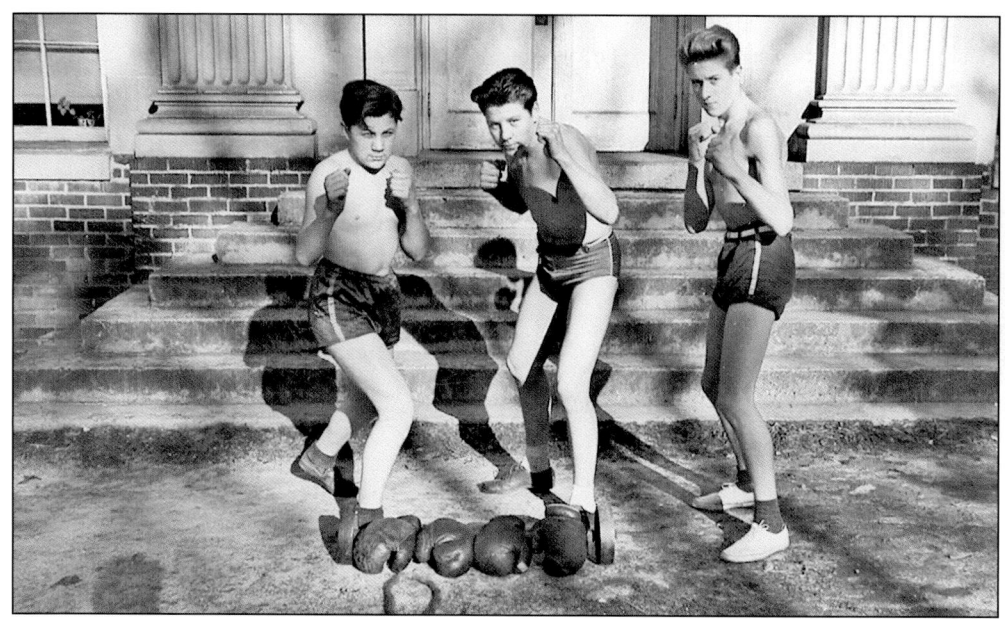

YOU WANNA GO. Three bare-fisted fighters from the Lincolnton High School boys' boxing team display a menacing growl in front of the school for this 1940s photograph. Baby Ray Cornwell's shadow can be seen the lower left-hand side of the photograph. The boxing team members are Rathmul Helms, Bill Milburn, and Walter Lineberger.

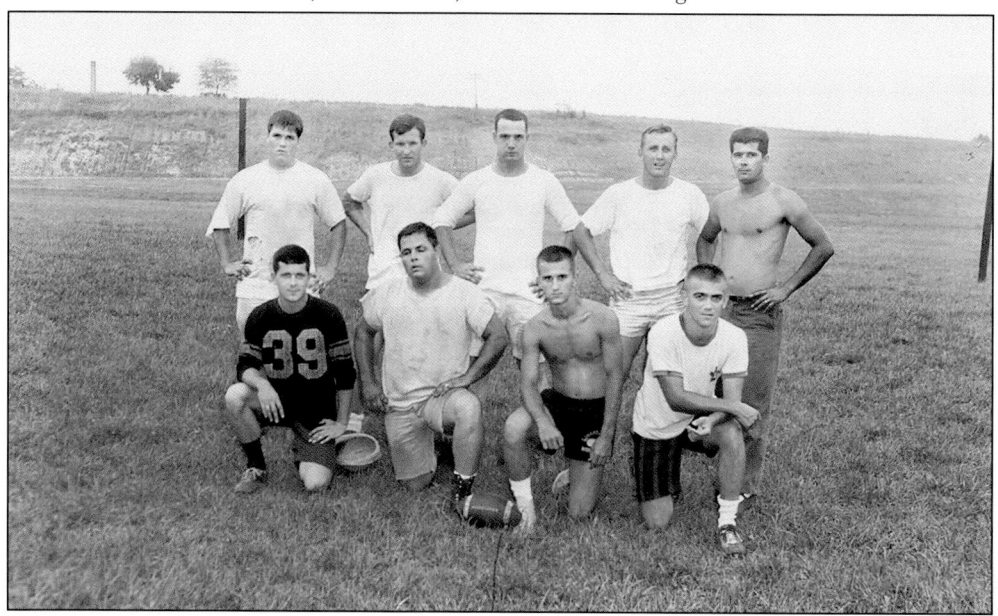

JAYCEES ALUMNI PLAYERS. On August 14, 1964, the local Jaycees sponsored an alumni football game at Lincolnton High School's Battleground Stadium. Lincolnton High School's 1961 and 1963 conference championship teams squared off to raise money for the stadium fund. Players shown in this photograph are, from left to right, as follows: (front row) Eddie Hovis, Nelson Beam, Rodney Dedmon, and Bob Beal; (back row) John Gorbin, Don James, Butch Hallman, Roby Jetton, and Larry Hovis. Those players not in attendance are Harold Billings, Judson Devine, John Froneberger, Jerry Barkley, Steve Gantt, and Rafe Howell.

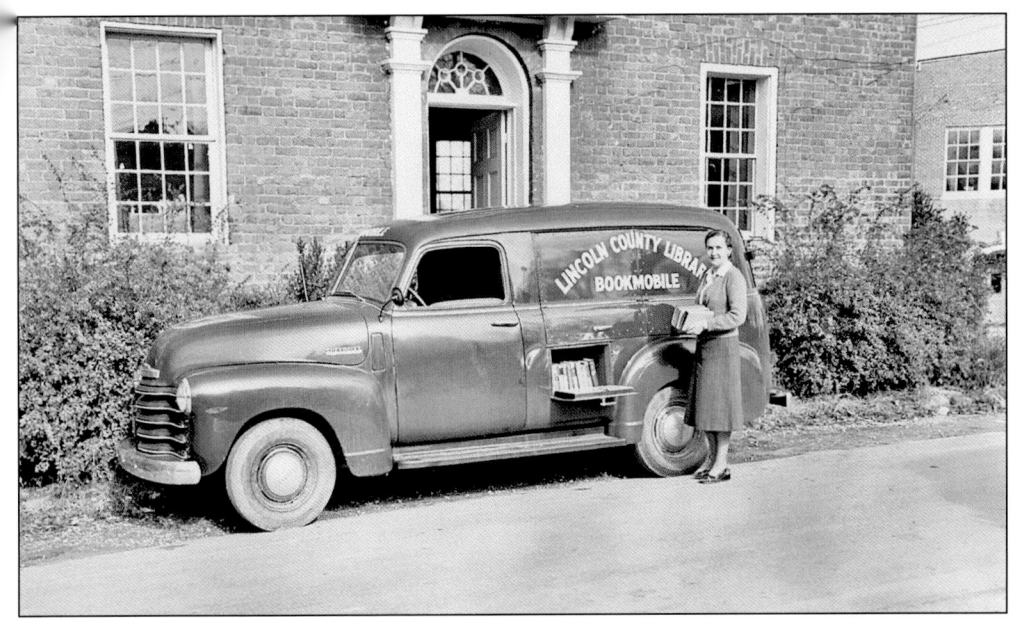

Mrs. Estelle Ross and the Library Bookmobile, 1948. Librarian Estelle C. Ross stands beside the first county-owned bookmobile for this photograph captured by her brother, Baby Ray Cornwell. The bookmobile participated in the Lincolnton Christmas parade in 1948 and was on display at the library following the parade. The county purchased the vehicle through state aid and offered adult fiction, adult nonfiction, and fiction, nonfiction, and magazines for children.

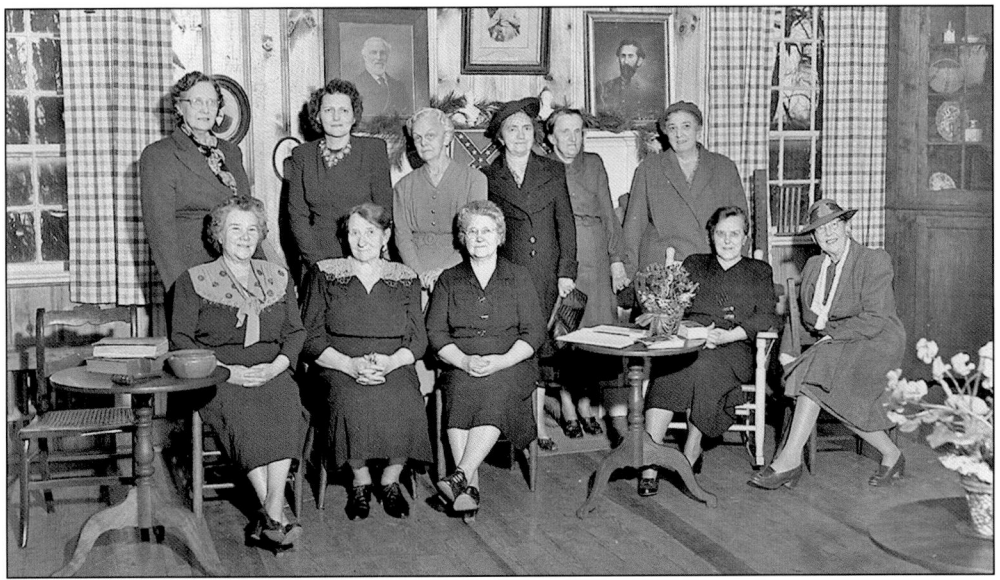

Ladies of the UDC. In January 1949 a group of Lincolnton's distinguished ladies associated with the United Daughters of the Confederacy gathered to pose for this image. This shot, taken by Baby Ray on the second floor of the library in the UDC's meeting area, includes, from left to right, the following: (front row) Lena Graham, Mrs. Heim Hoover, Mary Shuford, Mrs. Paul Rhyne, and unidentified; (back row) unidentified, Ruby Miller, Myra Sumner, unidentified, Addie Barineau, and Mrs. Miller.

45

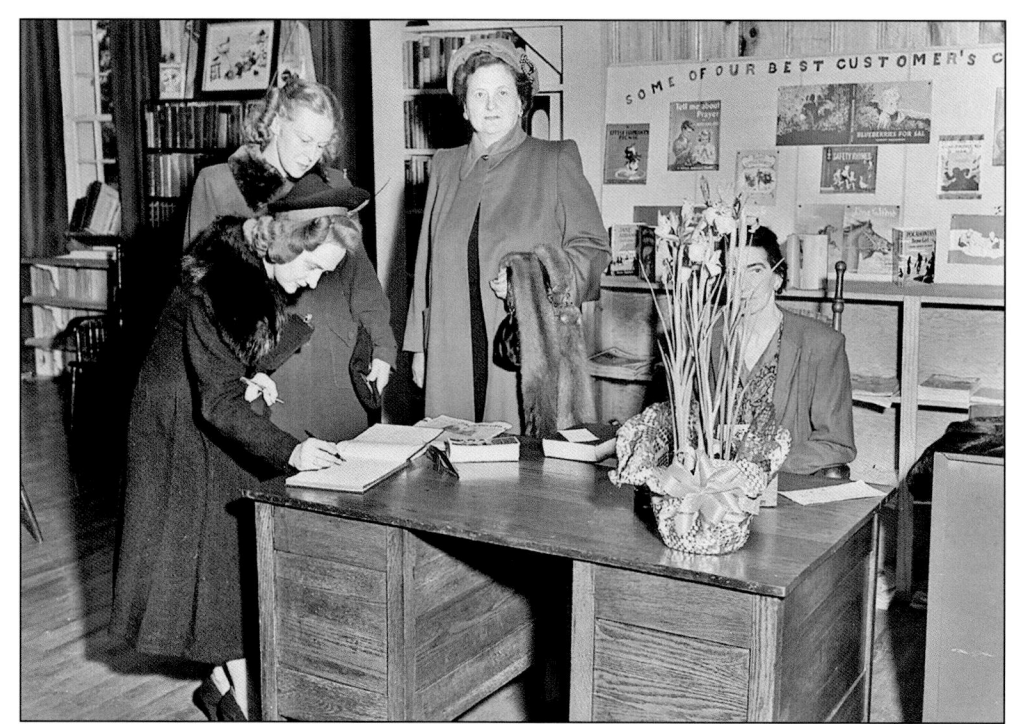

TWENTY-FOUR YEARS OPEN. On January 15, 1949, Rubylee Cline and Virginia Rhyne sign the guestbook as the library's special event, 24 Years Open, is captured by Baby Ray Cornwell. Mrs. John Cline (standing) looks on from the behind the desk where librarian Frances Fair sits and waits to assist Lincolntonians with possible reading selections. On this special day, the library held an open house from 3:00 to 5:00 p.m.

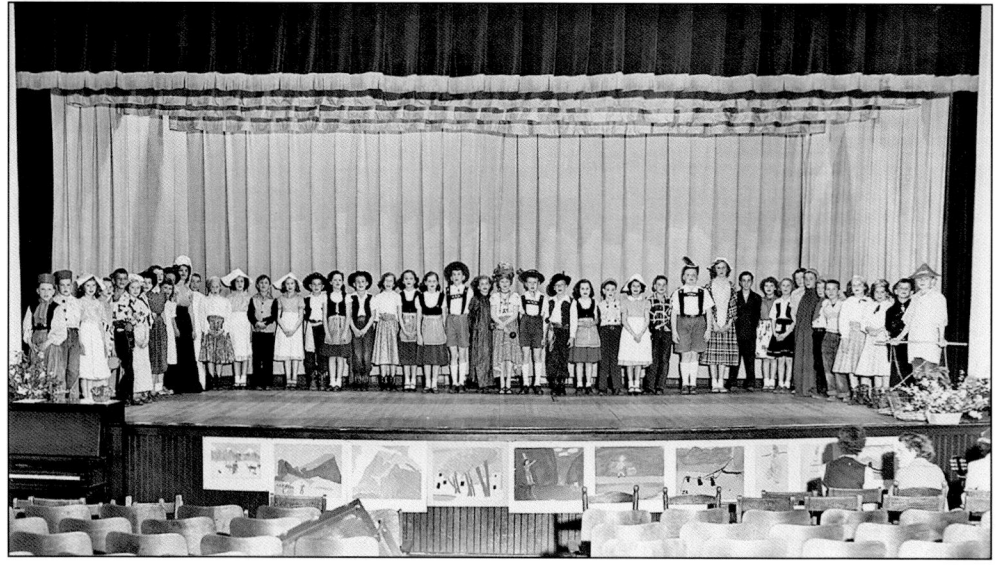

DRESSED FOR THE OCCASION. Captured by Baby Ray on April 4, 1952, two ladies are shown talking in the bottom right hand corner as student of Lincolnton's Grammar School pose for their picture. The grammar school students from several classes presented artwork and wore costumes that represented various cultures from around the world.

DOWN, SET . . . In 1942 LHS class historian Helen Wise wrote, "As we face the outside world there is a mingled feeling of regret in our hearts, as we think of trying our wings in a broad, open world and leaving behind us forever the sheltered friendliness of our high school years." This same year Cecil "Brat" Stroupe prepared for an action-packed year of football. Shown in this photograph, taken sometime between 1942 and 1944, Brat Stroupe poses in a three-point stance. As a Lincolnton High School football player, Brat carried the pigskin as a tailback on offense and roamed the defensive side of the ball as a linebacker. He played in the 1944 Shrine Bowl, when North Carolina's team overtook an equally formidable team from South Carolina. He left for World War II in 1944 to serve in the Pacific for the navy on a destroyer escort. Upon returning to Lincolnton, Brat took a post-graduate class and played one more season of football.

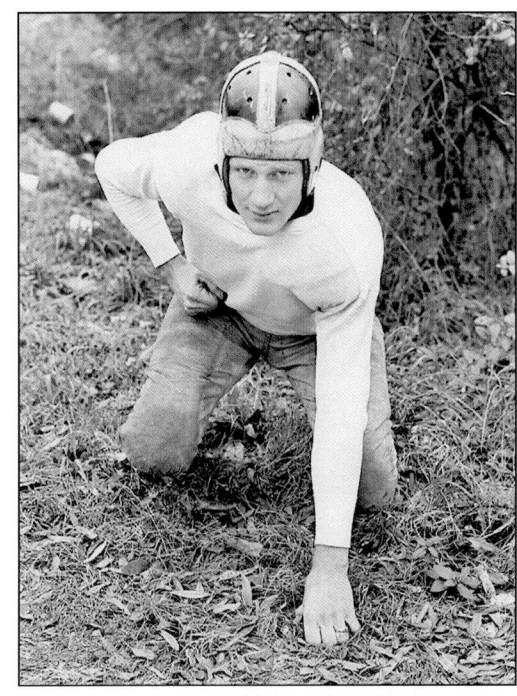

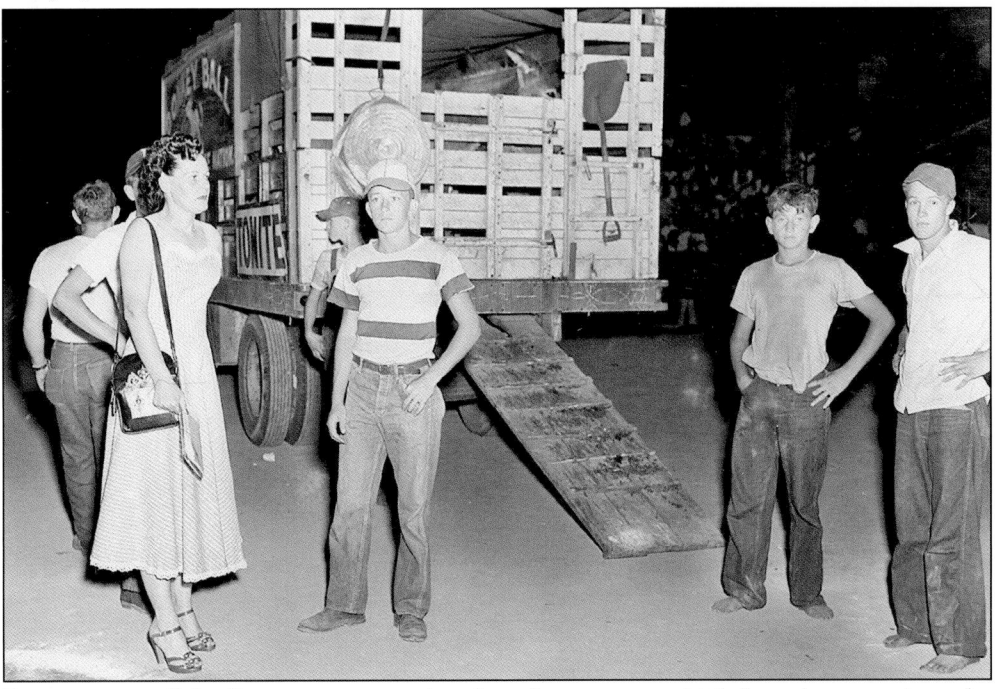

FUND-RAISER. Baby Ray captures two barefooted young men (right) as they peer into the camera anxiously awaiting the guest of honor—a donkey. On this evening in 1949, folks in Lincolnton held a Donkey Ball Game as a local fund-raiser. Hauled into the stadium in a truck labeled "Donkey Ball—Tonite," the donkey provided more than just the entertainment. One of the most memorable games in Lincolnton history featured Judge Sheldon M. Roper falling off the donkey and shattering the bones in his elbow.

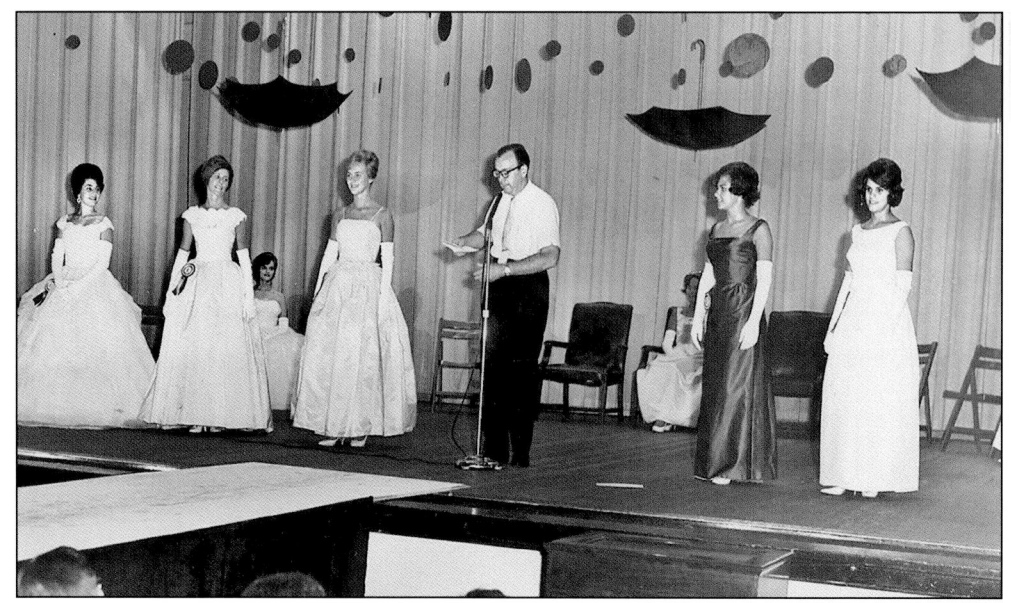

DOUG MAYS AND MISS LINCOLN COUNTY PAGEANT FINALISTS. Doug Mays, WBTV Channel 3 television personality and master of ceremonies, stands behind the microphone for the Miss Lincoln County Beauty Contest on August 22, 1964, held at Lincolnton High School. Sponsored by the local Jaycees, the pageant featured, from left to right, the following finalists: Vicki Turner, Betsy Mullen, Sandra Lucas, Peggy Helton, and Fondra Sherrill. Vicki Turner was awarded the 1965 Miss Lincoln County crown.

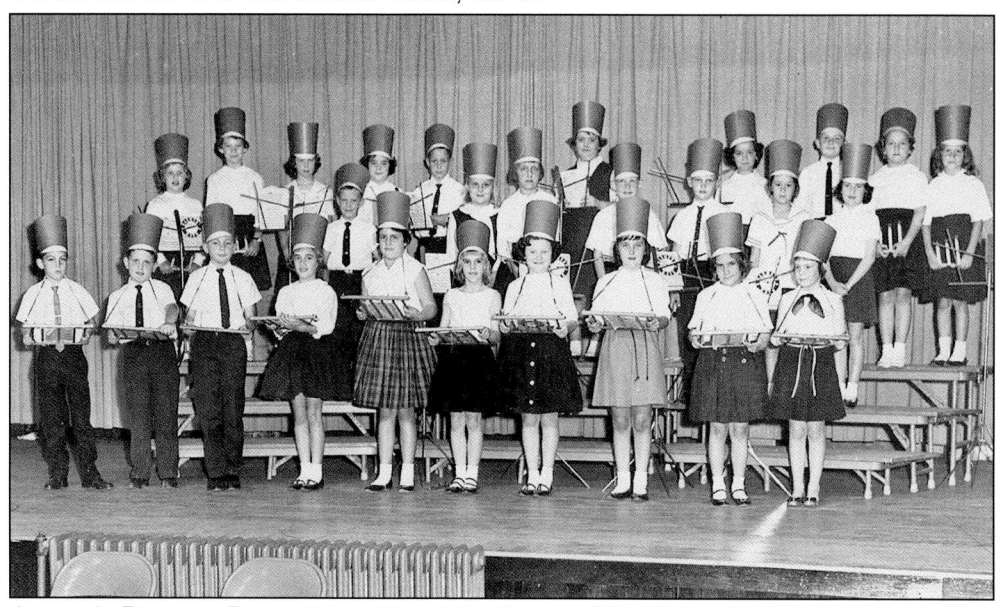

ASBURY'S RHYTHM BAND, MAY 21, 1964. Organized by Mrs. W.B. Goodson, the Asbury Elementary School's Rhythm Band stands equipped with both instruments and well-suited outfits for a Talent Night on Thursday, May 21, 1964. During the talent show Mrs. Goodson was sick at Crowell Hospital, and the band wanted Baby Ray Cornwell capture the moment for her. In addition, the students had a recording made of their performance to play for Mrs. Goodson during her hospital stay.

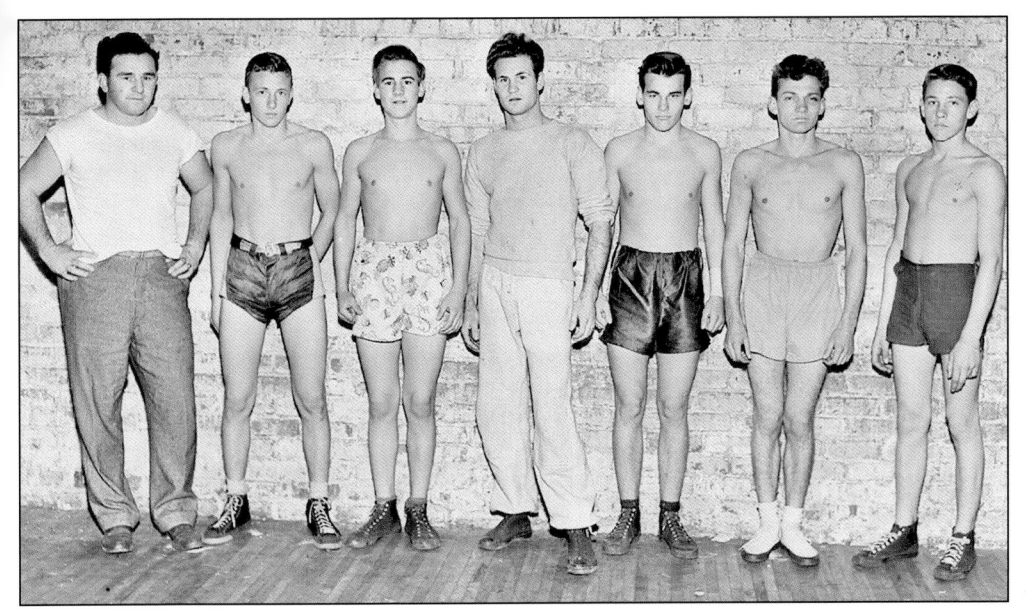

THE BEST OF THE BEST. Coach Arnold Tarr and six golden gloves boxers from Lincolnton pose for this photograph as they prepare for Charlotte's Golden Gloves Tournament February 13–17, 1947. Coach Tarr was a former Golden Gloves Champion in the middleweight division, and he predicted that he would "bring at least one and maybe two champions back to Lincolnton" after the tournament. The boxers are identified, from left to right, as follows: Coach Arnold Tarr, Steve Gabriel, Joe Fortenberry, Ray Little, Rathmul Helms, Carl Rudisill, and Jim Carter.

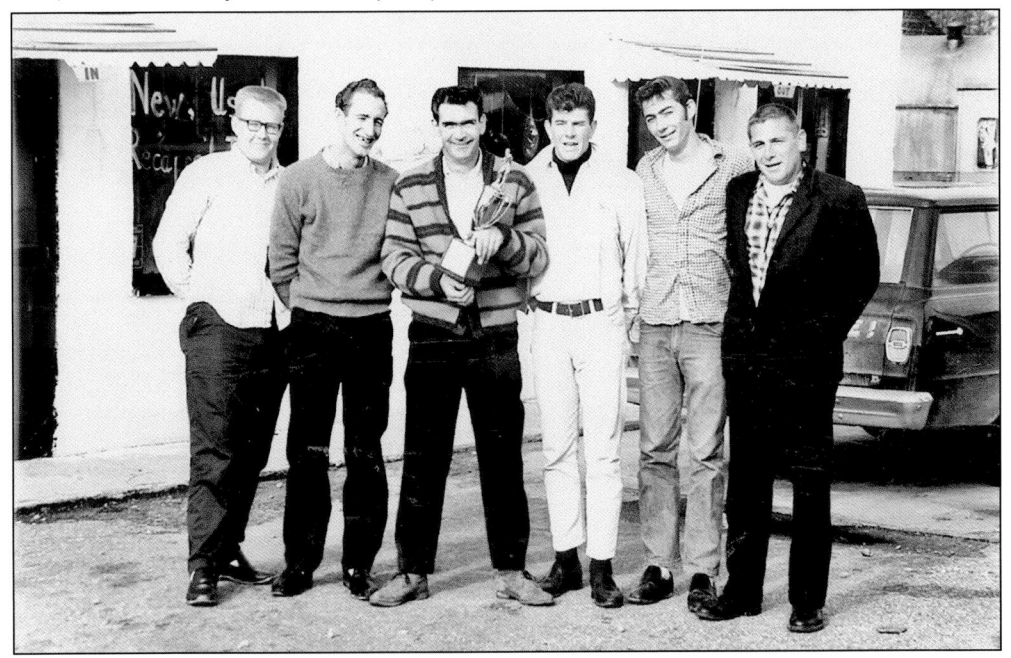

SIX PACK. A prized trophy held by Jim Bost spawns ear-to-ear smiles from the Bear Ridge Boxing Team in 1965. Baby Ray Cornwell chose the Bear Ridge Pure Oil sign as a suitable backdrop for his photograph session. Members of the boxing team are identified, from left to right, as Junior Keener, Jerry McGill, Jim Bost, Johnnie Houser, Ronnie Houser, and Bruce Martin.

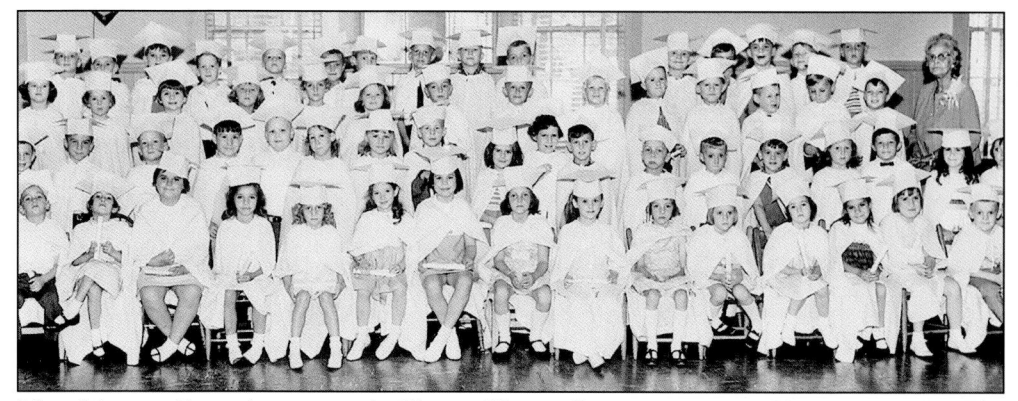

MISS MATTIE LOU ALEXANDER'S HAPPY HOUR COMMENCEMENT, MAY 16, 1967. The members of Miss Mattie Lou's commencement exercise, held at St. Luke's Episcopal Church are, in no order, as follows: David Gibson, David McKinnon, Dale Finger, David Harrill, Chuck Lippard, John Mark Beam, Jeffrey Peek, Kenny Dodgin, Larry Houser, Mart Plaxico, Alan Reid, Kirk Houser, Todd White, Robin Houser, Donald Reynolds, Tommy Ewing, Conrad Paysour, Daniel Boyd, Jerry Owen, Chad Saine, Ricky Keener, Gregg Houser, Barry Schronce, Don Pendleton, Van Chapman, Billy Henkel, Lynn Hedgspeth, Jimmy Eury, Todd Rash, Gregg Mosteller, Kenneth Gregory, Charles Jones, Nathan Smith, Larry Waynick, Keith Heavner, Beau Hodge, David Beaver, Betty Carter, Sara Friday, Charlotte Rhyne, Donna Mosteller, Leah Wilkinson, Anita Smith, Billie Watts, Sara Cronland, Tammy Cannon, Lisa Sherrill, Ellen Freeman, June Smith, Crystal Dameron, Leslie Rhyne, Connie Bradshaw, Paula Saine, Debbie Hawkins, Robin Propst, Paula Self, Dianne Thomas, Susan Snipes, Jane Blackwell, Rhoda Drum, Susan Robinson, Heather Huitt, and Jeri Jordan.

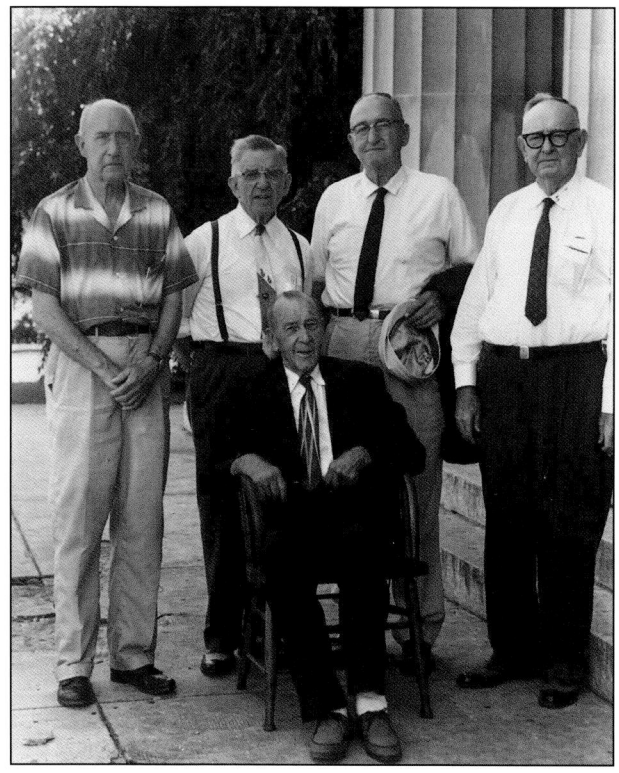

GRIDIRON GREATS. Five of Lincolnton's first football players gather at the Lincoln County Courthouse in Lincolnton to have a photography session with Baby Ray Cornwell on August 31, 1960. Joe B. Johnston, operator of Lincolnton's ice plant, recruited the "biggest and strongest young men in Lincolnton" for a game with Catawba College in 1907. The newly organized Lincolnton team only had baseball uniforms to wear for the game. Members of the team shown in the photograph are, from left to right, as follows: Jim Shuford, Vaughan Padgett, Howard Leonard, Kemp Nixon, and Frank Ramseur (seated). Members of the team not pictured were Bob Hinson, Barron F. Caldwell, Oscar Shuford, and Mason Pressley.

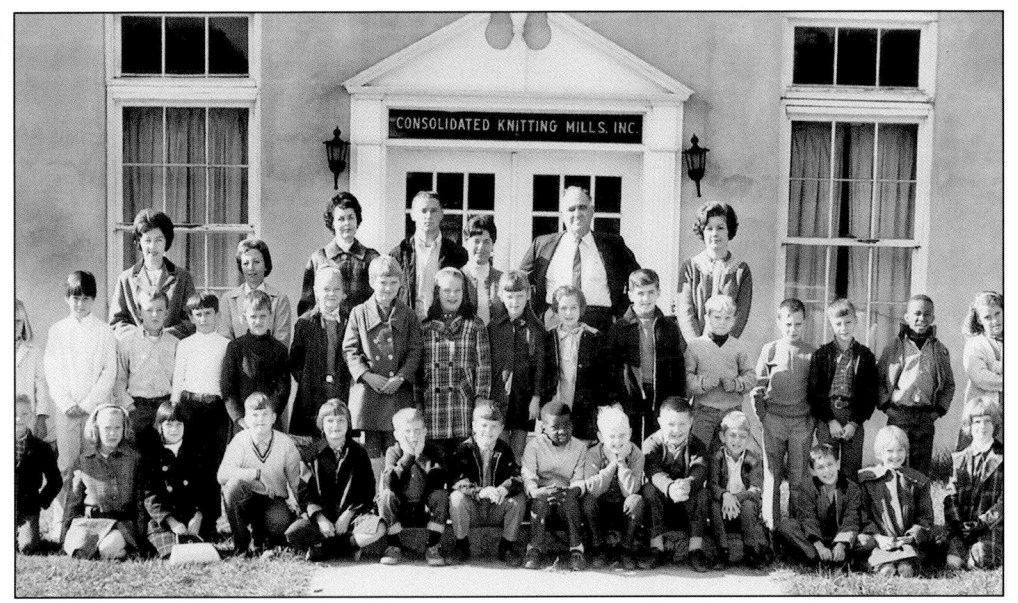

Rock Springs School's Field Trip, October 30, 1968. Students from Rock Springs School in Denver (Lincoln County), North Carolina enjoyed a field trip to Long Shoals on October 20, 1968. Baby Ray Cornwell photographed the group and their "room mother," teacher Karen Johnson, in front of Consolidated Knitting Mills. Consolidated Knitting Mills president E.E. Suttle is included in photograph wearing a shirt and tie.

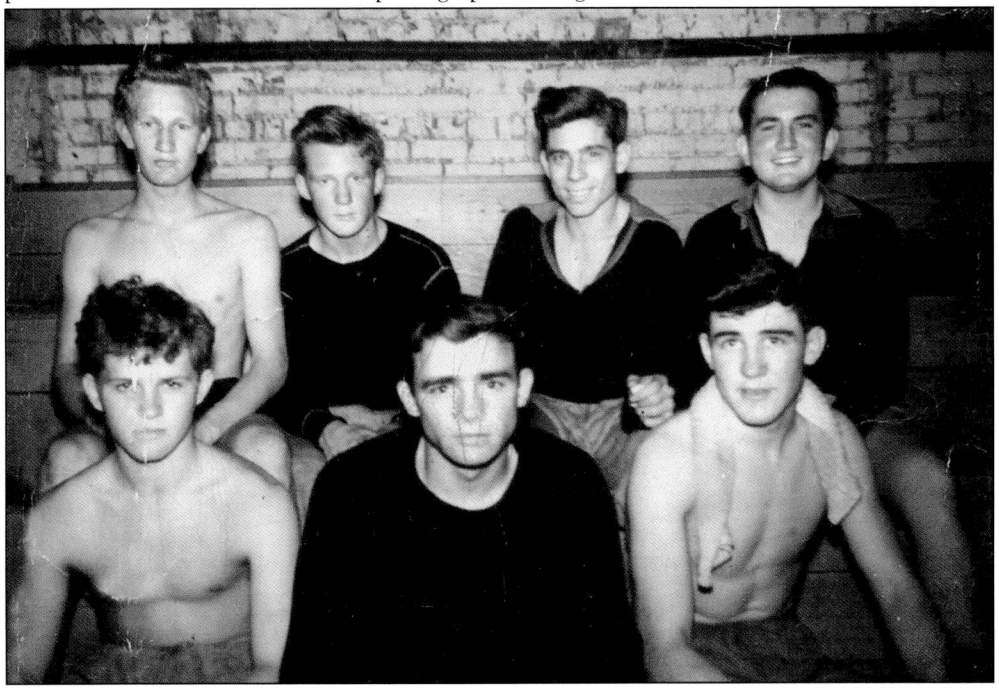

Prize Fighters. A group of prize fighters from Lincolnton pose for Baby Ray's camera after a workout. The 1942 Golden Gloves Team members are identified, from left to right, as follows: (front row) W.C. Cornwell, Jack Dellinger, and Ralph Connor; (back row) Junior Seagle, Cecil "Brat" Stroupe, Herbert Lester, and Bud Warlick. (Courtesy of Jack L. and Carolyn Dellinger.)

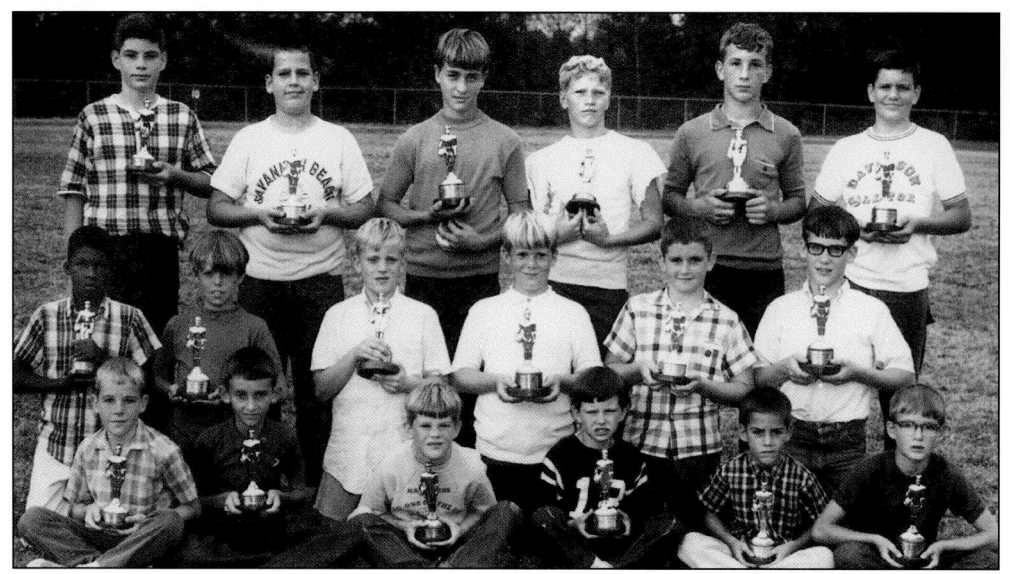

EIGHTH ANNUAL PP&K EVENT. On Sunday, October 13, 1968, 137 boys participated in the eighth annual Punt, Pass, and Kick Event at Memorial Stadium. Hoyle Motor Company and the Lincolnton Sports Boosters Club sponsored the event, which featured six divisions for boys ages 8 to 13. The first place winners from the Lincoln County competition advanced to the zone competition at Bryant Park in Charlotte the following week. The first place winners from the group shown above were Jeffrey Harrill, Mark Medlin, David Eaker, Jonathan Rhyne, Robert Pope, and John Shuford.

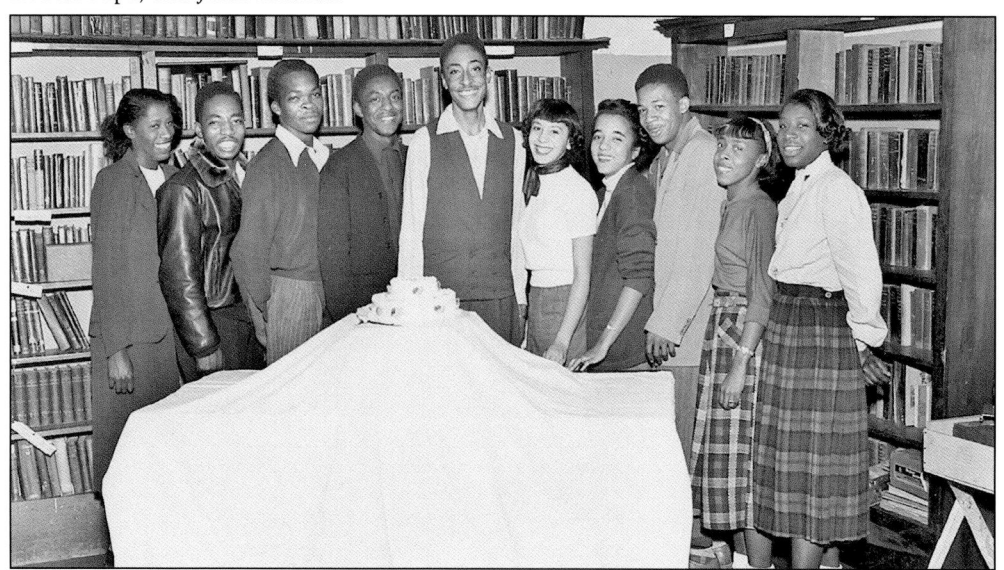

A NEW BEGINNING. In April 1952 the Newbold High School Class of 1952 became the last graduating class of Oaklawn High School and the first graduating class of Newbold High School. Not only was the group embarking on a new course in their young lives, but they set a new course for Lincolnton's African-American community. Members of the graduating class of 1952 are identified, from left to right, as follows: Gwendolyn Lewis, Haywood Killian, Sherman Davis, Frank Cobb, Ervin Reinhardt, Emma Hill, Jane Beam, Hugh Herndon, Hattie Cobb, and Erma True Lewis.

Three
SUN UP TO SUN DOWN

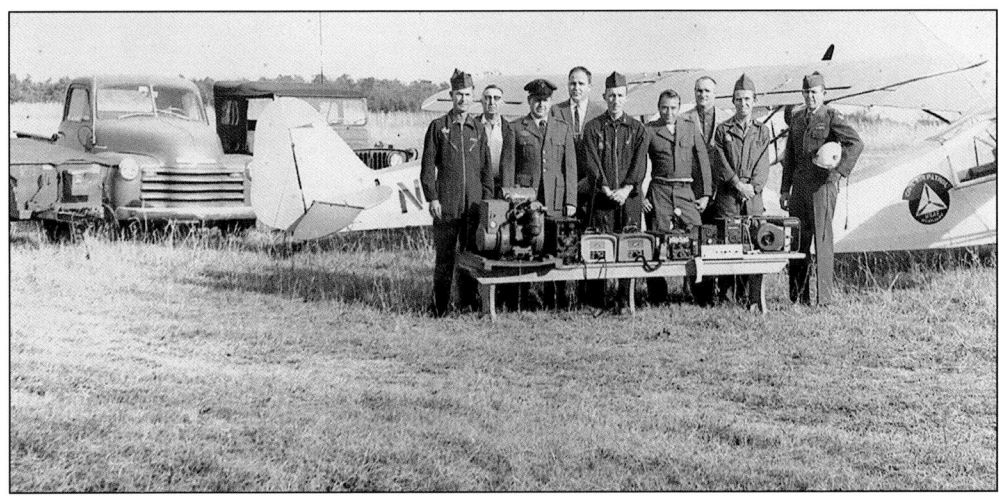

FLYING HIGH. Members of the Boger City Civil Air Patrol Unit stand in front of their planes while Baby Ray Cornwell photographs them. Taken on November 20, 1960, the photograph commemorates the 19th anniversary of this unit. Members of the unit are identified, from left to right, as follows: (front row) James Long, first lieutenant and commanding officer; Floyd Painter, captain; Mack Glover, executive officer; John Painter, second lieutenant; Archie Causey, and Ralph Sisk, second lieutenant; (back row) J.J. Canipe; W.A. Abernethy, second lieutenant; and Joe Chaffin.

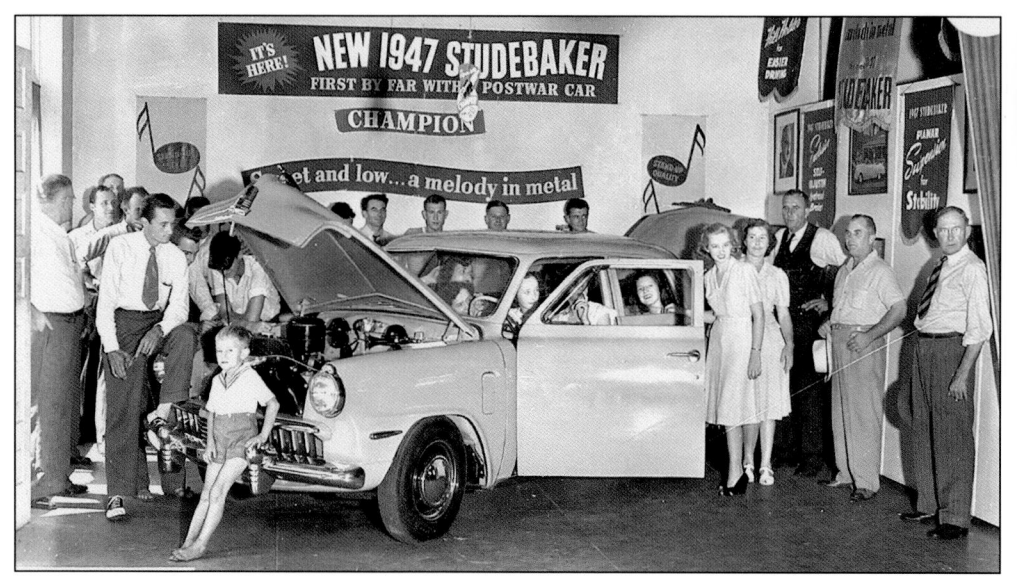

YOU SEE MORE . . . YOU GET MORE. Piedmont Motor Company included this catchy slogan in their local newspaper advertisements during 1947. Piedmont Motor Company, located on South Academy Street in downtown Lincolnton, finds a large group of excited and anxious car buyers in their showroom as Baby Ray Cornwell captures the "thrilling new postwar Studebaker."

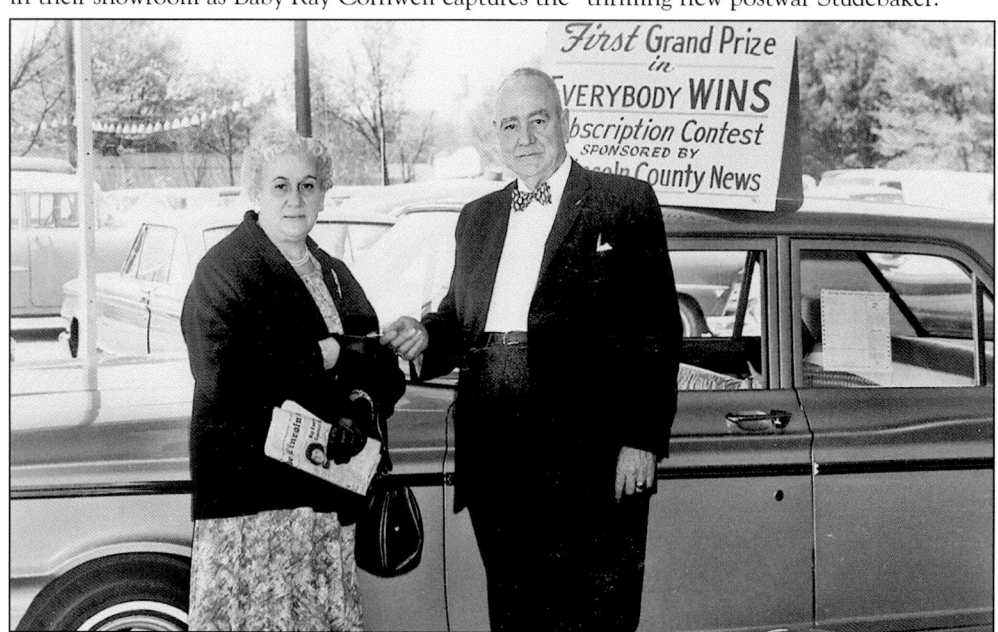

THE LINCOLN COUNTY NEWS EVERYBODY WINS SUBSCRIPTION CONTEST. On Friday morning of April 12, 1963, Alton Claytor, publisher for *The Lincoln County News*, presents Mrs. B.M. Bolinger the keys to a new 1964 Ford Fairlane Sedan. The car, the grand prize of the "Everybody Wins" contest, was designed by Liner Circulation Services and their manager Mrs. Ural Everett to increase new and renewal subscriptions to the paper. Other prize winners in the contest include the following: Mrs. Marvin S. Beam, who received a $750 check for second place; Mrs. Henry Huss, third; Mrs. C.L. Lineberger, fourth; Mrs. Hettie Locke Johnson, fifth; and Mrs. W.B. Roberts, sixth.

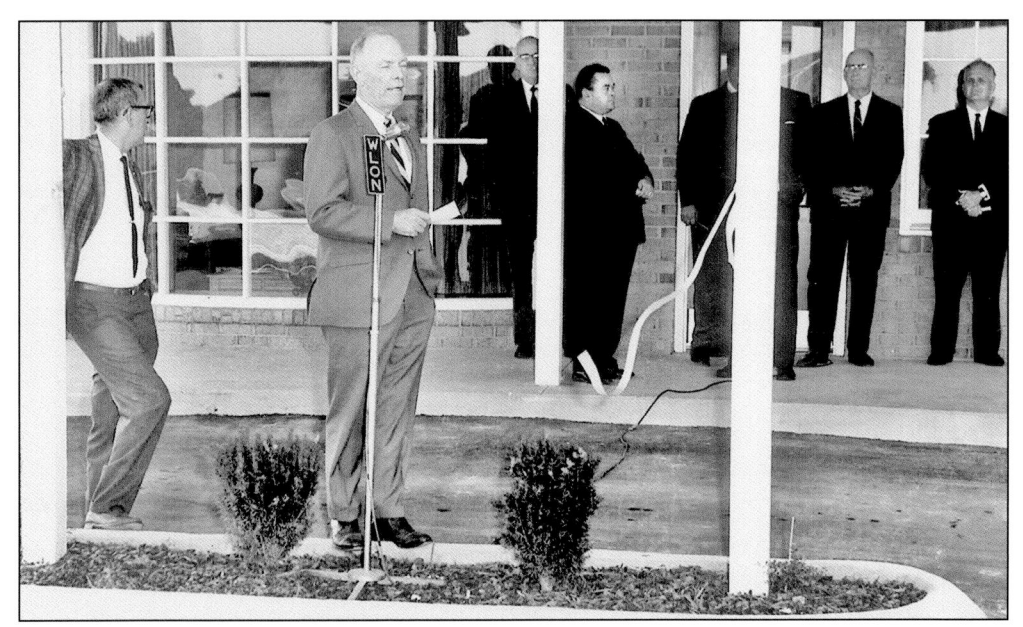

TOWN AND COUNTRY INN RIBBON CUTTING CEREMONY, THURSDAY, SEPTEMBER 14, 1967. Mayor William M. "Buster" Lentz speaks into a WLON microphone during the ribbon-cutting ceremony held at the Town and Country Inn in Lincolnton. To construct their motel, the inn's owners utilized funds from the Small Business Administration (SBA). In addition to Mayor Lentz, a number of other officials attended the ceremony, including David Clark; Ray Shaw, regional coordinator of the SBA; Herman Howard; Howard McKenzie, regional director of the SBA; Hal Hoyle Jr.; J.L. Beam, architect; Grier Beam; Hal Hoyle Sr.; Dr. John Gamble; and S. Ray Lowder.

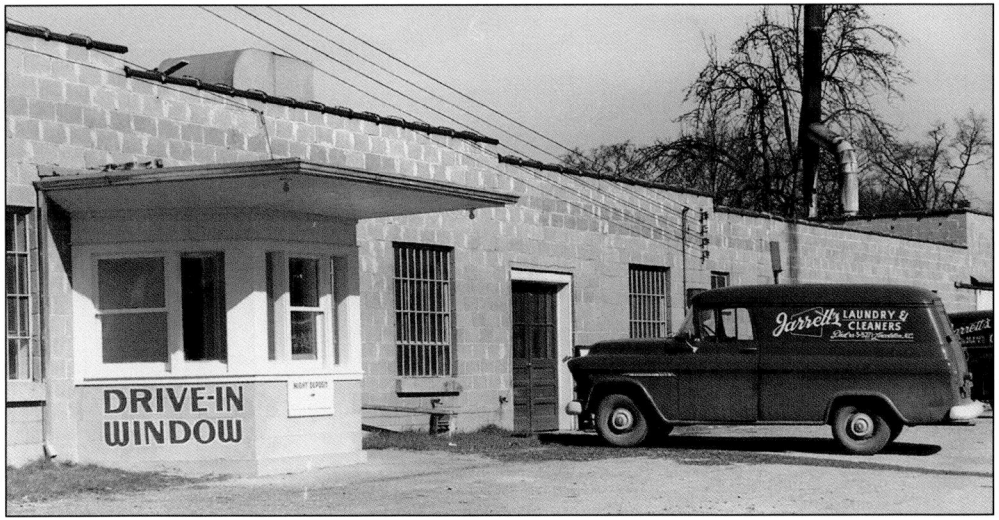

SPIC 'N SPAN. Jarrett's Laundry of Lincolnton was founded in the 1950s when C.C. Jarrett bought out Lincoln Dry Cleaners on the west side of South Academy Street. The photograph above was taken c. 1955. From the early days of the operation until 1990, Jarrett's Laundry and Cleaners owned the only cold storage vault between Hickory and Charlotte, and they used this to store valuable furs. Fred Jarrett, son of C.C. Jarrett, grew up in the business, delivering clothes in a Model-A Ford during high school. He still operates the business at the same location today.

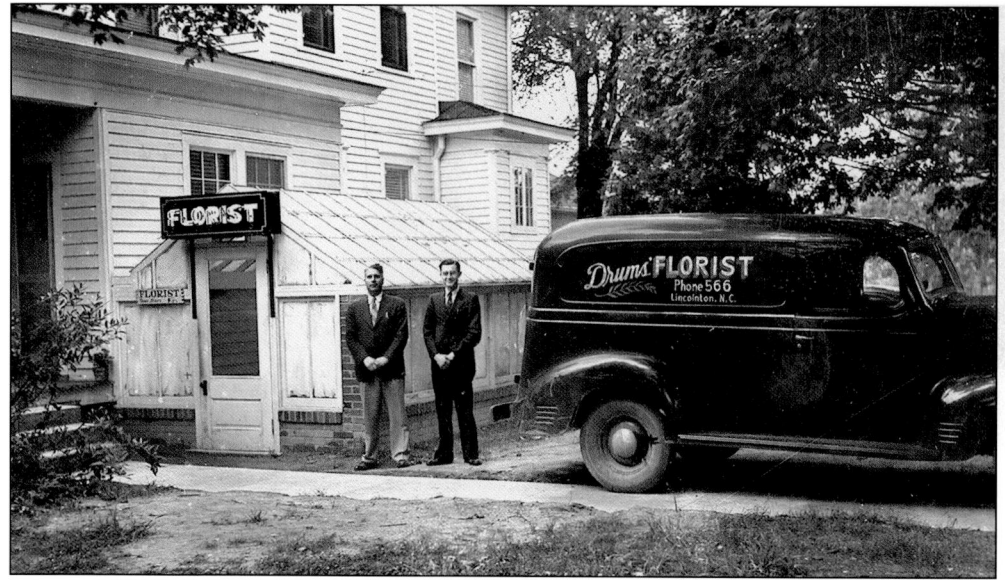

DIAL 566 FOR FLOWERS. E.F. Drum (left) and an unidentified man stand ready to deliver beautiful flowers to a local Lincolnton resident. The staff at Drum's Florist during the 1940s and 1950s included Florence Proctor, Mrs. T.V. Lineberger, Mrs. Bryan Dellinger, and Mrs. E.F. Drum. The home just to the left of the florist is Drum's Funeral Home, owned and operated by Mr. E.F. Drum. E.F. Drum, the son of A.S. and Blanche Drum, was born in Catawba County on November 11, 1904. He opened the funeral home in Lincolnton after working for the Maiden Chair Company and Goodin-Drum Furniture Factory.

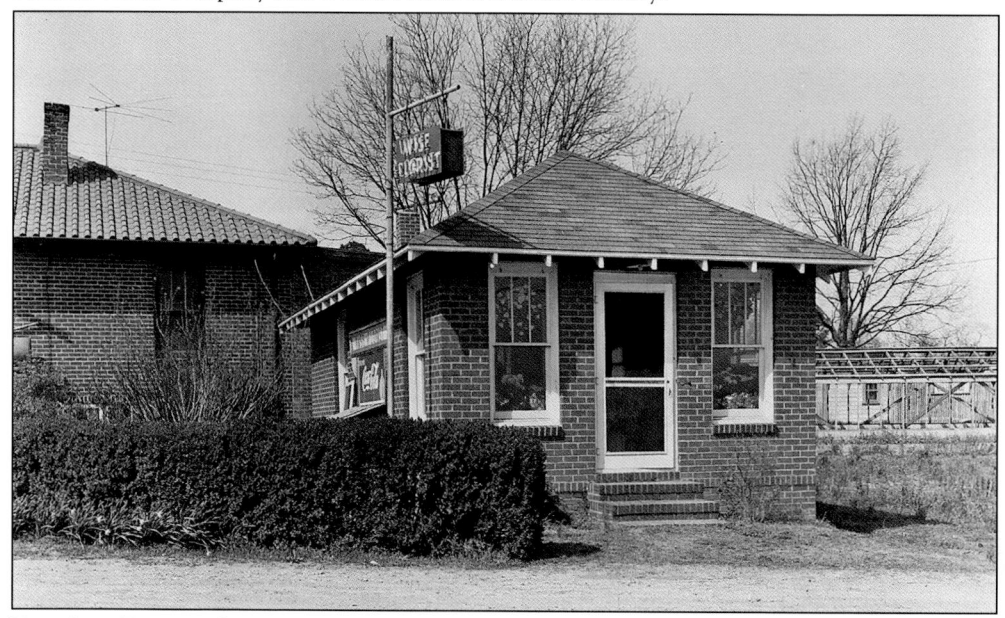

FOR ANY FESTIVE OCCASION. Wise Florist stands along Highway 27 east in Lincoln County ready to provide the finest flowers imaginable. Located on the same corner as the Wise Tourist Court (a grouping of small one-room motels), Wise Florist dressed many chapels and churches for weddings and other special occasions in Lincolnton. Blanche Wise (1907–1985) owned and operated Wise Florist, which is now part of Gas Station Antiques.

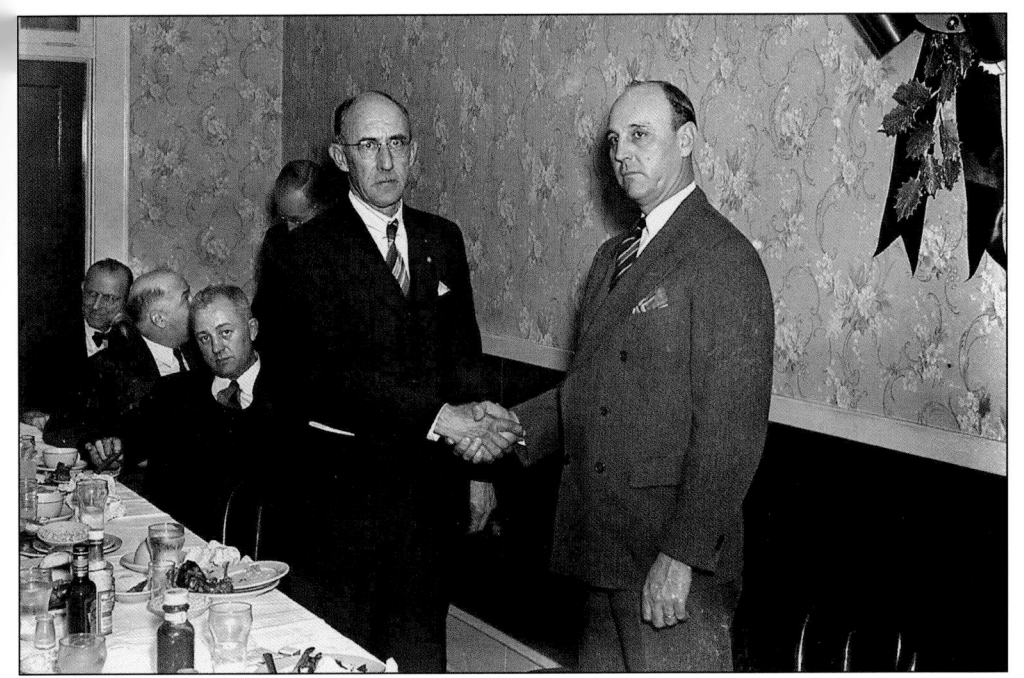

Good to See You. James "Jim" Shuford, Lincolnton's first electrician, shakes the hand of G.W. Myrick (right) at the Bell Telephone Dinner in the 1940s. The officials of Bell Telephone chose the dining room at Lincolnton's North State Hotel for this dinner with their city and county officials.

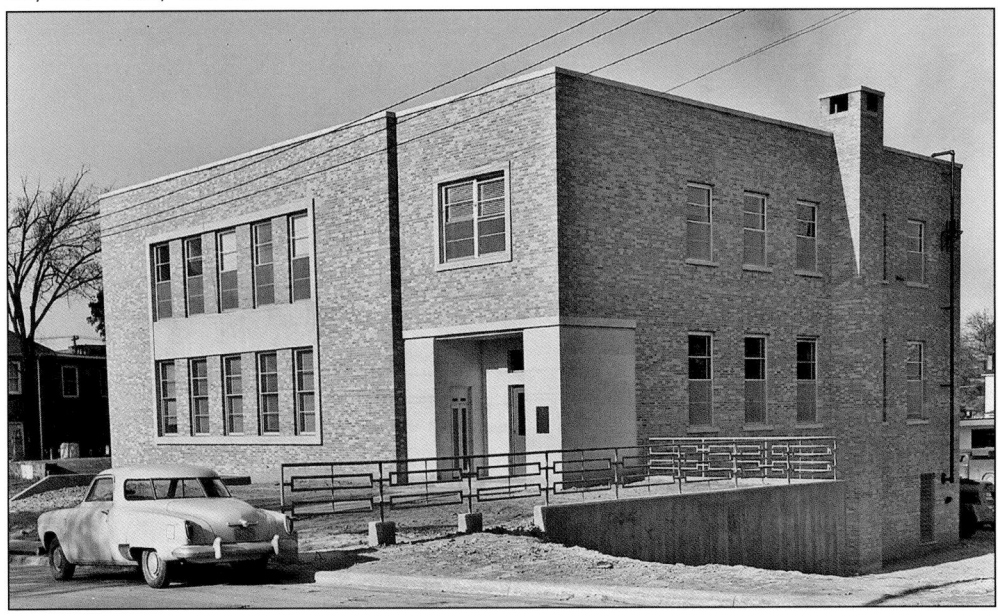

Making the Call. The Southern Bell building, located on South Aspen Street in Lincolnton, is part of Baby Ray Cornwell's collection of images featuring local business and industry. Dated March 27, 1953, this photograph shows the building in its early years. When Southern Bell constructed their Lincolnton office building, they had to relocate graves and stones from the Emanuel Lutheran Church Cemetery (Old White Church) to the back of the plot.

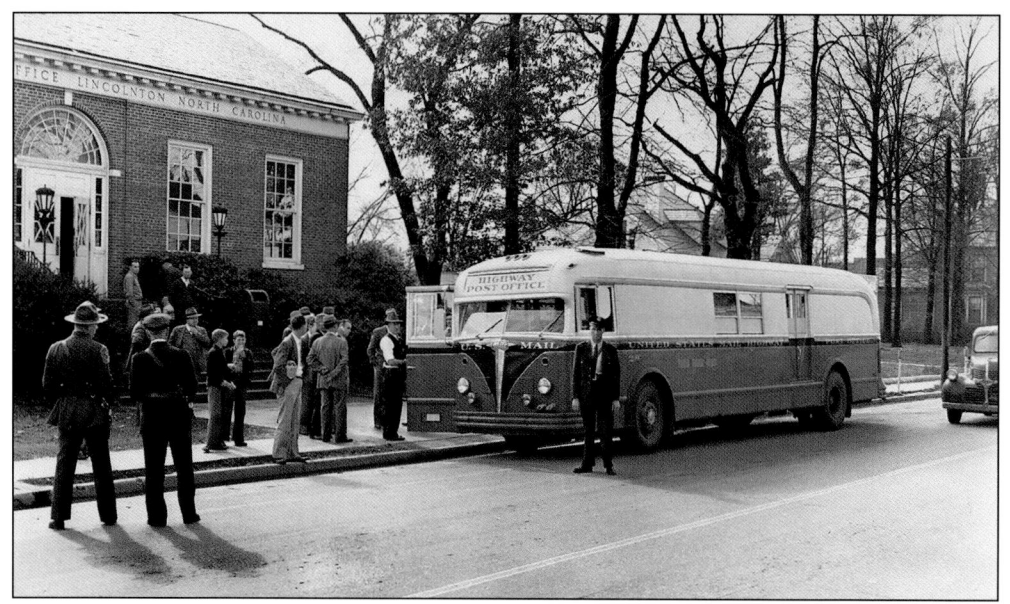

THROUGH RAIN, SLEET, OR SNOW. Joe Biggerstaff, Lincolnton city policeman, stares at Baby Ray Cornwell's camera with an authoritative gaze for this 1940s photograph. The Lincolnton Post Office opened on Monday, May 17, 1937, and was built by the Bonded Construction Company of New York of stone, brick, and steel. The building, located on East Main Street at the former site of the Childs home, was constructed at a cost of $65,000 and measured 58 by 45 feet. Rep. A.L. Bulwinkle of the 10th Congressional District worked diligently to see that Lincolnton was the first to receive a new building, ahead of Kings Mountain, Newton, and Belmont. A 7,094-square-foot addition was made to the post office building in August 1964.

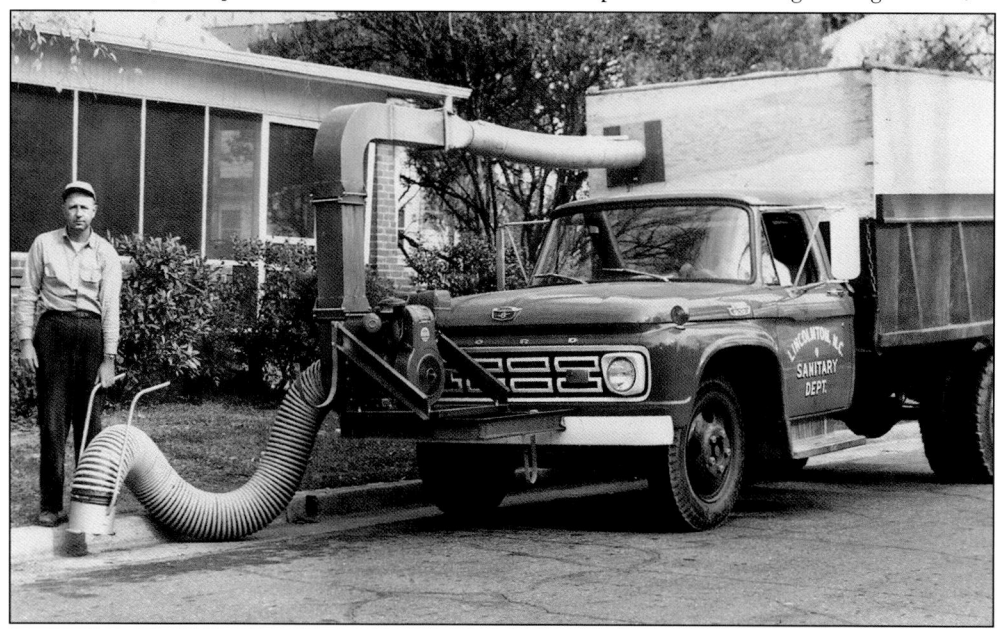

CLEANING UP THE CITY. City employee Rife Leonard takes a much-needed break while working on West Sycamore Street in Lincolnton. Brandishing the hose of a leaf shredder, Leonard ensures that Lincolnton's Sanitation Department keeps the city's streets neat and clean.

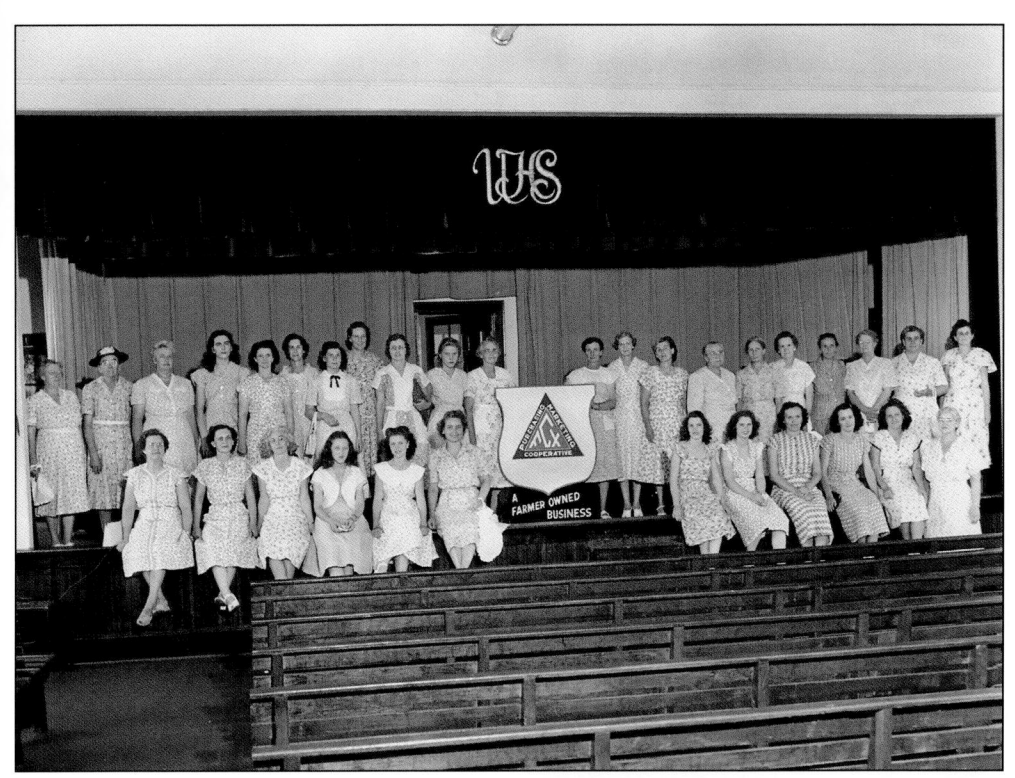

LINCOLN FCX SERVICE ANNUAL MEETING AND BARBEQUE, THURSDAY, JULY 22, 1948. Between 400 and 500 patrons of the Lincoln FCX Service attended the annual meeting, barbeque, and fashion show held at Union High School. M.G. Mann, general manager of the Farmers Cooperative Exchange, served as the principal speaker from Raleigh and reported on the past year's business. Thirty-three ladies took part in a dress revue that featured dresses made from FCX feed sacks, and Mrs. Robert Warlick won first place in the contest.

RAMSEUR HARDWARE, DOWNTOWN LINCOLNTON. David C. Heavner, owner of Ramseur Hardware, stands at the store's counter with Mrs. Richard Slaughter for Baby Ray Cornwell's camera on August 17, 1964. Richard Slaughter met his wife, Didi Alseema, while he was on leave from the military in Amsterdam. The couple fell in love and when Richard returned to the United States, he sent for Didi. She arrived in Lincolnton on January 24, 1964, and they were married two days later.

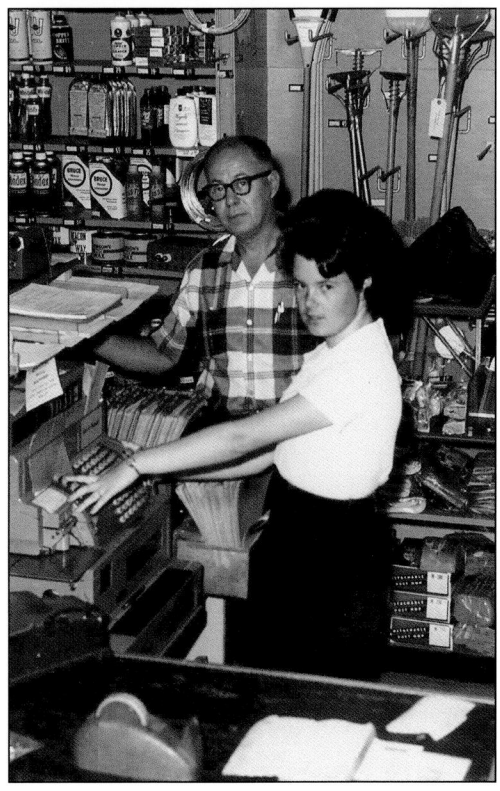

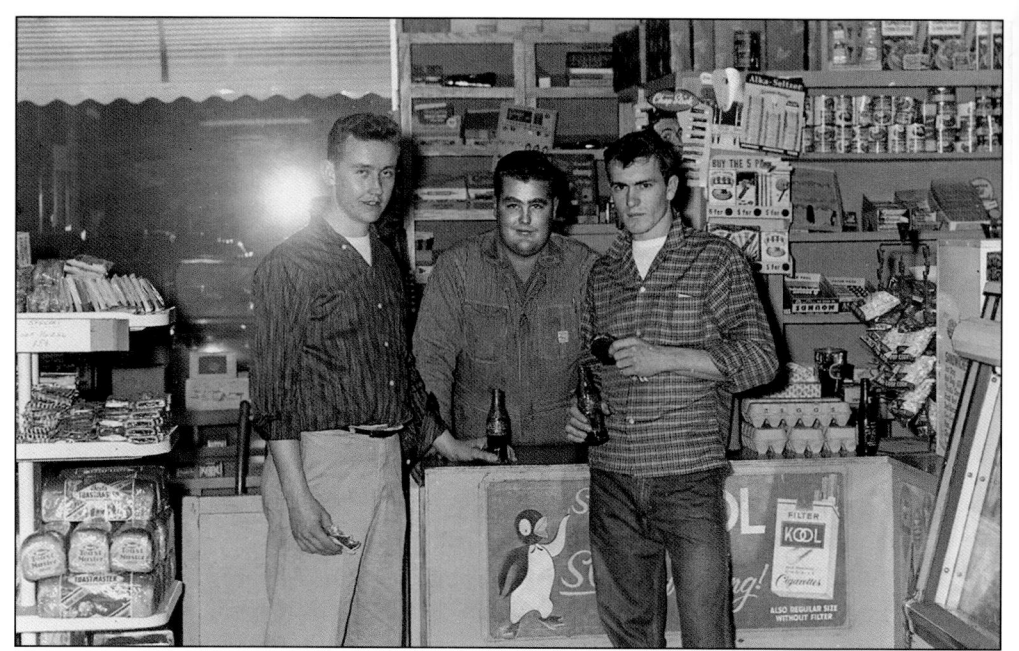

IN THE STATION. Baby Ray Cornwell gets a half smile from an employee (center) of Hoyle Service Station on East Main Street in Lincolnton as two customers take a break from their bottled cokes. Hoyle Service Station supplied Lincolntonians with food, drinks, gas, and other necessities for many years. The station was located across East Main Street from the present-day Kentucky Fried Chicken.

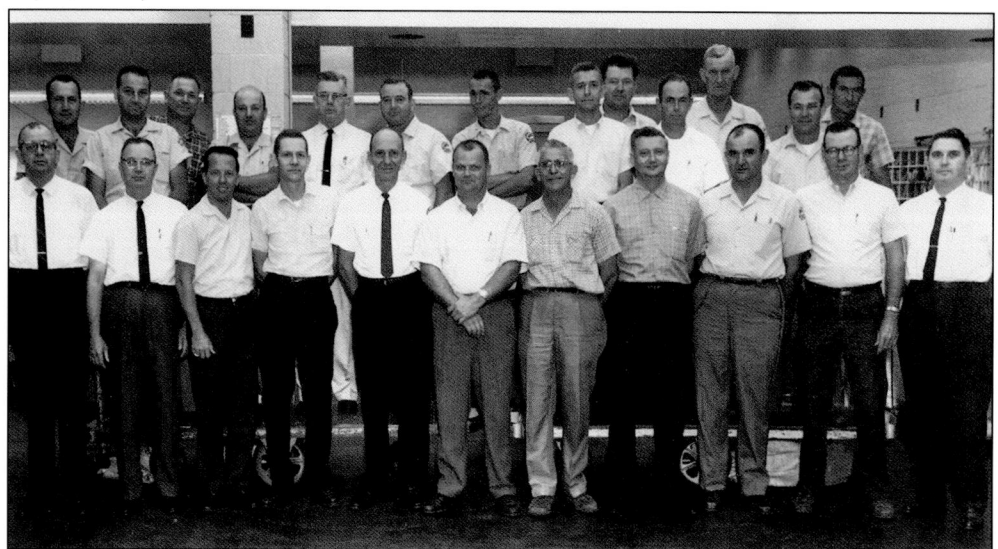

POSTAL TEAM. The men of the Lincolnton Post Office assemble for this photograph in the building's new addition on September 17, 1964. The men are identified, from left to right, as follows: (front row) Joe Ross, postmaster; Frank Killian, assistant postmaster; Bob Buff; Bill Keener; Jake Wyckoff; Robert Hallman; Robert Warlick; Lee Rhodes; Hugh Houser; Gene Ross; and Fred Rudisill; (back row) Harold "Bud" Warlick; Garmon Schrum; Wade Shuford; Fred Carpenter; J. Thomas McLean; Joe Barkley; Don Lackey; Vernon Knuckles; Jack Cagle; John Yoder; Arthur Sellers; Rathmul Helms; and Blair Wilkinson. (Courtesy of Betty G. Ross.)

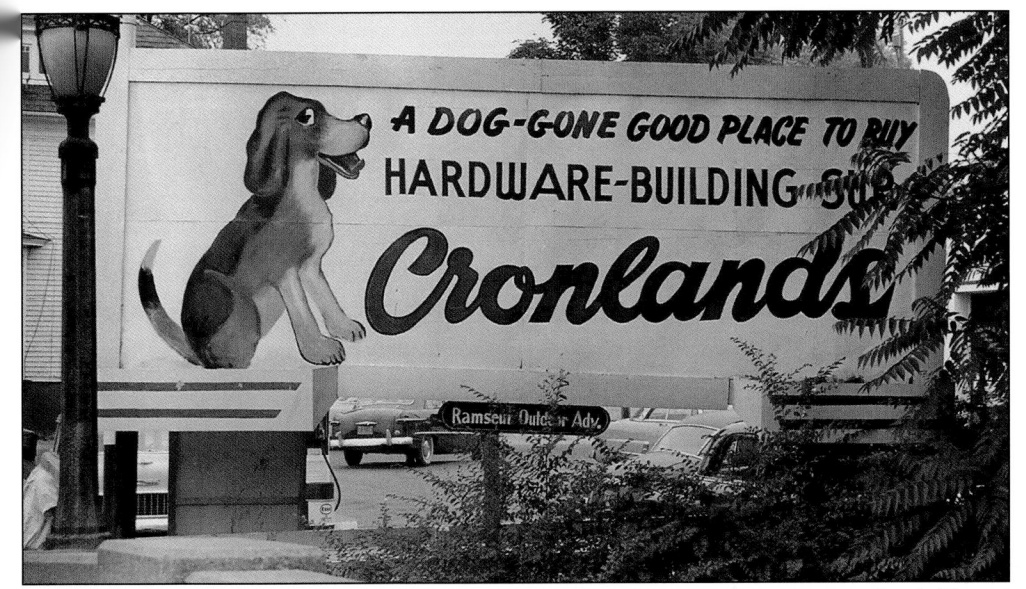

BUD THE BILLBOARD ARTIST. Visible from East Main Street in Lincolnton, this billboard encourages Lincolntonians to visit Cronlands because it is "A Dog-Gone Good Place to Buy." Billboard artist "Bud" Ramseur owned and painted this sign, shown here in June 1956. Ramseur started painting billboards in 1950 and owned billboards in Wilkes County, North Carolina, where he painted for Holly Farms. He also lettered trucks for Holly Farms and the race cars they sponsored.

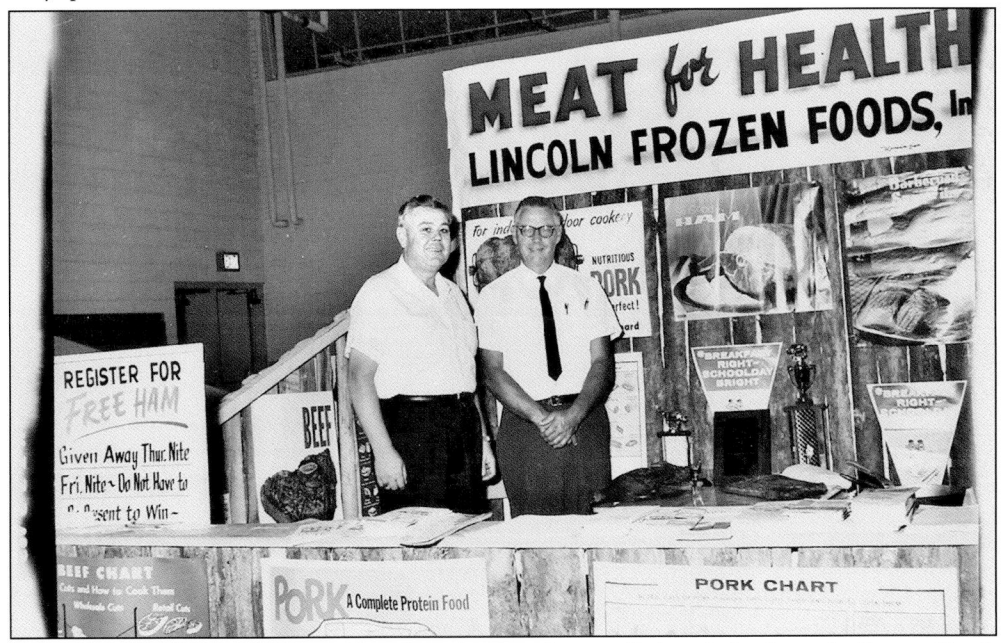

TOO COLD. On September 30, 1965, Baby Ray Cornwell found the Lincoln Frozen Foods display an excellent composition for capturing Gus Carter (left) and a man believed to be Hap Abernethy standing under the "Meat for Health" banner and behind the Lincoln Frozen Foods Inc. counter awaiting customers. Owned by Frank Crowell and Dewey Hoyle, the freezer locker was located at the intersection of East Main Street and Flint Street.

61

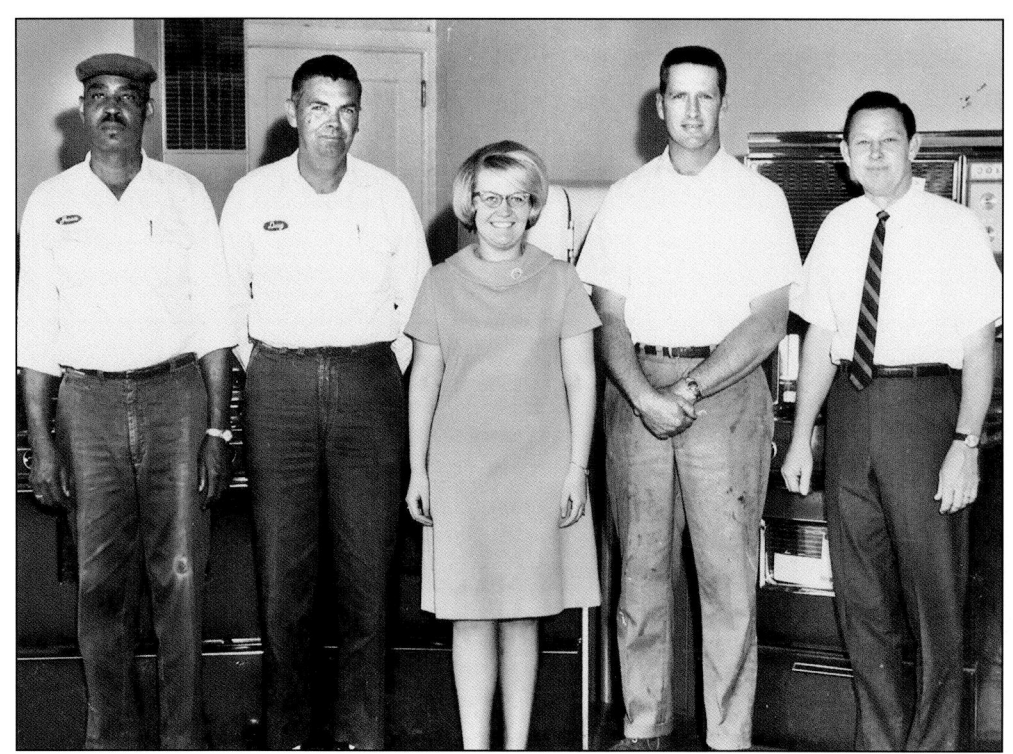

ON THE JOB. Baby Ray Cornwell made an impromptu stop at Santane Gas Company in Lincolnton on April 8, 1968. The employees of Santane Gas Company are, from left to right, Jessie Ashe, Doug Brackett, Gwynn Rudisill, Charles Crowell, and John Anderson.

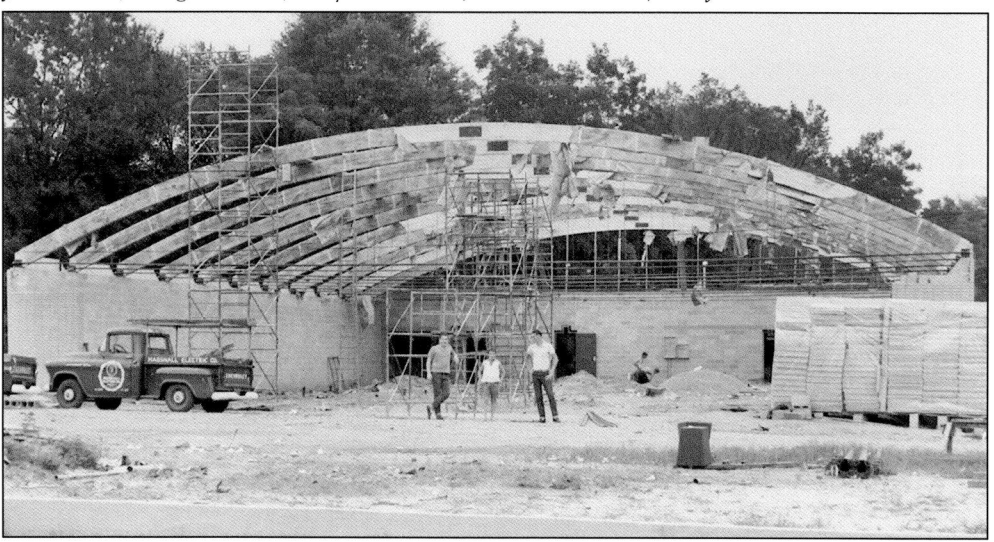

COMING ALONG. Scaffolding provides a good resting point for three people who were the focus of this August 14, 1959 Baby Ray photograph. The Marshall Electric Company's truck and pallets of building materials stand unattended during construction of Winn-Dixie. This building, located on E. Water Street in Lincolnton, was the site of Winn-Dixie for many years and is now the home of First Charter Bank. Winn-Dixie is now located on Highway 27 West in Lincolnton.

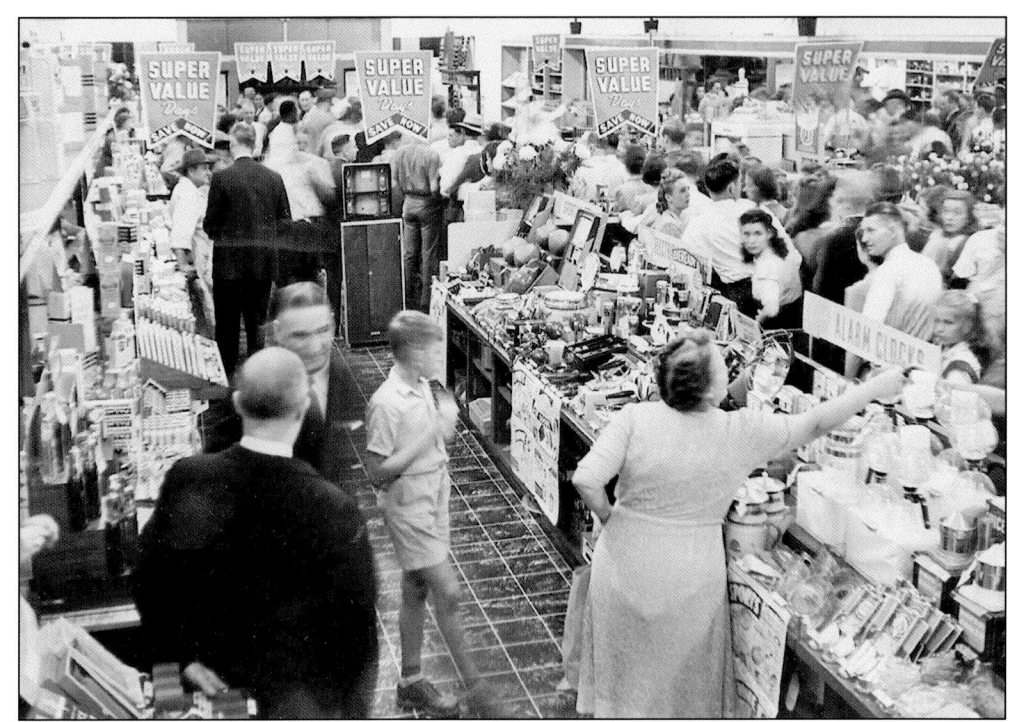

TRAFFIC JAM. A lady reaches for an alarm clock as a large group of people shop at the Eagle Variety Store in downtown Lincolnton. Baby Ray Cornwell was on hand to grab another piece of life in Lincolnton during the 1950s. The Eagle Variety Store was located in the first block of East Main Street in building now occupied by Classic Art & Framing.

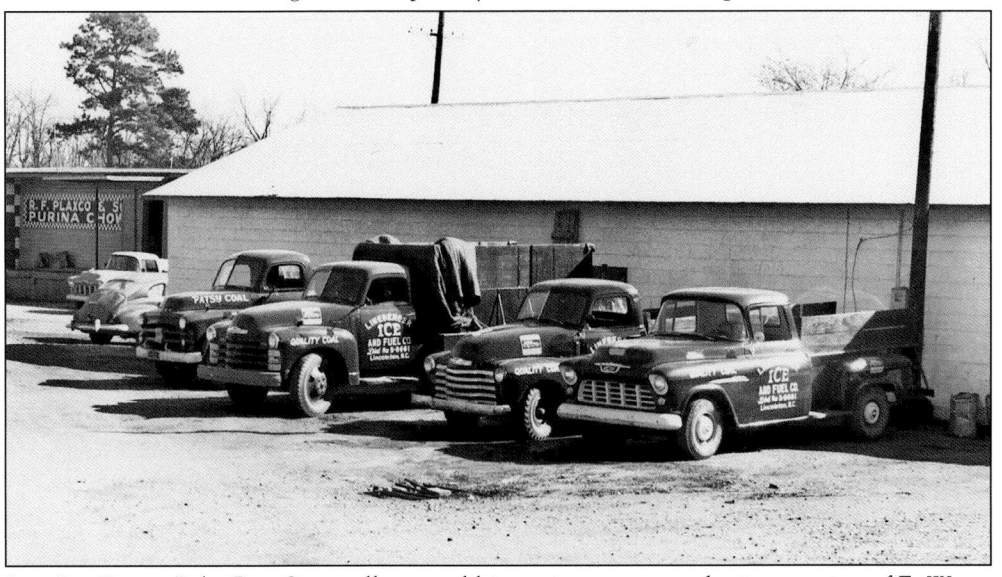

ICE, ICE BABY. Baby Ray Cornwell stopped his station wagon at the intersection of E. Water Street and N. Laurel Street to get the perfect shot of Lineberger Ice and Fuel Co. on November 22, 1958. Many residents of Lincolnton still have their old ice cards from Lineberger Ice & Fuel Company. The Lineberger delivery men used these cards to determine the amount of ice to drop at each home.

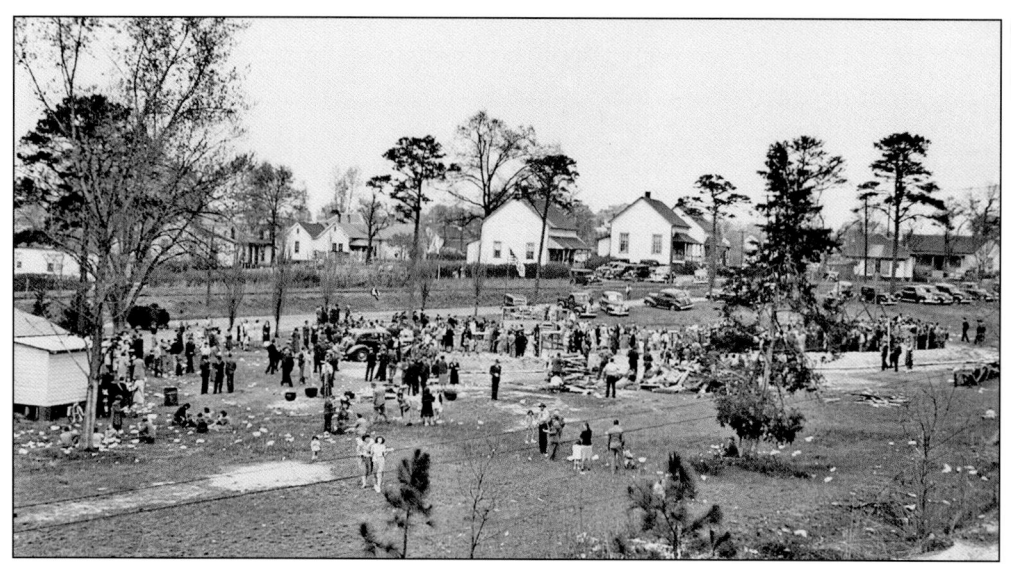

FIELD DAY. The Carter Mill community in Lincolnton was filled to capacity for the Annual Field Day during the 1940s. Members of the community enjoyed games, festivities, special events, and the delicacies cooked in a pit barbeque. The Boger and Crawford Mill communities in Boger City, previously Goodsonville, also held field days during this period.

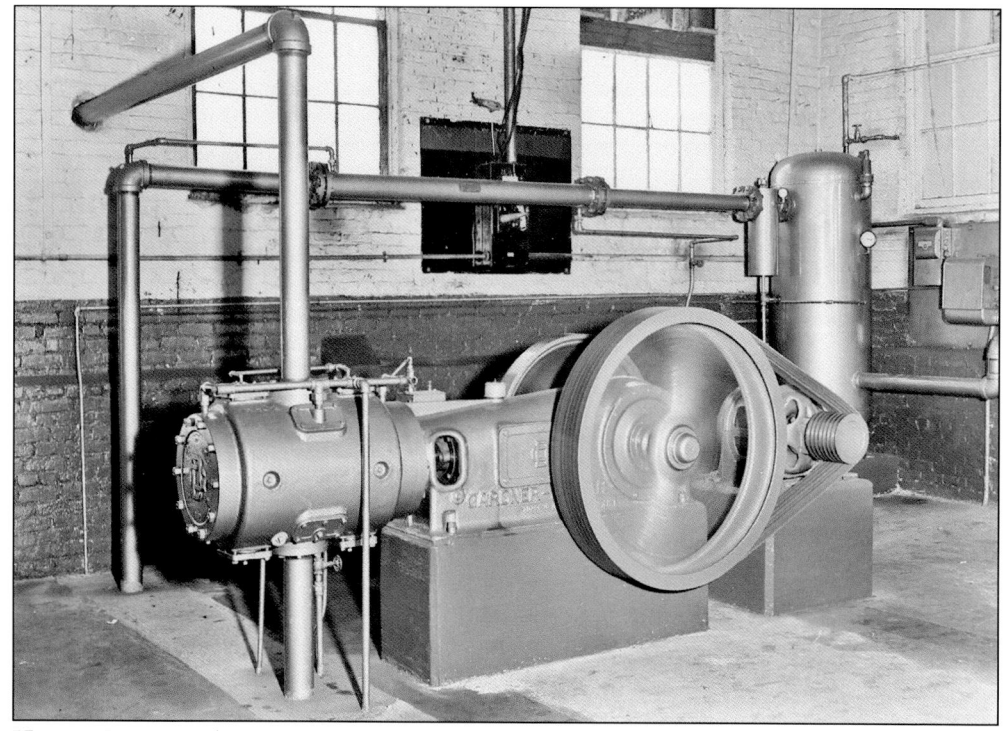

HEAVY DUTY. Baby Ray Cornwell took this shot in April 1948 at the Carter Mill in Lincolnton. It can be assumed that the owner of the mill hired him to document a new and innovative piece of machinery, vital to the growth of the facility. This image is another example of the varying types of photographs that Cornwell took throughout the 1940s, 1950s, and 1960s.

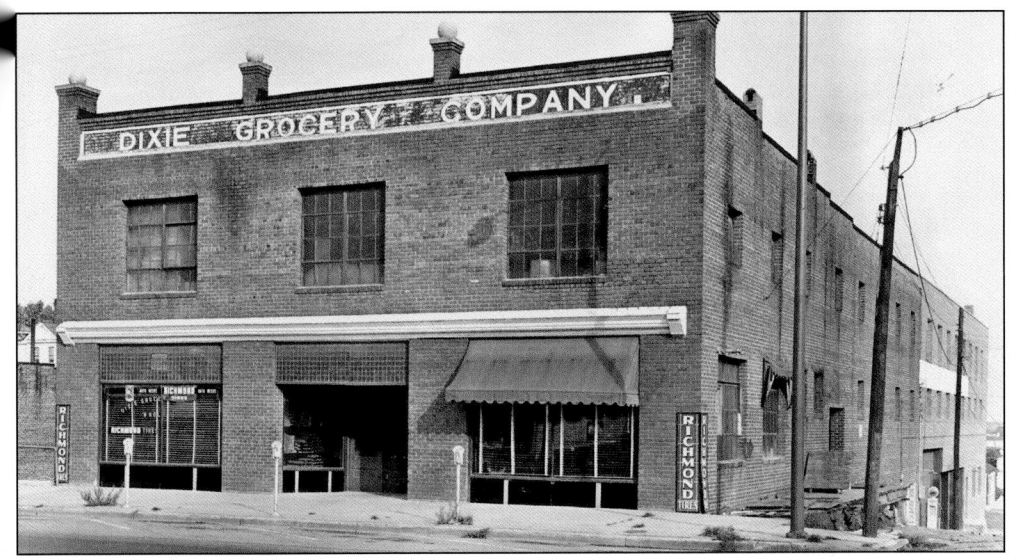

THE NAME SAYS IT ALL. The Dixie Grocery Company of Lincolnton, incorporated on January 1, 1924, occupied the lot at the corner of East Main Street and North Poplar Street until the late 1980s. The large brick structure is still part of the architectural character of downtown Lincolnton, but today it is owned by John Anderson and labeled Anderson Building. The first officers of Dixie Grocery Company were R.C. Goode, president; Herbert Miller, vice-president; and Plato Miller, both secretary and treasurer.

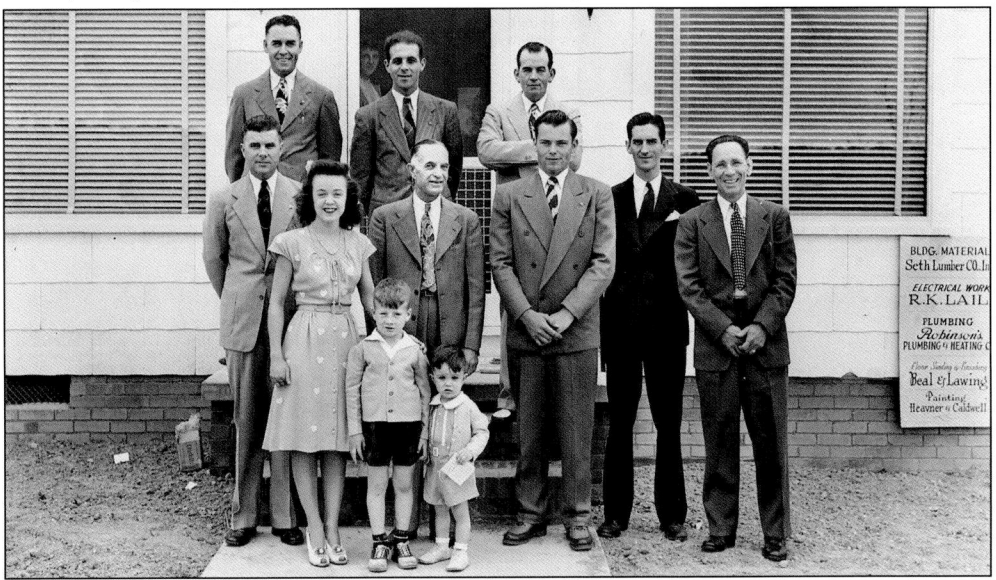

LATEST THING IN HOME COMFORT. During the 1940s and 1950s, many companies participated in the presentation and advertisement of a new model home. Baby Ray Cornwell photographed this group in front of a model home on South Aspen Street in Lincolnton. The structure was built and furnished by Goodin-Burris Furniture Company, Seth Lumber Company Inc., R.K. Lail, Robinson's Plumbing and Heating Company, Beal and Lawing, and Heavner and Caldwell. The people are identified, from left to right, as follows: (front row) Steve Burris and unidentified; (middle row) Leonard Bynum, Joyce Chronister, ? Jackson, Harry Morrison, Fred Ellis, and Victor Rudisill; (back row) Bill Parker, Joe Bondurant, and Zeb Burris.

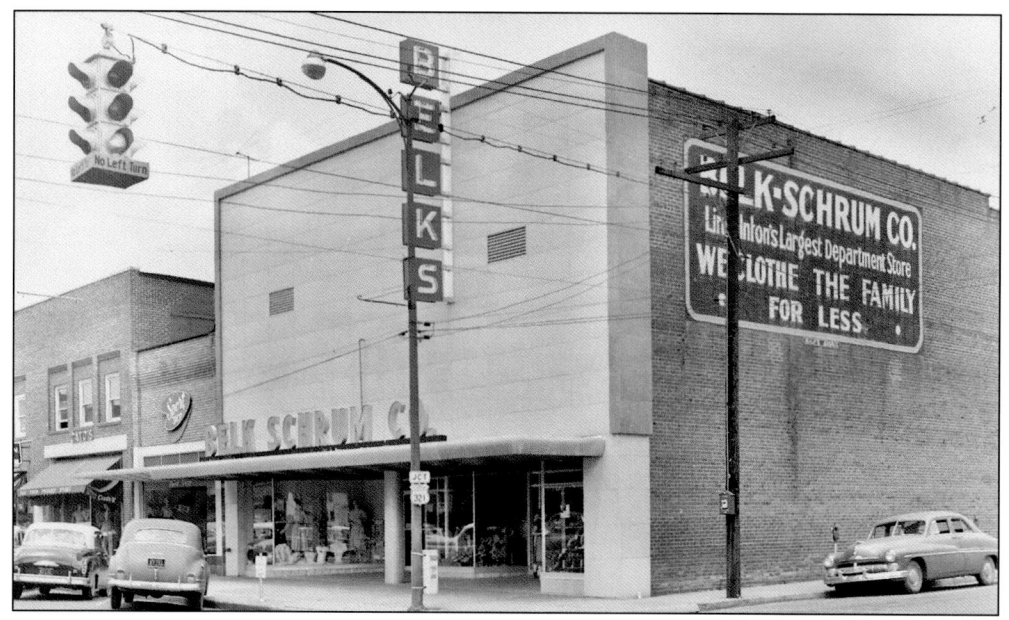

BELK-SCHRUM COMPANY BUILDING. Belk-Schrum Company, shown above at the corner of East Main Street and North Academy Street in downtown Lincolnton, was originally known as Belk-Johnson Company in 1921 when it first opened locally at 112 East Main Street. As shown here on June 16, 1957, the store had doubled in size from its 1950 specifications and incorporated a new parking lot. Belks was relocated to the Lincoln Center Mall in April 1989.

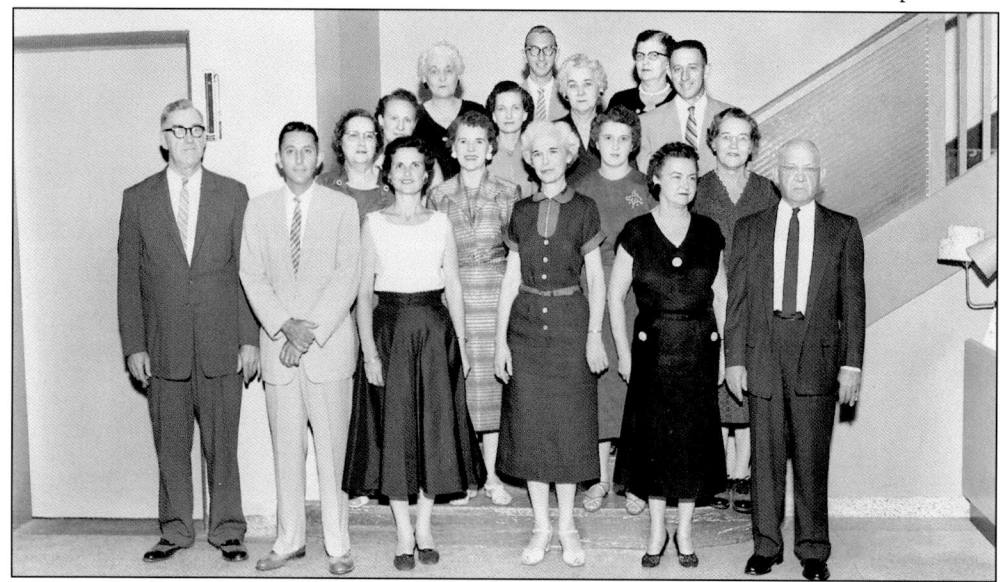

EMPLOYEE LINEUP. Employees of Belk-Schrum Company of Lincolnton pose for this August 1957 group photograph inside their building. The employees are identified, from left to right, as follows: (first row) John R. Schrum, Wilford "Bill" Shidal, Mable Seagle, Annie Heavner Shidal, Belle Rhyne, and Bernard Hamell; (second row) Pearl Mitchem Rhyne, Coleen Burns Rudisill Outlaw, Lib Seagle, and Mae Quickel; (third row) Mae Schrum Honeycutt, Ruth Childers Davis, Lenora F. Campbell Mauney, and Robert Boyles; (fourth row) Edna Graham, Glenn Lanier, and Prue Workman Shidal.

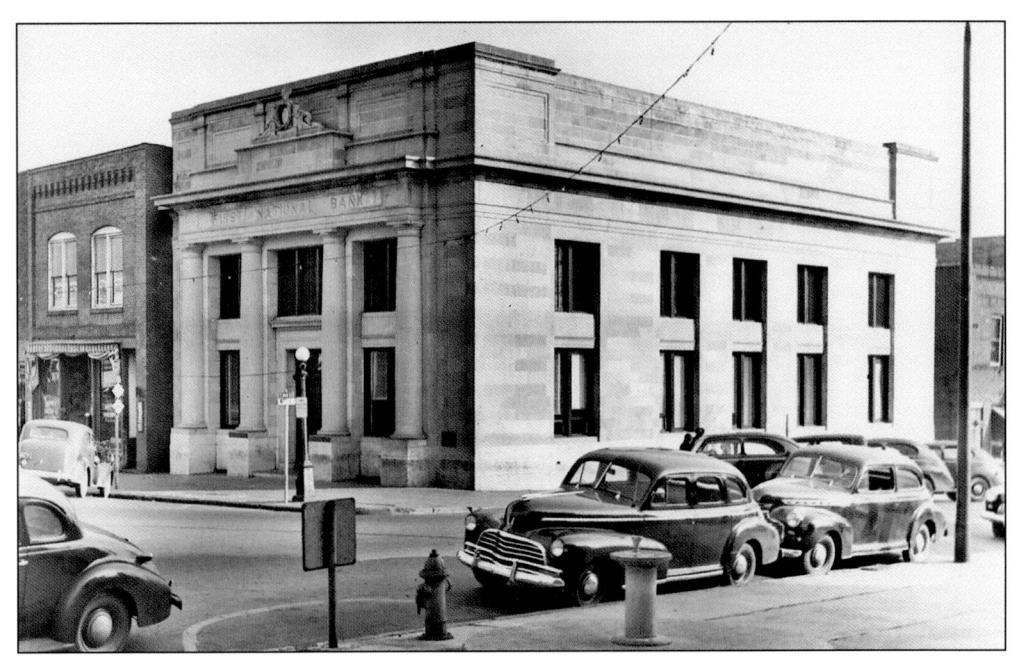

HOVERING ON THE COURTSQUARE. The imposing structure on the southeast corner of Lincolnton's Courtsquare served the banking needs of Lincolnton and Lincoln County's citizens for almost 70 years. Its architectural elegance and strength provided a stable and sturdy foundation for the Courtsquare. The First National Bank was originally located across the street on the northeast corner of the Courtsquare before it was relocated after the stock market crash of 1929. The building was razed in 1976. (Courtesy of Paul Dellinger.)

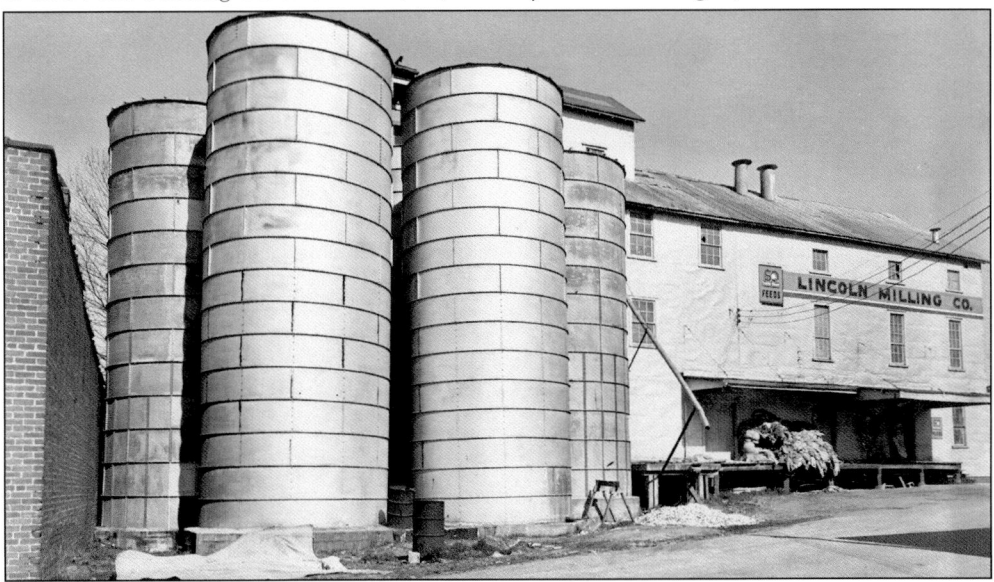

MILLIN'. Standing strong at two blocks from East Main Street, along the railroad between South Cedar and South Poplar Streets, the Lincoln Milling Company was photographed on February 25, 1954. The company played a crucial role in the agricultural life-span of Lincoln County—buying grain, grinding flour for local farm families, and making high-grade flour for local stores. E.C. Baker built the Lincoln Milling Company during the 1910s.

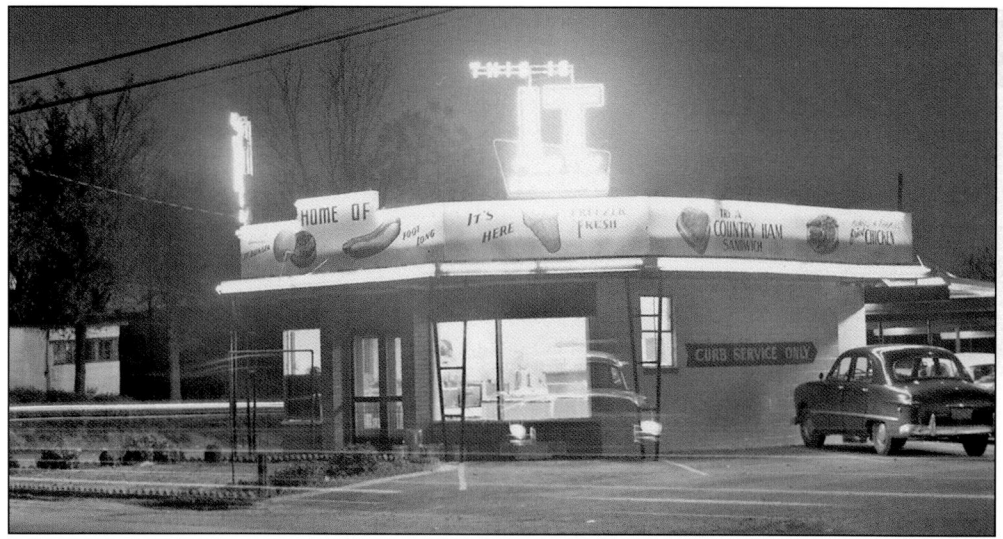

POOR BOY AND POOR GIRL. It's Grille on East Main Street has been a staple in Lincolnton since Earl Elmore built it in 1956. Hazel Cherry, an employee since 1956, remembers the landmark as "one of the only drive-ins from the time." Specializing in Poor Boy and Poor Girl sandwiches, the grille has hardly changed its menu in over 45 years. The grille is currently owned by Sandy Hudson and maintains the same charm and character from its founding days.

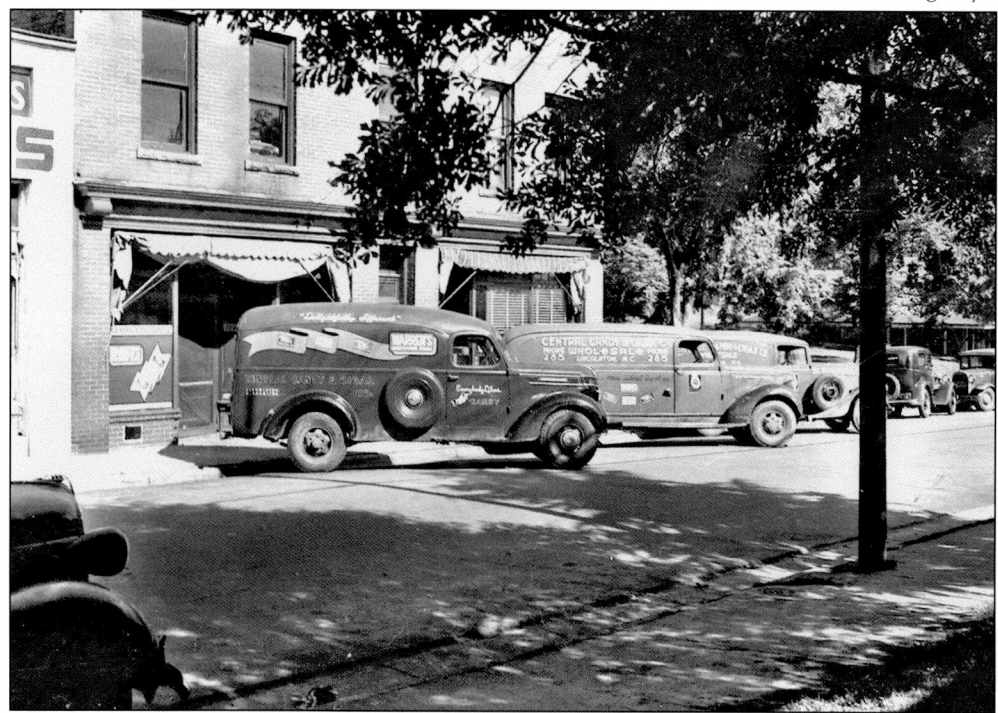

WHAT A MIX! The trucks of Central Candy and Cigar Company in Lincolnton are backed up with tires against the curb as they head out and deliver products in Lincolnton. Baby Ray Cornwell stands across from the store under the shade of an oak tree for this 1950s shot. The company was located on the south side of Academy Street in downtown Lincolnton and was run by Randolph Shives Sr. and Dewey Hoyle.

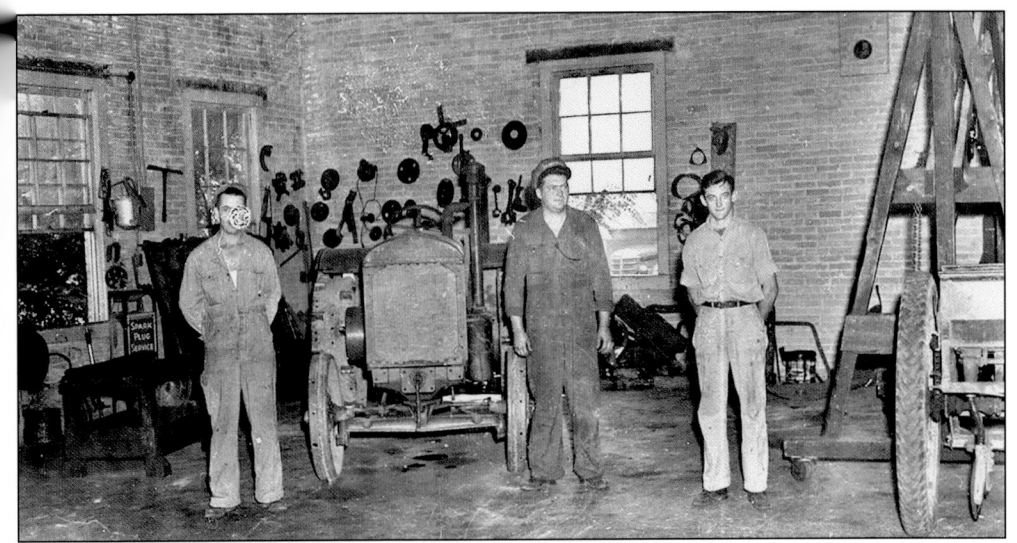

WISE IMPLEMENT COMPANY. Located on West Water Street in Lincolnton, present location of *Lincoln Times-News*, Wise Implement Company handled International Harvester Company products and new and used farm equipment, and it maintained a repair shop. Robert Guy Wise started the implement company and ran it for 19 years before his death in 1958. In the 1940s photograph above, Baby Ray Cornwell shows Elzy Wise (cousin of R.G. Wise), Grady Sisk, and Risden Burris beside a tractor.

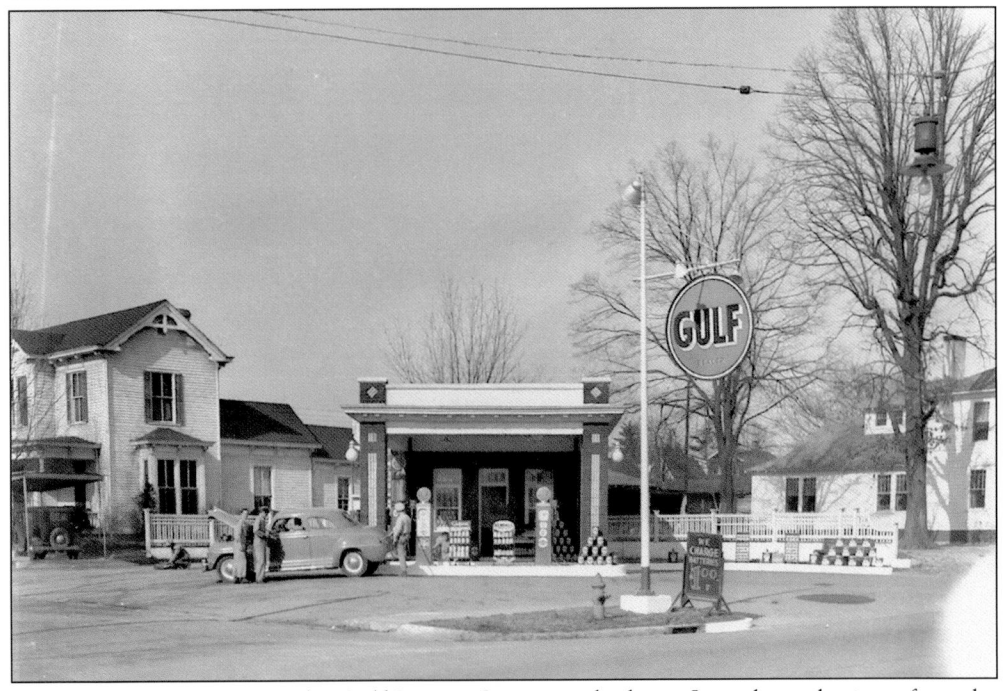

HERE TO PUMP YOU UP! The Gulf Service Station is the latest Lincolnton business from the 1940s to be photographed by Baby Ray. The image shows not only the service station but also the beautiful Victorian home of the late Alfred Nixon, Lincoln County's first public historian. The Gulf Service Station was located at the corner of East Main Street and North Laurel Street.

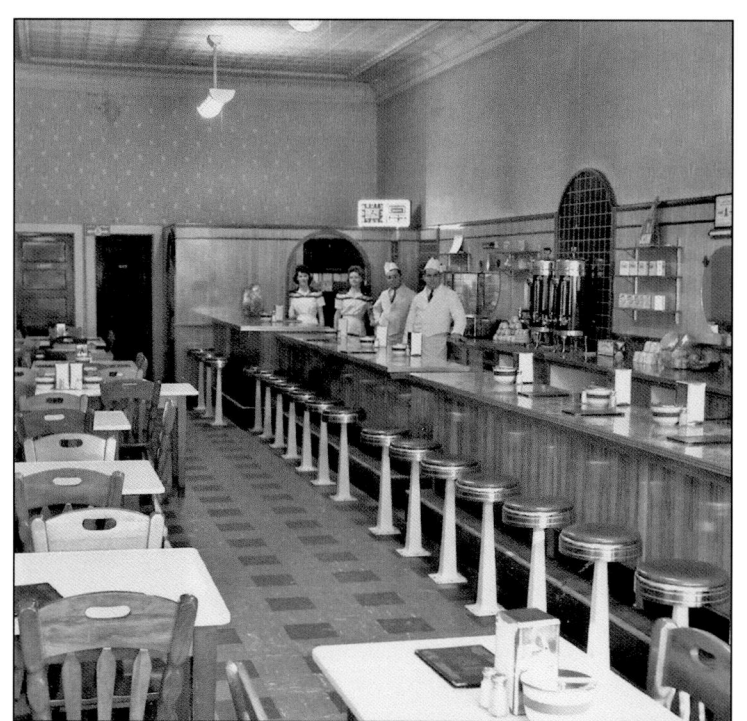

AWAITING THE LUNCH CROWD. With tables cleared, chairs upright, and counter glimmering, Elliott Howard and Harlee Ramseur stand with two unidentified waitresses for this 1940s photo. Howard worked at the café before moving to the Washington, D.C. area to operate another café. Ramseur purchased the building on East Main Street from L.C. Hovis. Central Café is visible in many of the parade photographs taken by Baby Ray and Frazier's Studio during the 1940s.

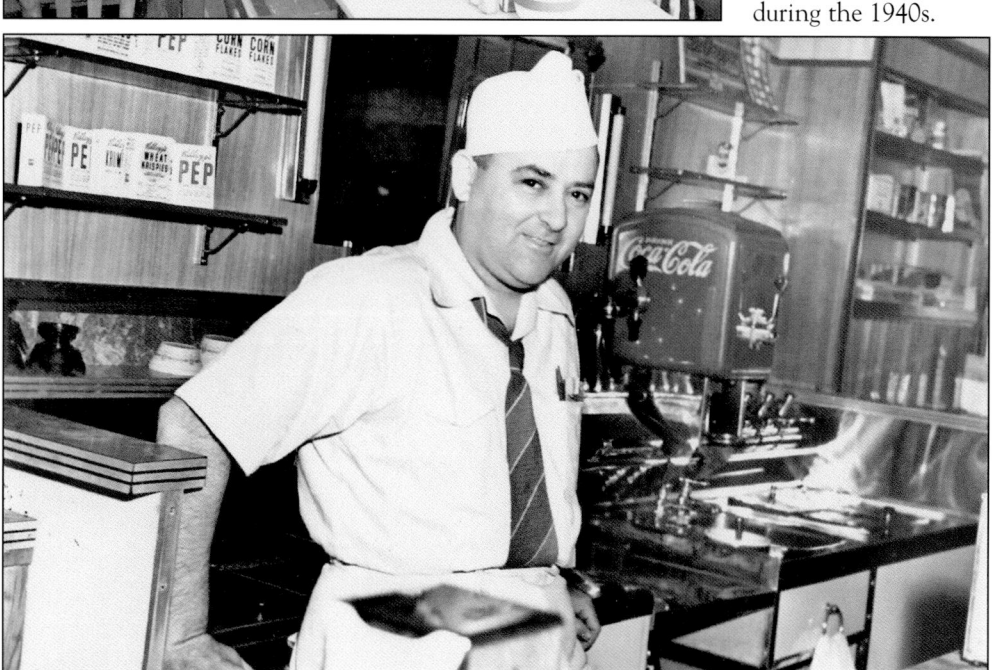

UP CLOSE AND PERSONAL. Central Café owner Harlee Ramseur loosened his tie and leaned against the back counter for this 1940s photograph in downtown Lincolnton. Ramseur (1900–1975), a World War II navy veteran, worked a number of different professions before operating Central Café in Lincolnton. He worked in Akron, Ohio, for a few years and sold real estate in Florida before running a café called Lady's Blue Bird in Lincolnton with his brother Marshall Ramseur.

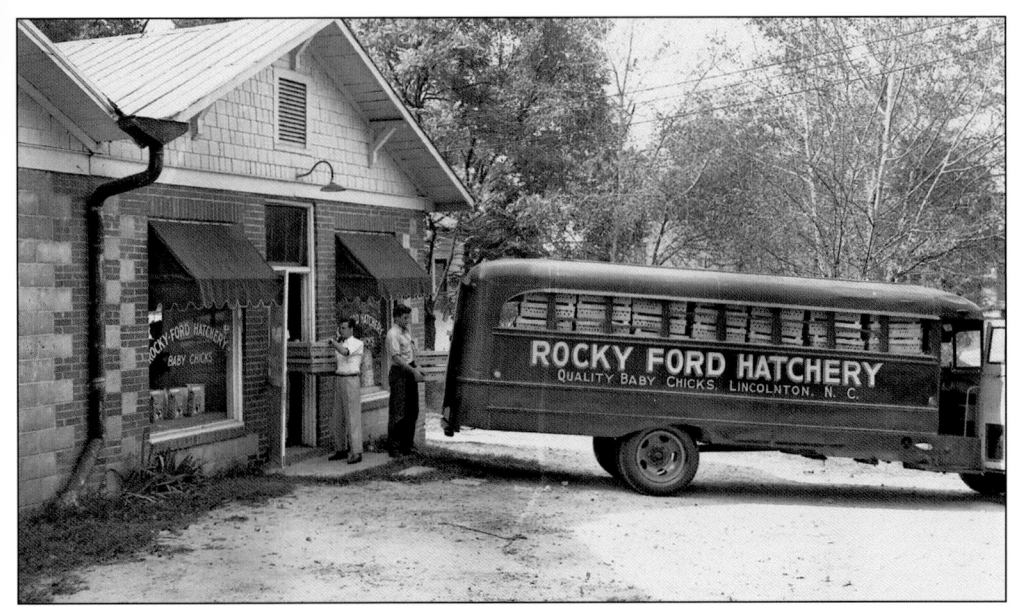

MASS VOLUME CHICKS. In this Baby Ray photograph from the 1940s, Joe Ford and Claude Reynolds pack the Rocky Ford Hatchery delivery bus full of baby chicks. Started in 1929 by R.L. Ford Sr., the Rocky Ford Hatchery delivered baby chicks to many sites in North Carolina, including farms as far away as North Wilkesboro. R.L. Ford's son, Joe Ford, says that "Dad had the first electric incubator in North Carolina . . . 1926." The company had a production volume of 100,000 baby chicks a week year round. The business was located at 316 East Pine Street in Lincolnton and closed in 1973.

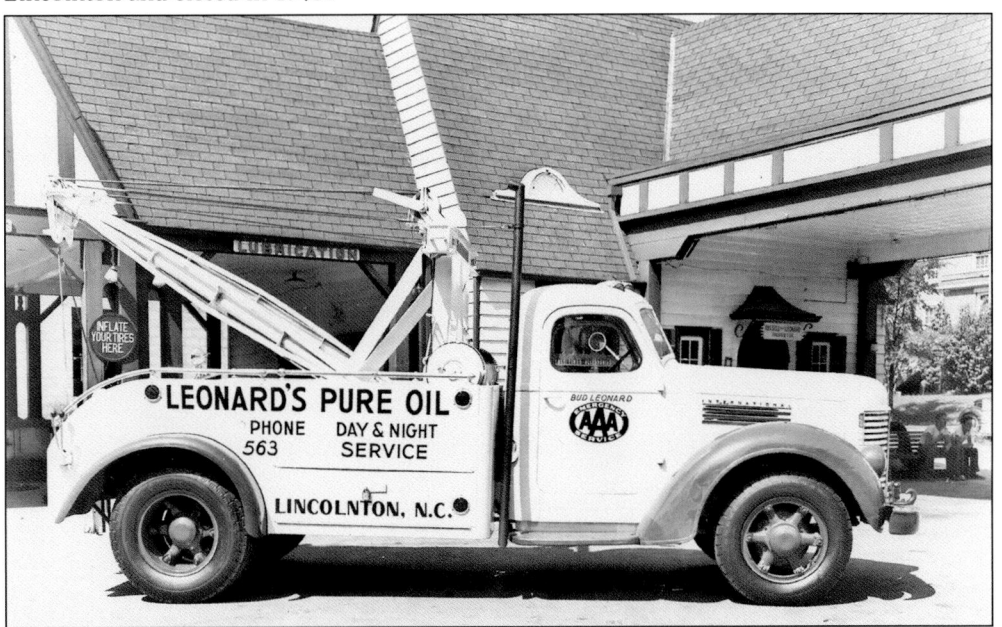

SERVICE 24/7. Leonard's Pure Oil and Wrecker is shown here on the corner East Main Street and North Cedar Street in Lincolnton. By simply dialing 563, one can be serviced by the company's wrecker day and night. Bud Leonard, the owner during World War II, has this wrecker personalized with his name on the passenger's side door.

71

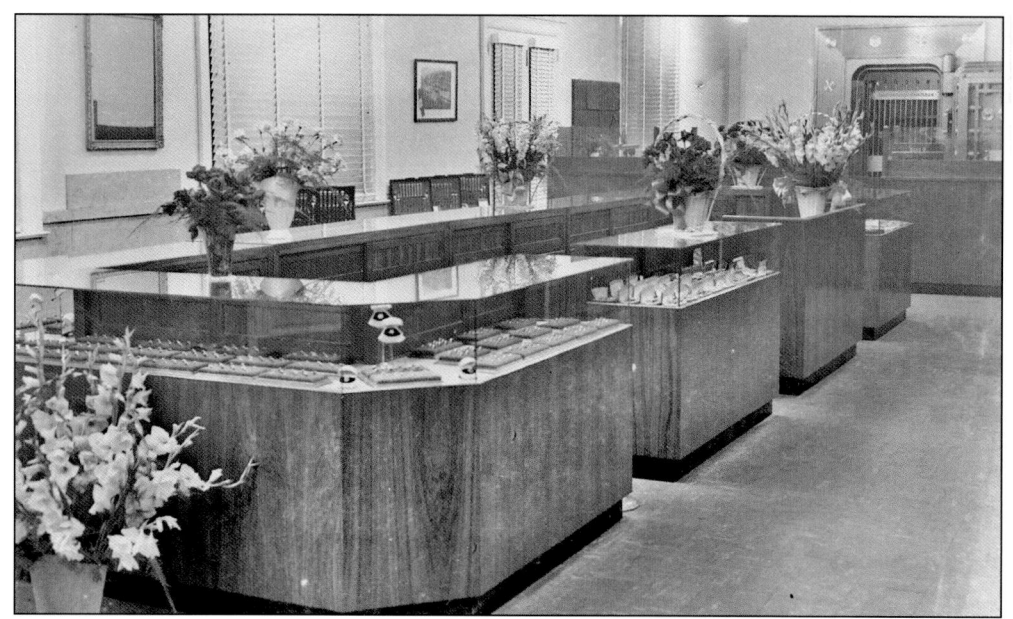

LEONARD BROTHERS JEWELRY STORE, DOWNTOWN. On Friday, February 21, 1947, W.H. Leonard Jr. opened Leonard Brothers Jewelry Store in downtown Lincolnton. Located in the former First National Bank building, the firm gave away a total of $700 or more in merchandise on opening day. The gifts included ladies diamond rings, dinner rings, watches, and a souvenir for each man and woman visiting the store. Leonard's son, W.H. Leonard III, managed the store in Lincolnton. The Leonard family name had been associated with the jewelry business throughout North Carolina since the 1880s.

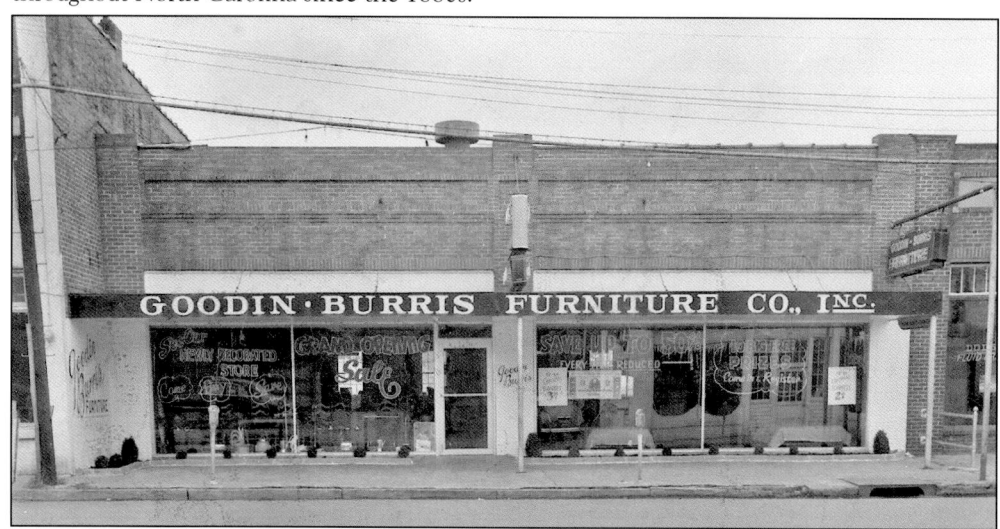

GOODIN-BURRIS FURNITURE COMPANY, DOWNTOWN. Goodin-Burris Furniture Company on W. Sycamore Street in downtown Lincolnton manufactured and marketed upholstered furniture—principally chairs, sofas, love seats, tables, and lamps. Founded in 1936 under a partnership by J. Alonzo Burris and E.B. Goodin, the company changed its name in 1948 to Burris Manufacturing Company and, on July 30, 1969, to Burris Industries, Inc. Wayne Burris, son of Alonzo Burris, managed the company after his father's death on June 1, 1977, until he sold the company to La-Z-Boy Chair Company in 1985.

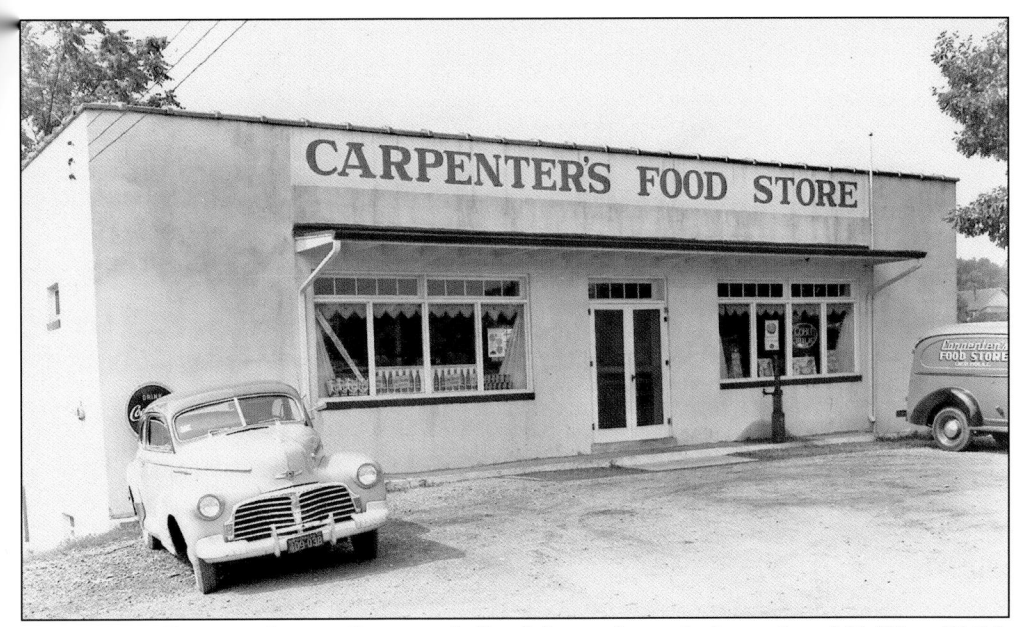

Just a Few Blocks Away. Carpenter's Food Store, formerly located at 552 West Childs Street in Lincolnton, was just a few blocks away from West Main Street and provided in town a convenient grocery stop. Brothers Cecil and Oracho G. Carpenter opened the food store in the late 1940s to serve the surrounding community. The store's 1,700 square feet of floor space provided ample room for any number of meats, vegetables, and beverages. Pilgrims Tabernacle currently occupies the building.

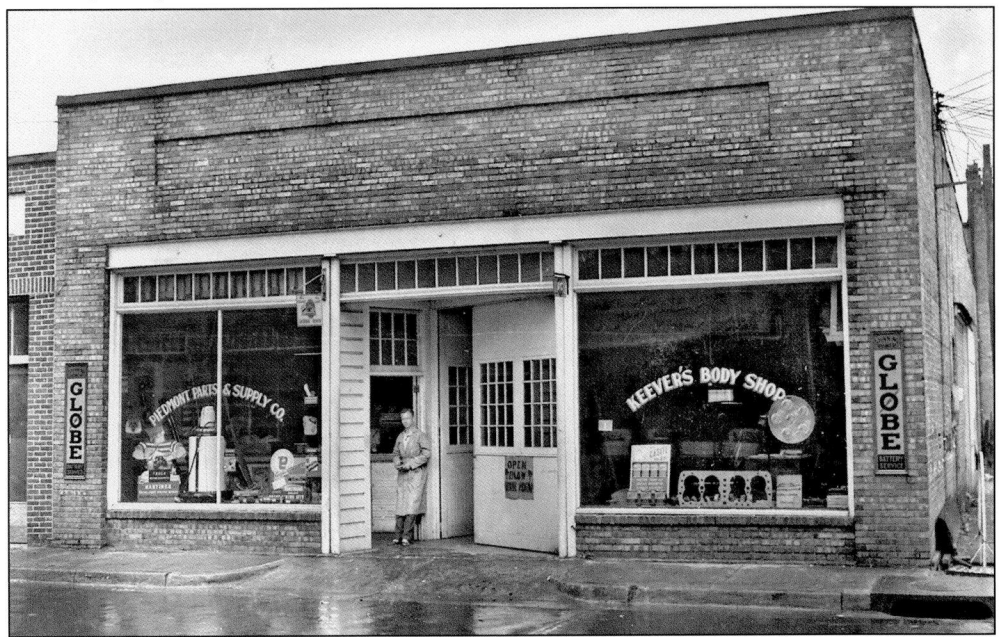

Body Work? Keever's Body Shop in Lincolnton was owned and operated by Zeb Keever during the second quarter of the 20th century. Tuning cars, fixing carburetors, and providing other valuable mechanical services, Keever's Body Shop received much traffic on East Sycamore Street in Lincolnton. The building is now owned by Dennis Williams, a Lincolnton architect.

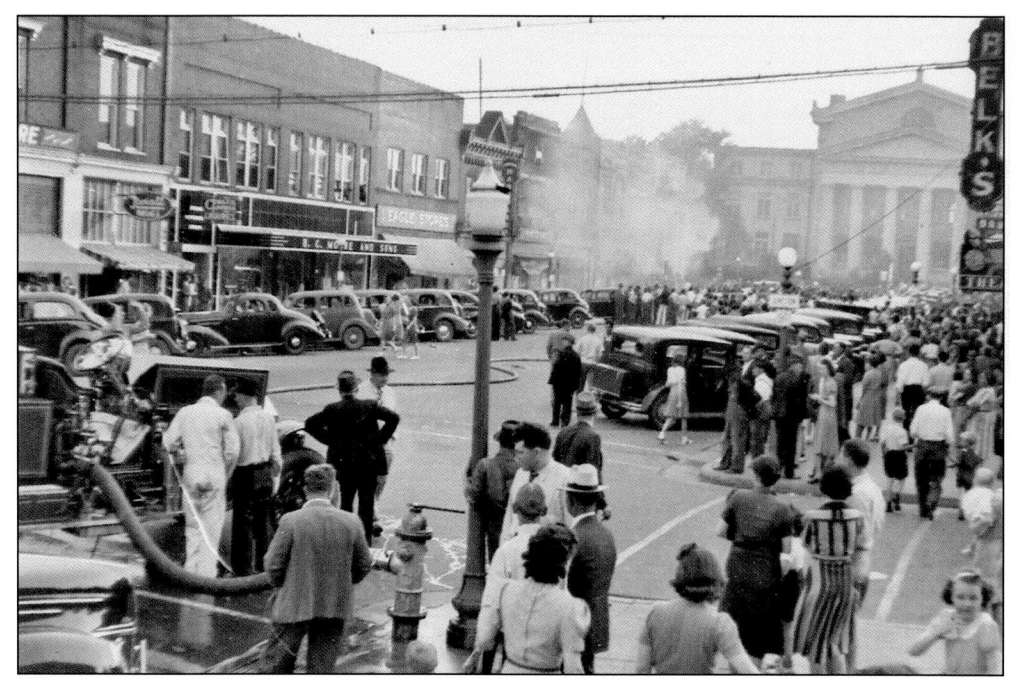

DOWNTOWN MAYHEM! A blazing fire beside Ramseur Hardware in downtown Lincolnton draws the attention of many residents and requires the support of the town's fire department. Some in this image are shown walking down East Main Street with shopping on the mind as others look on with fear in their eyes. A single hose runs down the middle of East Main Street, and the fire department deploys a single ladder up to the second story of the downtown building.

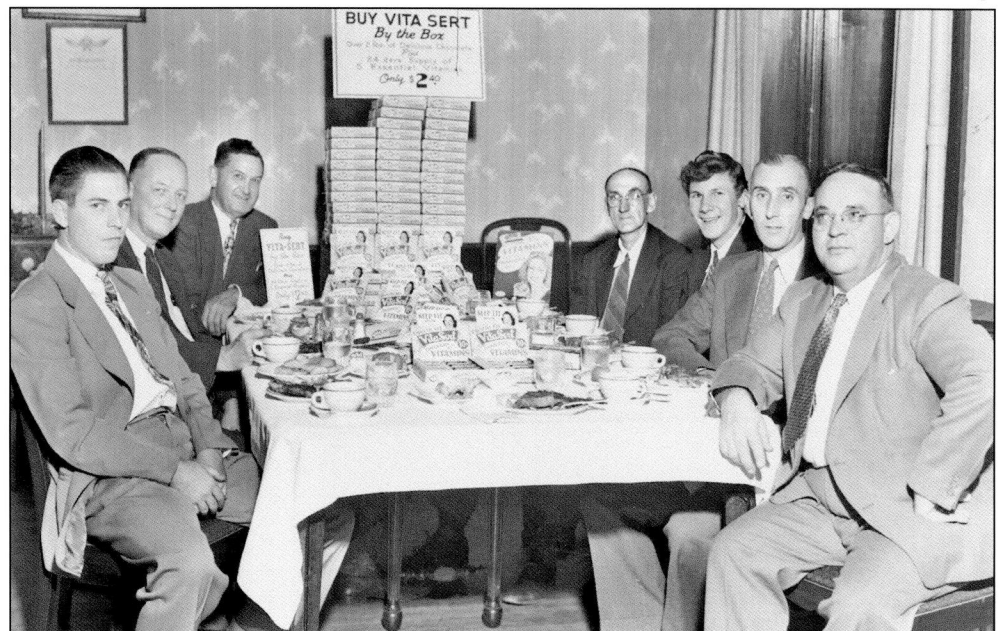

BY THE BOX. Salesmen for Vita Sert Vitamins sit around their products for Baby Ray Cornwell's camera during the 1940s. Dewey Hoyle, the first man on right, is the only identified member of the group, and the others are assumed to be from out of town.

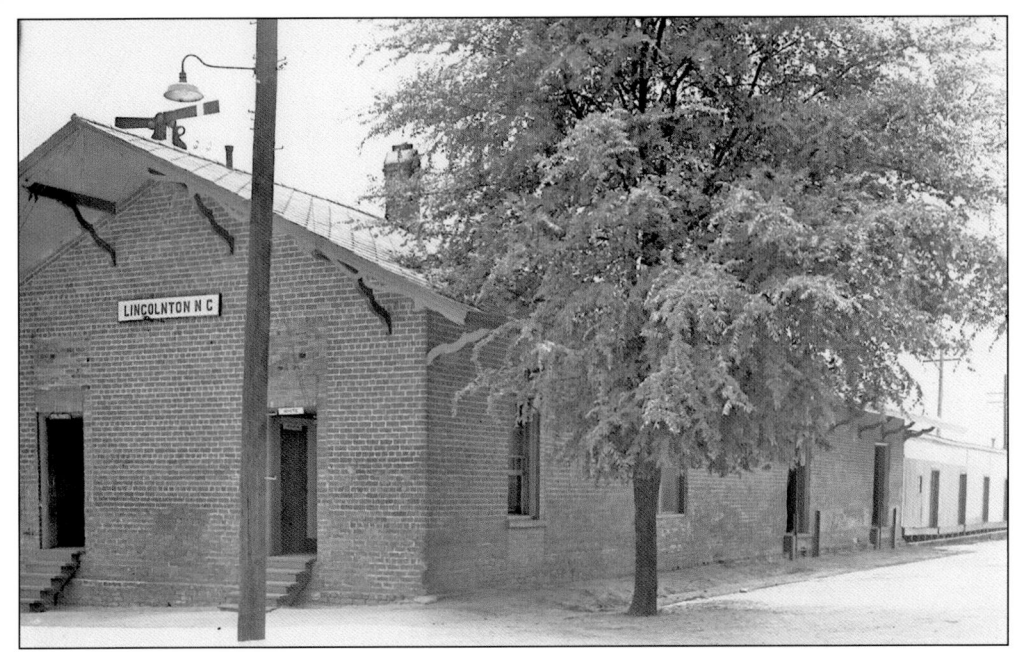

FROZEN IN TIME. One of the city's earliest landmarks, located on Water Street in Lincolnton, is shown here frozen in time. The Seaboard Air Line Railway Depot transported some of Lincoln County's finest soldiers across the Southeast to serve in the Civil War and both world wars. Some of Lincolnton's oldest citizens remember reading the names of Union soldiers that were inscribed on the depot's large structural beams.

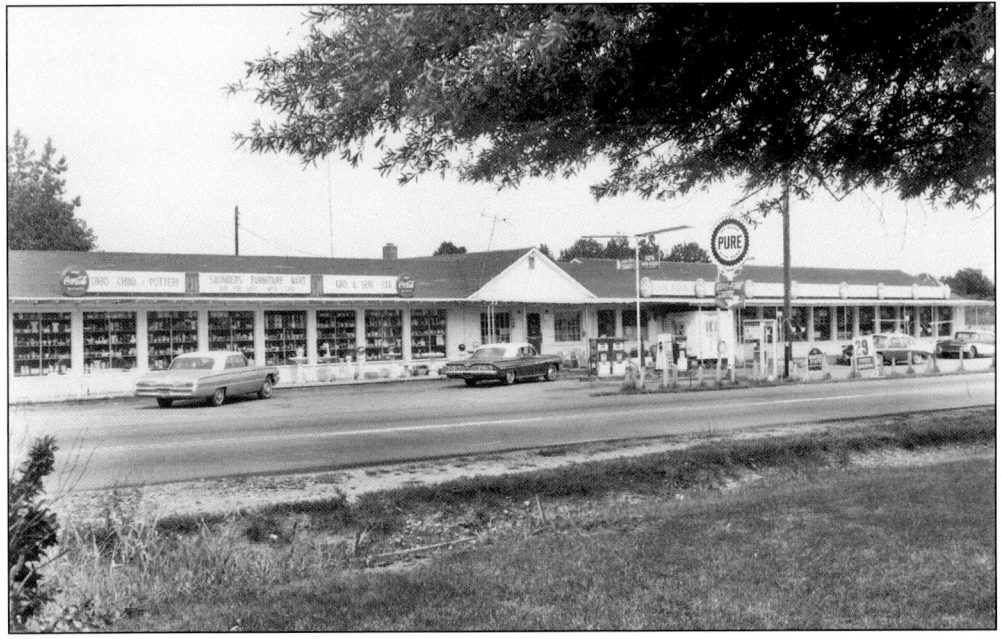

FURNITURE, POTTERY, GAS, AND MUCH MORE. The absence of traffic opens a brief window for Baby Ray Cornwell to capture this photograph of Saunders Furniture in Lincolnton. Saunders Furniture Mart sold more than just furniture; as you can see on their various signs, they sold Ohio China and Pottery, groceries, and gas.

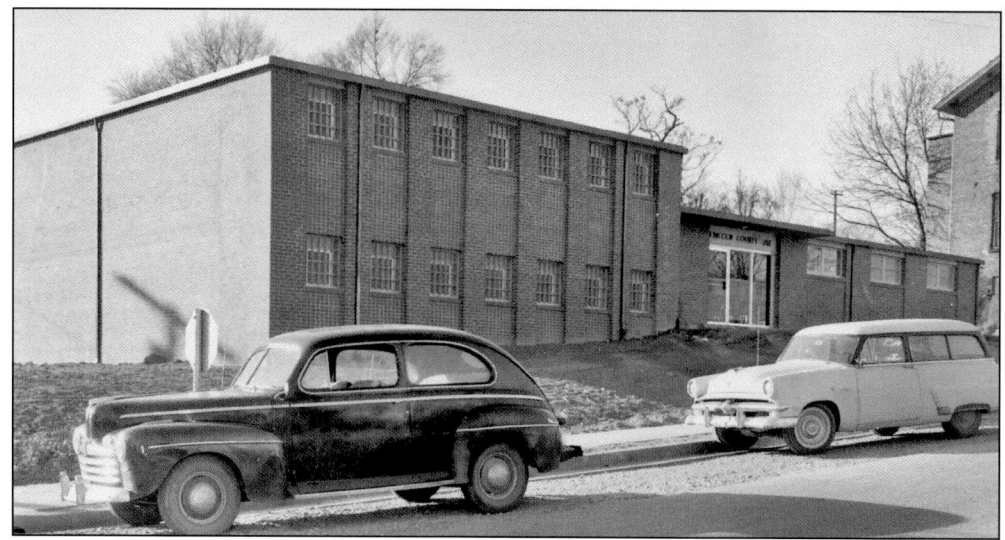

LINCOLN COUNTY JAIL. The old Lincoln County Jail (1849–1956) sits in the background as the new Lincoln County Jail, built in 1958, occupies the foreground of this 1958 photograph. Designed by architects Marsh and Hawkins, the new Lincoln County Jail was opened to the public for viewing and inspection on November 29, 1958. The event was held by the Lincoln County Board of Commissioners and Sheriff Frank P. Heavner. Work began on the new jail in September 1957. Completed at a cost of $130,000, it officially opened on December 1, 1958.

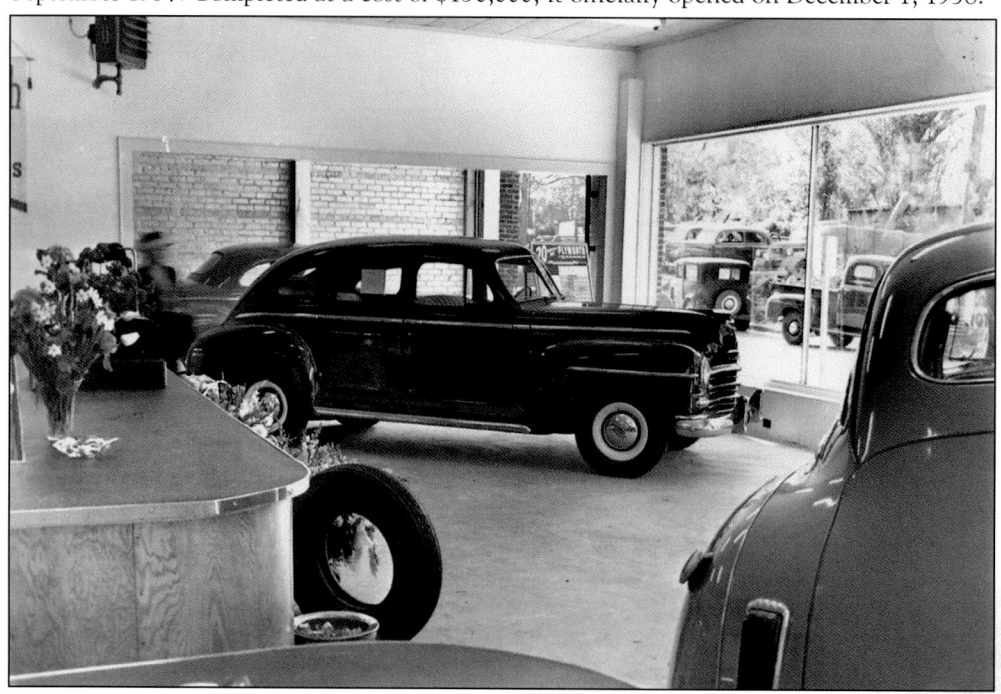

NEW AND MODERN. *The Lincoln County News* featured the Lincoln Motor Company's opening on April 17, 1948, with the announcement that the dealership would have a "new and modern home." The owners, K.D. Heavner and E.H. Williams, believed that they now "had one of the very best equipped garages in this part of the country." Two De Sotos rest in Lincoln Motor Company's showroom on West Water Street in Lincolnton.

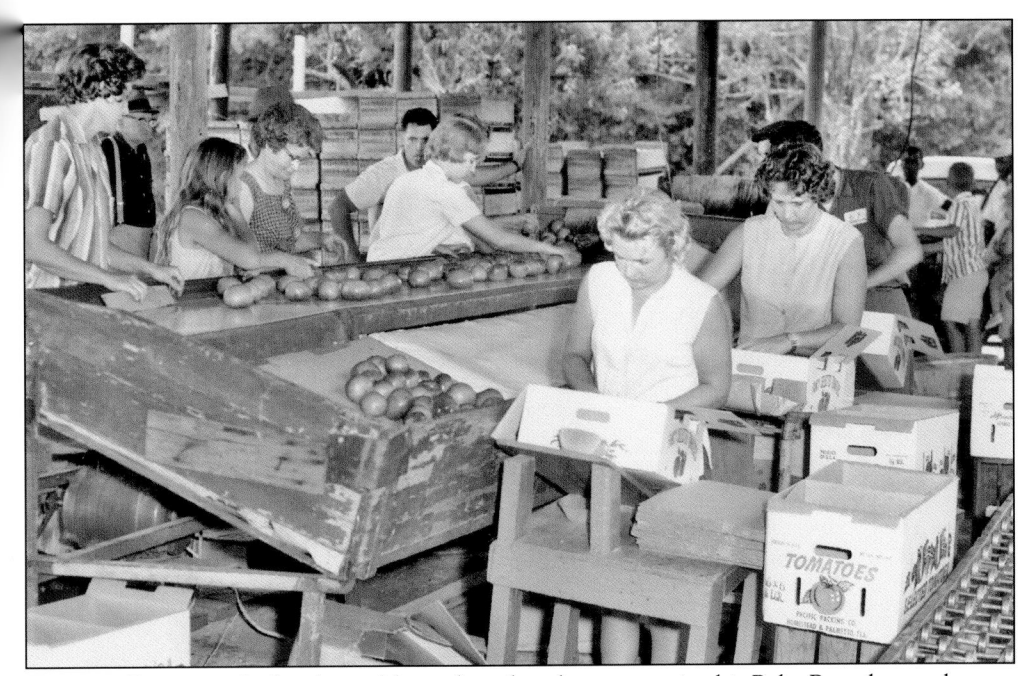

TOMATO PACKING. Ladies feverishly wash and pack tomatoes in this Baby Ray photo taken on Monday, July 6, 1964. Vernon Boyles operated the tomato packing shed, located on Highway 27, for S&S Produce Company. According to *The Lincoln County News*, farmers in Lincoln County had been awaiting such a facility to enable them to process their crops locally. The photograph shows the ladies at machines that washed the tomatoes before packing.

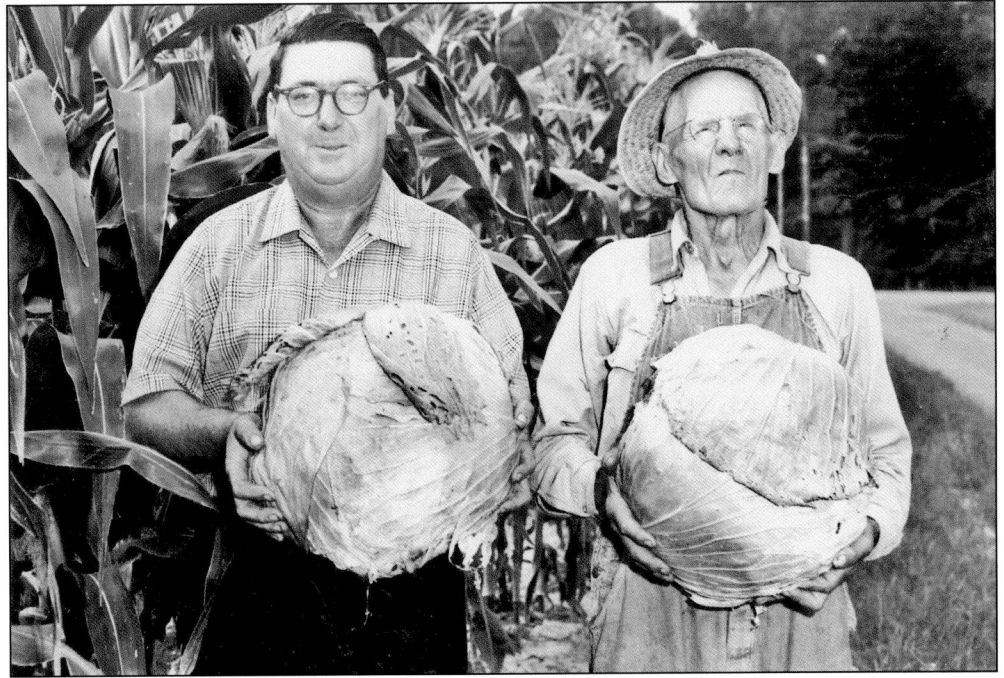

BIG HEADS. Holding their prize cabbages, these two men from Lincolnton pose for Baby Ray Cornwell. One man was identified by Cornwell as "Mr. Reel, cabbager."

77

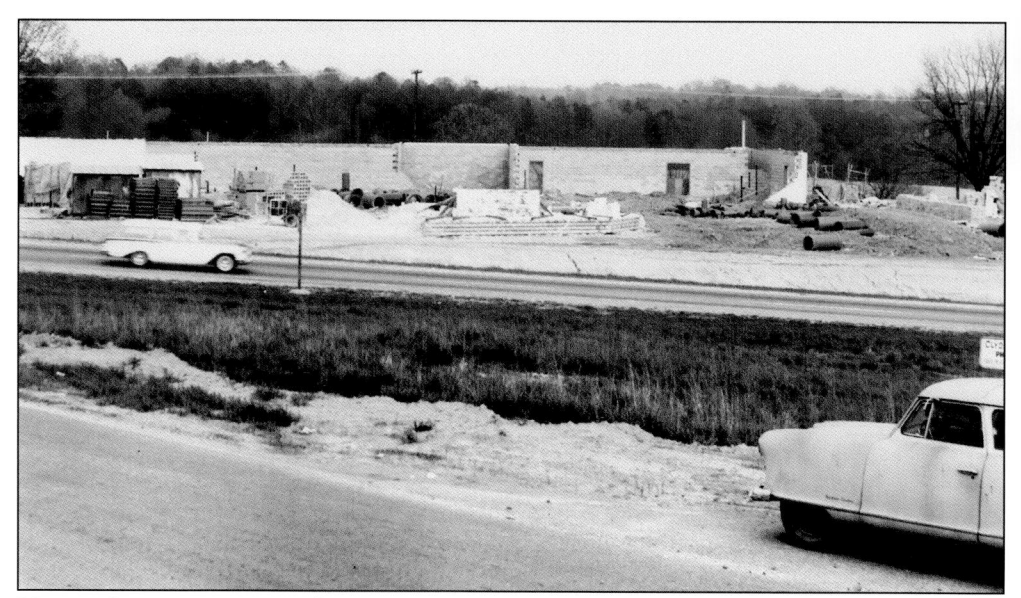

UNDER CONSTRUCTION. Baby Ray Cornwell gets an early shot of Warlick's Funeral Home in its infancy. Solomon Rhodes Warlick started the funeral home in 1911 as part of Warlick and Barkley Furniture and Undertakers on the Courtsquare in Lincolnton, currently the site of Courtstreet Grille. Years later, they moved the business to 301 South Aspen Street on the former site of Lincolnton's Old White Church. In December 1965 Sol and his son, Dave, moved the funeral home to the site shown in the above photograph. Warlick's Funeral Home is currently in its fourth generation of operation.

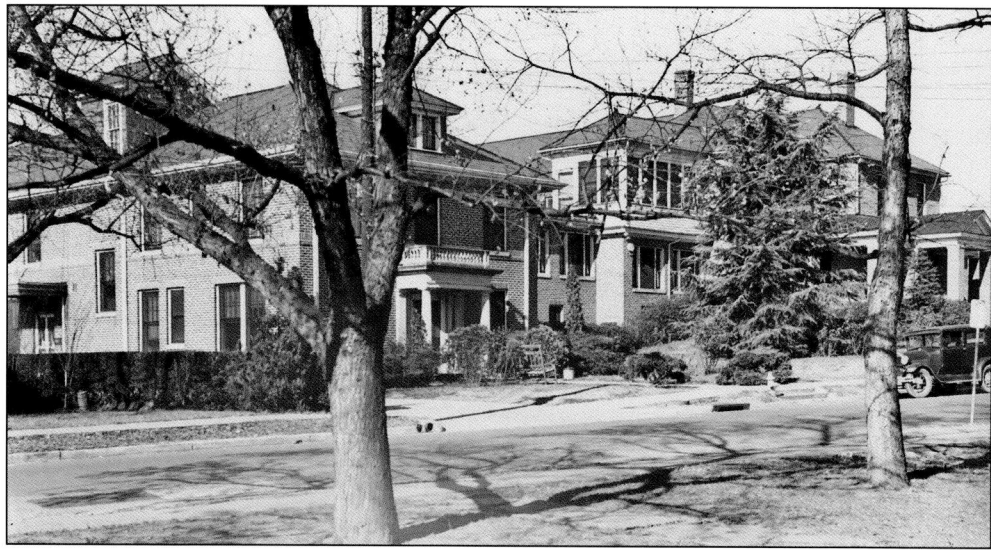

LINCOLNTON'S HOSPITAL. Nestled in the historic and quaint neighborhood along South Aspen Street in Lincolnton, Crowell Hospital stands as a local landmark. The Lincoln Hospital opened on March 11, 1907, under the supervision and leadership of Dr. L.A. Crowell and Dr. R.W. Petrie. In 1936 the Crowell family incorporated the hospital and changed the name to Crowell Memorial Hospital in honor and memory of Dr. Crowell's son, Dr. Gordon Bryan Crowell, who died in 1926. The hospital became Brian Nursing Centers in 1985 and is now owned by Ralph Carpenter.

Four
FLOATS, DEBUTANTES, AND COTTON CANDY

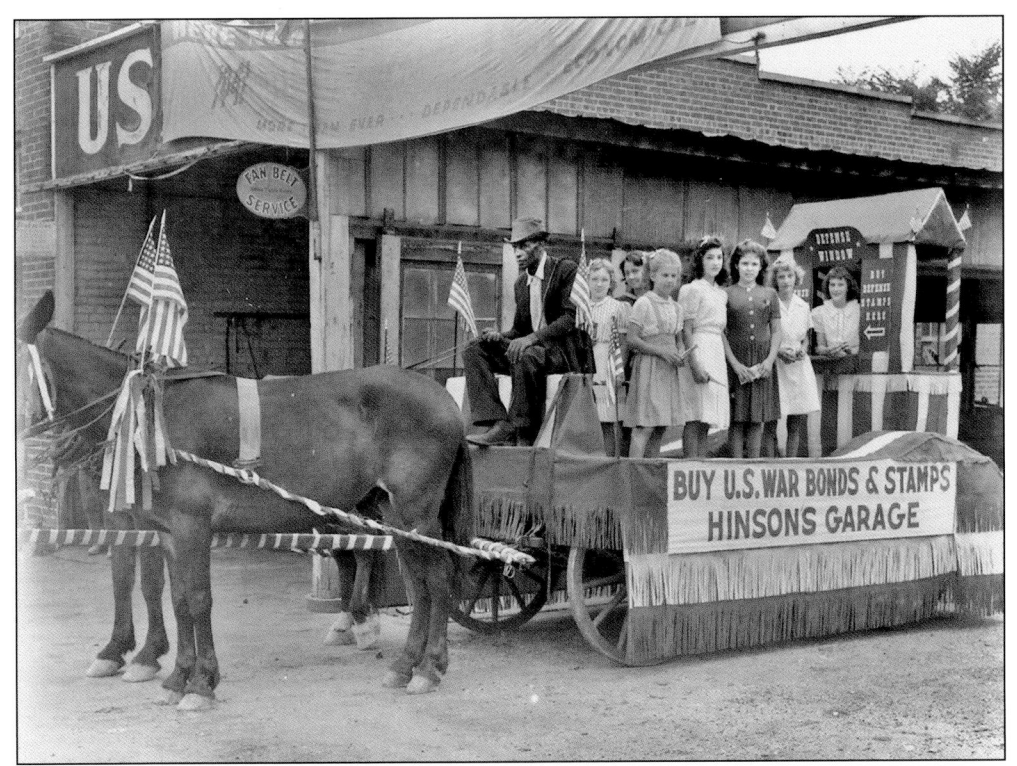

HINSON GARAGE PARADE FLOAT, C. 1940S. Betty Kincaid peeks out from inside the "defense window" on the Hinson's Garage float that promotes U.S. war bonds and stamps. The young girls riding on the float are, from left to right, as follows: Barbara Kiger McNeill, Betty Jane Rhyne Saunders, Laura Hoffman, Doris Crowell, Mary Miller, Bobby Joe Belch Paysour, and Betty Kincaid. (Courtesy of Paul Dellinger.)

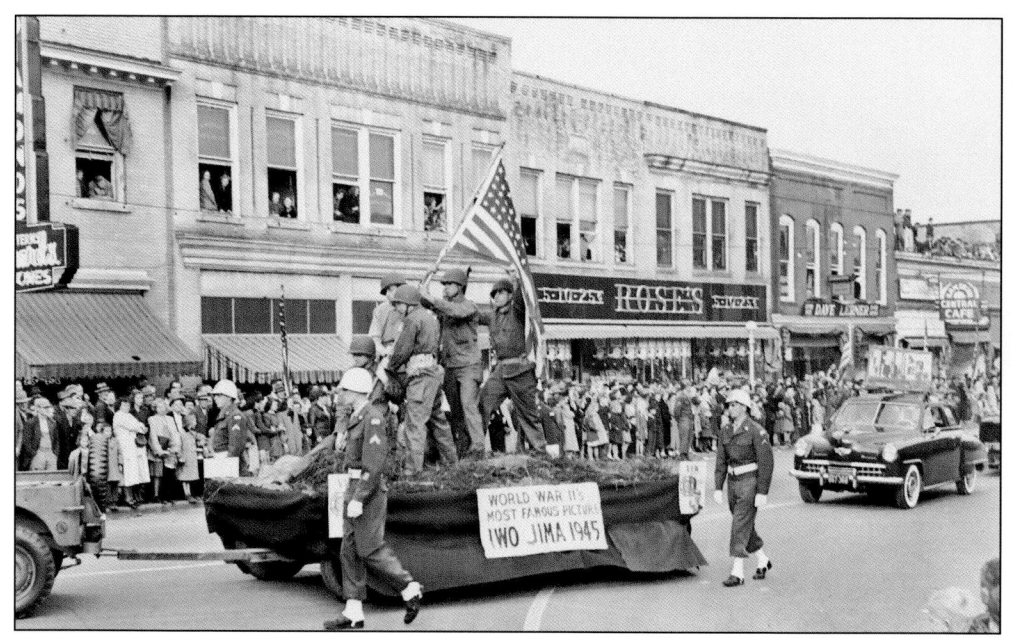

RAISING THE FLAG. Participating in an annual Lincolnton parade, a number of men from Lincolnton portray the raising of the flag on the Iwo Jima float during the late 1940s. The participants assumed the following positions of the six flag raisers from left to right: (front row) Ira Hayes, Franklin Sousley, John Bradley, and Harlon Block; (back row) Michael Strank (behind Sousley) and Rene Gagnon (behind Bradley).

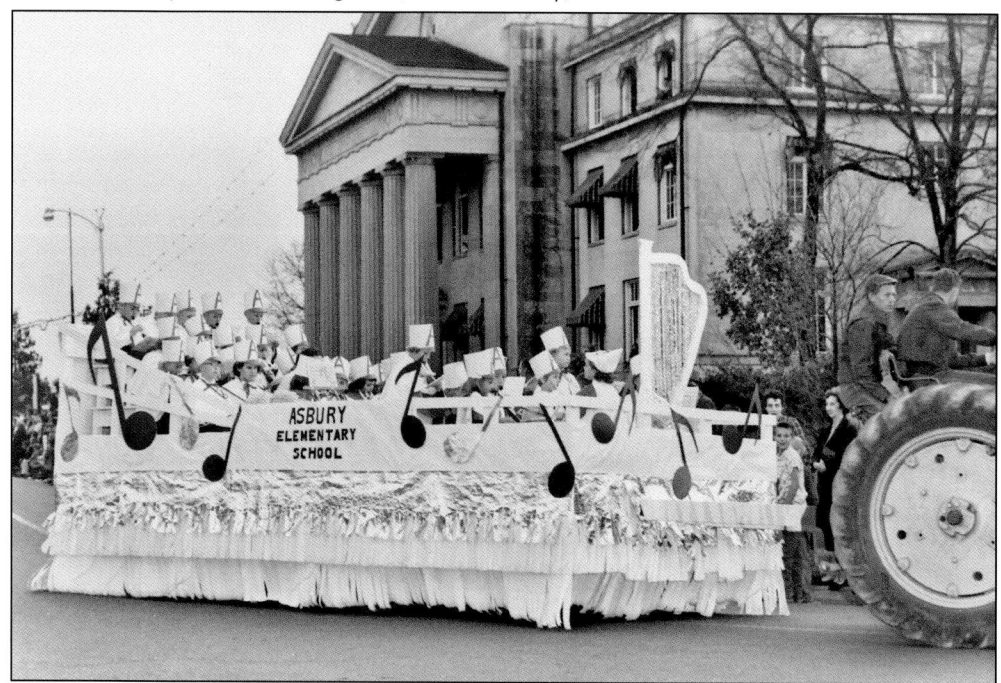

ASBURY ELEMENTARY SCHOOL PARADE FLOAT, NOVEMBER 25, 1958. A large harp and treble clefs provide the theme of music as the Asbury Elementary School Harmony Band parade float makes its way around the Courtsquare in Lincolnton.

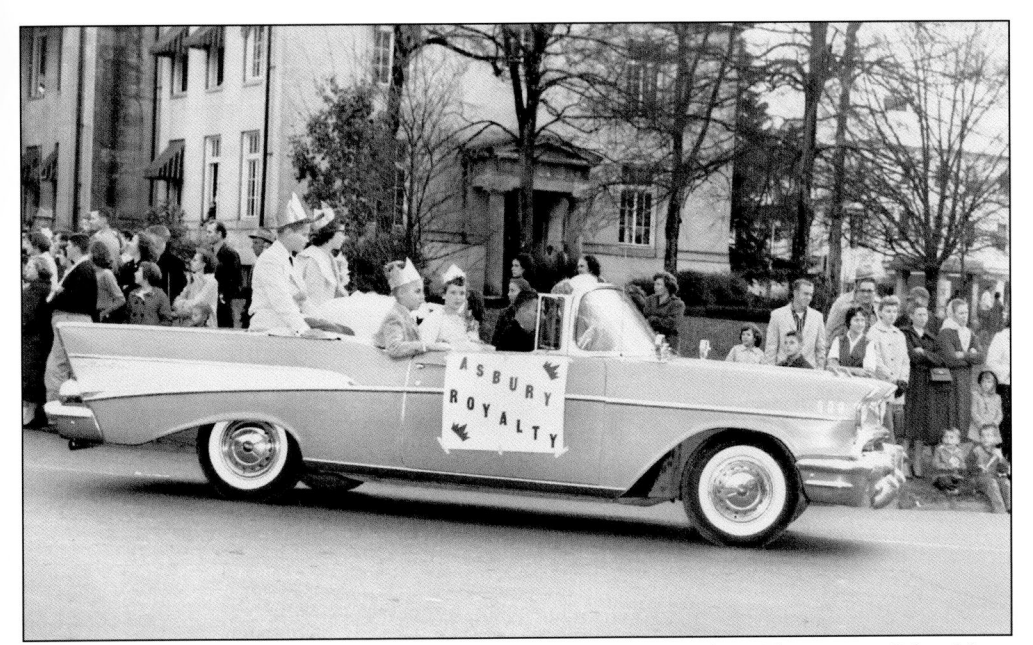

ASBURY ROYALTY, NOVEMBER 25, 1958. Four students from Asbury Elementary School bear paper crowns as their school's royalty and head around the Courtsquare in Lincolnton. Touted as the "biggest show in Lincolnton," the procession of parade floats "was thrilling to the labyrinth of excited children and their elders," explained *The Lincoln County News*.

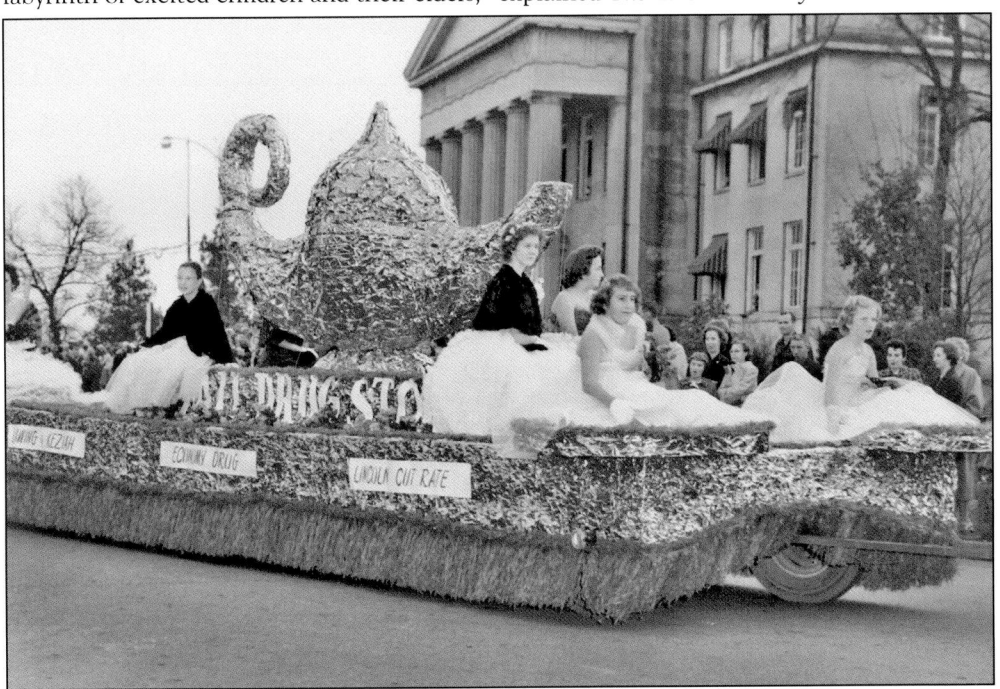

LINCOLNTON DRUG STORES' PARADE FLOAT, NOVEMBER 25, 1958. Lawing-Keziah, Economy, and Lincoln Cut Rate Drug Stores combine resources for their parade float that carries a genie's lamp and a group of young girls. An estimated crowd of 10,000–20,000 spectators crowded Main Street and the Courtsquare for the Christmas parade of 1958.

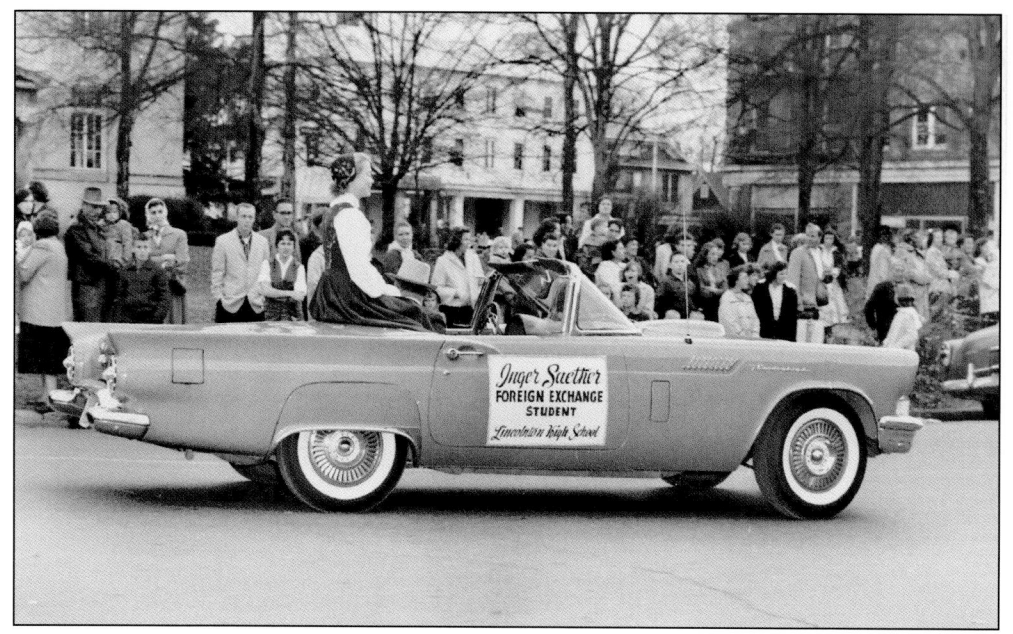

INGER SAETTNER, LINCOLNTON HIGH SCHOOL EXCHANGE STUDENT, NOVEMBER 25, 1958. Inger Saettner rides atop a Ford Thunderbird in the annual Merchants Association Christmas Parade in this shot taken by Baby Ray from East Sycamore Street.

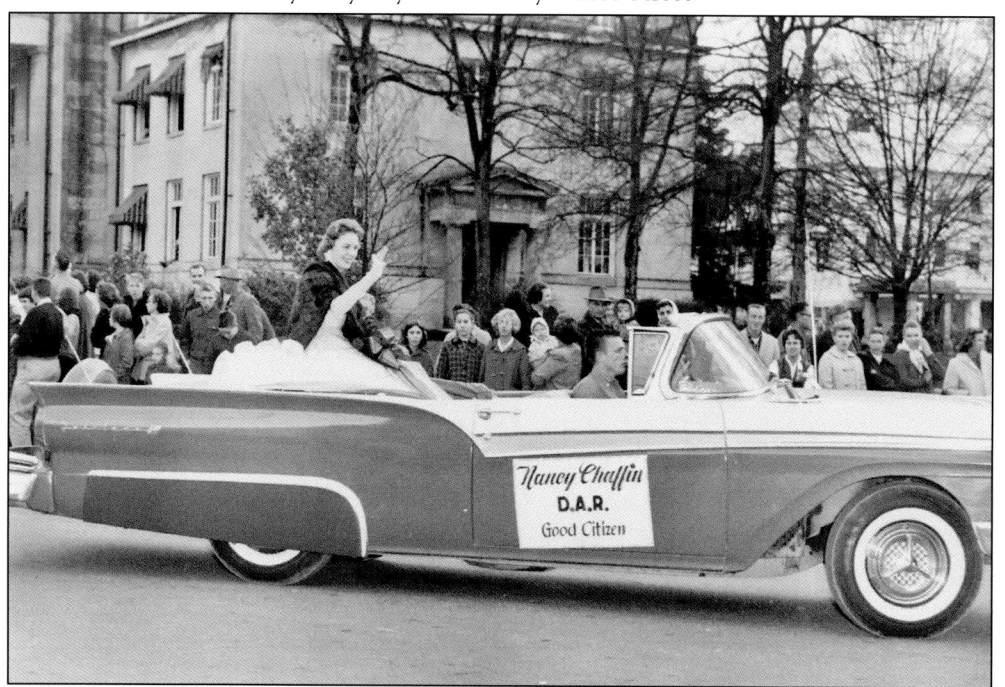

NANCY CHAFFIN, DAUGHTERS OF THE AMERICAN REVOLUTION GOOD CITIZEN AWARD WINNER, NOVEMBER 25, 1958. Nancy Chaffin is escorted around Lincolnton's Courtsquare as onlookers admire her attire and await the next parade float in the procession. The Lincolnton Fire Department's sirens sounded to alert everyone that the parade was approaching between 4:00 and 4:30 p.m.

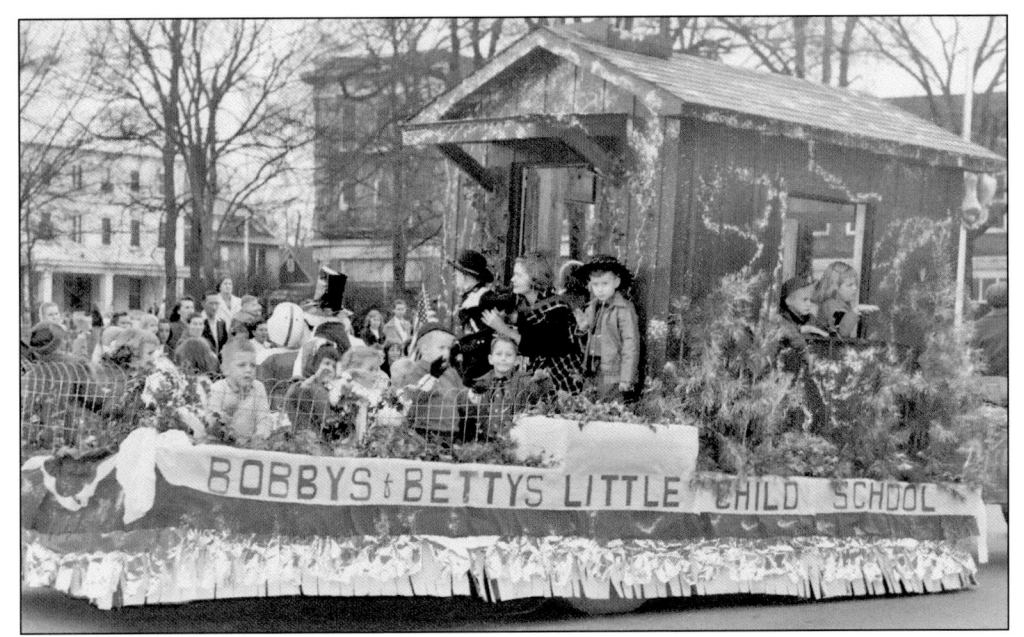

BOBBY'S AND BETTY'S LITTLE CHILD SCHOOL PARADE FLOAT, NOVEMBER 25, 1958. The children of Bobby's and Betty's Little Child School peer out from behind their gated parade float. This float was one of 65 units that took part in Lincolnton's Christmas Parade of 1958. The floats began moving at 4:00 p.m. from Hoyle Motor Company on East Main Street.

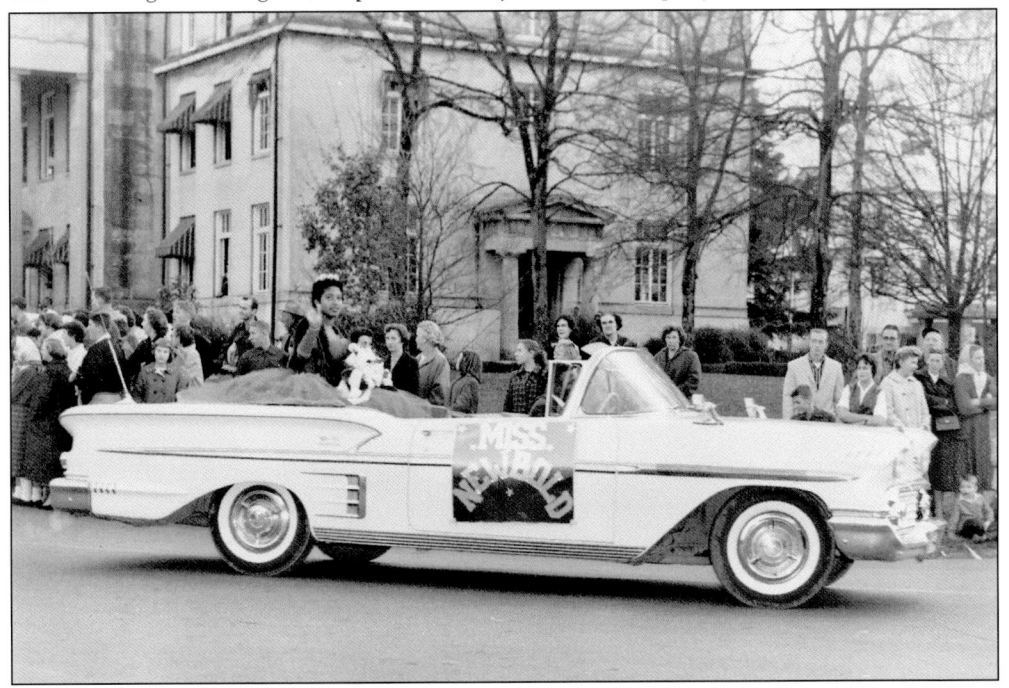

MISS NEWBOLD HIGH SCHOOL, NOVEMBER 25, 1958. Miss Newbold High School takes an easy ride in the annual Christmas Parade as one of the featured parade guests. She was just one of the many featured queens in a procession that also included Betty Lane Evans, Miss North Carolina 1958–1959.

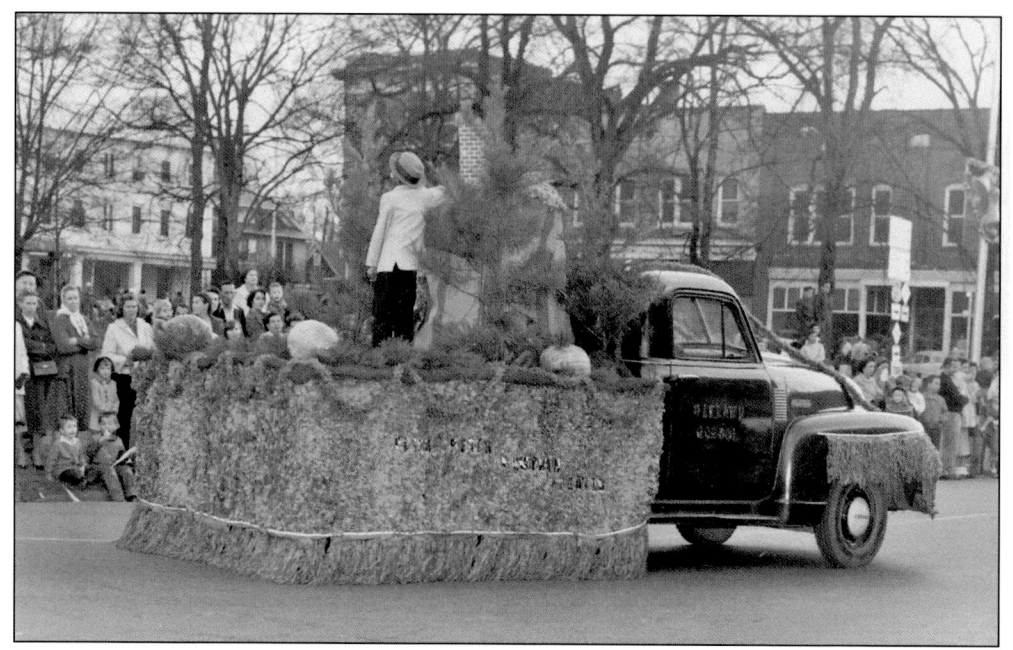

OAKLAWN SCHOOL PARADE TRUCK, NOVEMBER 25, 1958. A single child stands in the bed of an old truck float decorated with a Christmas tree, pumpkin, and garland. The Oaklawn School Parade Truck was one of two African-American schools in Lincolnton that participated in the parade. Newbold High School was the other African-American school.

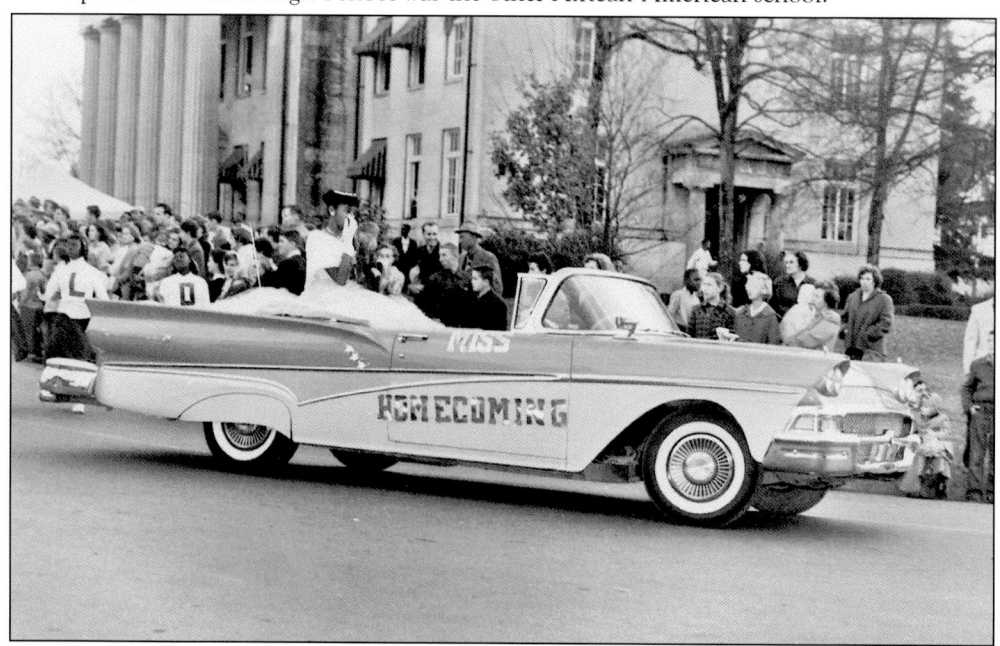

MISS HOMECOMING, NEWBOLD HIGH SCHOOL, NOVEMBER 25, 1958. A few members of the Newbold High School cheerleading squad can be seen cheering and dancing behind their school's Miss Homecoming. Other participating schools' homecoming queens and carrousel princesses included Miss Lincolnton, Carrousel Princess, Miss North Carolina, Miss Hi-Miss, and Miss Lincoln Lion.

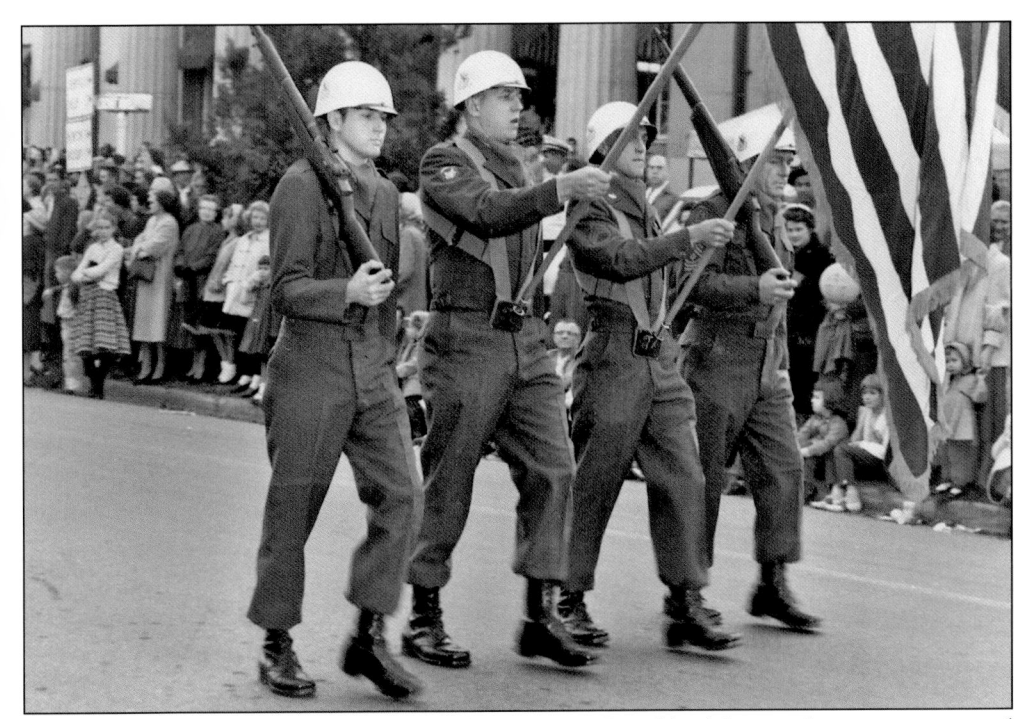

FLAGS HELD HIGH. Members of this Lincolnton Honor Guard lead the parade procession around the Courtsquare in Lincolnton for another large crowd of citizens from all over Lincoln County.

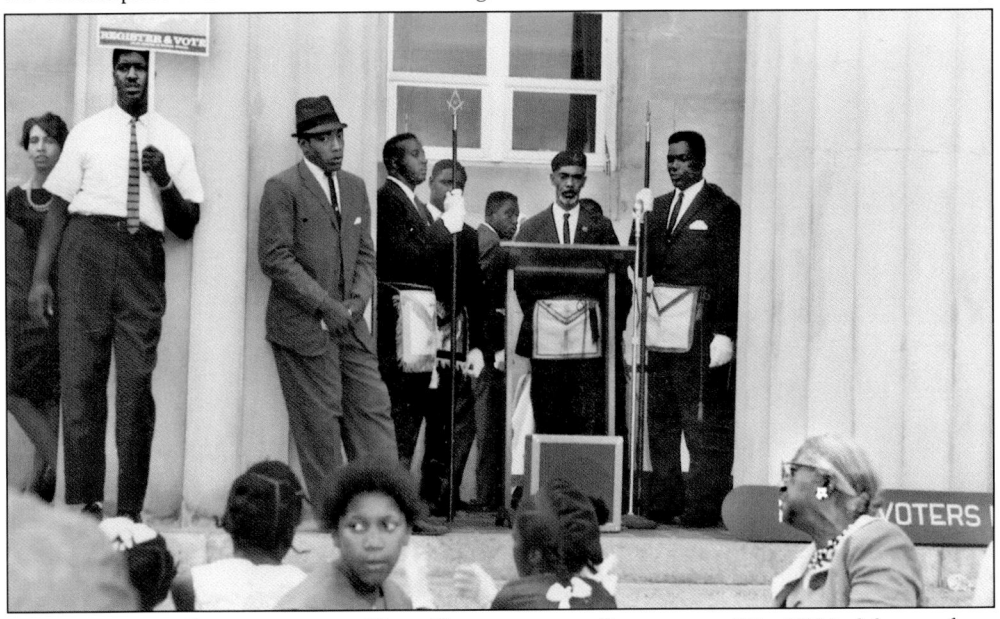

EMANCIPATION PROCLAMATION DAY CELEBRATION, SEPTEMBER 29, 1964. Masons from Lomax Lodge and members of the Negro Voters League assembled on the Lincoln County Courthouse steps for the celebration of Emancipation Proclamation Day. Those members in attendance are, from left to right, as follows: Shelia Holloway, Buddy Lee Friday, John Shuford Jr., Calvin Scruggs, unidentified, Darell Odoms, Lysander Price, Leonard Holloway (Master of Lomax Lodge), George Reinhardt, and Hattie Shuford.

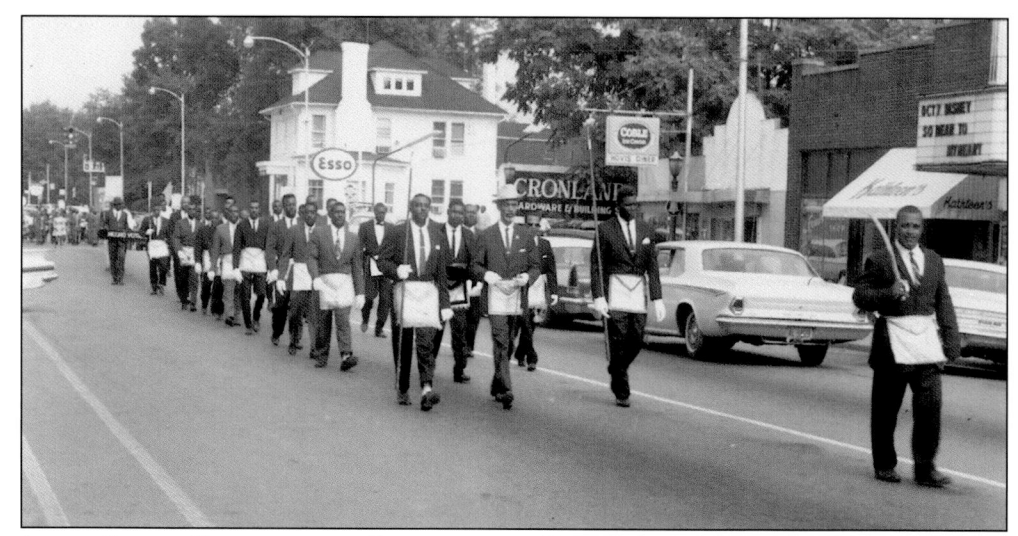

LOMAX LODGE, EMANCIPATION PROCLAMATION DAY CELEBRATION, SEPTEMBER 29, 1964. Members of Lomax Lodge proceed past the Esso Service Station in downtown Lincolnton for the celebration of the Emancipation Proclamation Day. The purpose of the event was, according to Leonard Holloway, to "revive interest in Emancipation Proclamation Day," which corresponded with National Constitution Week. Members of the procession in the first row are, from to right, as follows: Millard Link, senior deacon; Leonard Holloway, Master of Lodge; and George Reinhardt, junior deacon.

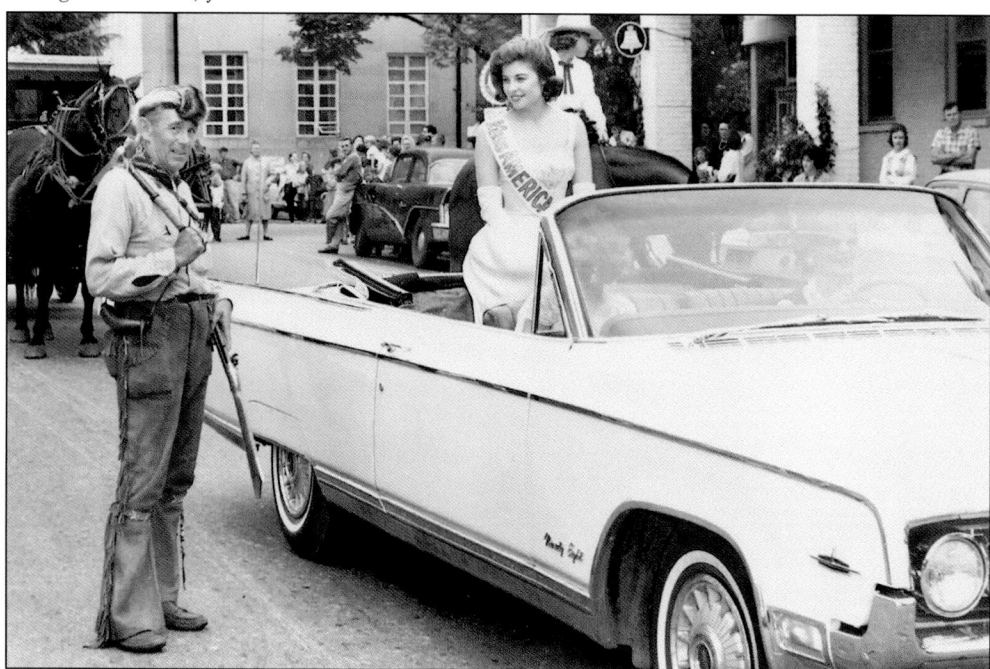

MISS AMERICA 1964, DONNA AXUM. Donna Axum, Miss America 1964, was in Lincolnton for the horse show at the "Ponderosa" and parade sponsored by the Lincoln County Horsemen's Association on Friday and Saturday, September 18 and 19, 1964. Axum was a rising senior at the University of Arkansas when she came to Lincolnton. Accompanied by her mother, Axum stayed at the North State Hotel and was interviewed by Pat Borden of the local paper.

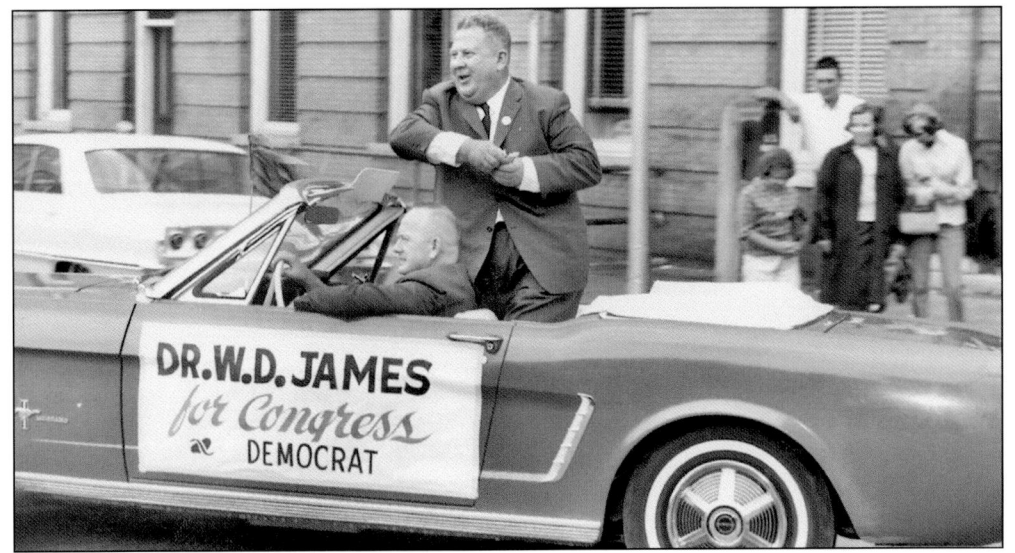

DR. WILLIAM "BILL" JAMES. "Dr. Bill" James, Democratic candidate for Congress, participated in the parade in Lincolnton on Saturday, September 19, 1964. According to reports in the local paper, he was in Lincolnton with his nephew, Mark Lindsey Jr., the Wednesday before the parade "making some friends and getting some votes." James, a Presbyterian minister and deacon from Hamlet, North Carolina, fought to unseat C.R. Jonas of the eighth congressional district in the November 1964 election. Bryan Craig, chairman of the Lincoln County Democratic Executive Committee, drives Dr. James past the Reinhardt Building as he distributes campaign mementos.

GITTY UP. Featured in *The Lincoln County News* on Thursday, September 24, 1964, William W. Modlin and his two sons are dressed in appropriate western attire. The Modlins participated in the three-day horse show at the "Ponderosa," which was developed by the Lincoln County Horseman's Association. The Horseman's Association received much praise from the attendees, even with occasional rain and a conflicting football game between Lincolnton and Belmont that weekend.

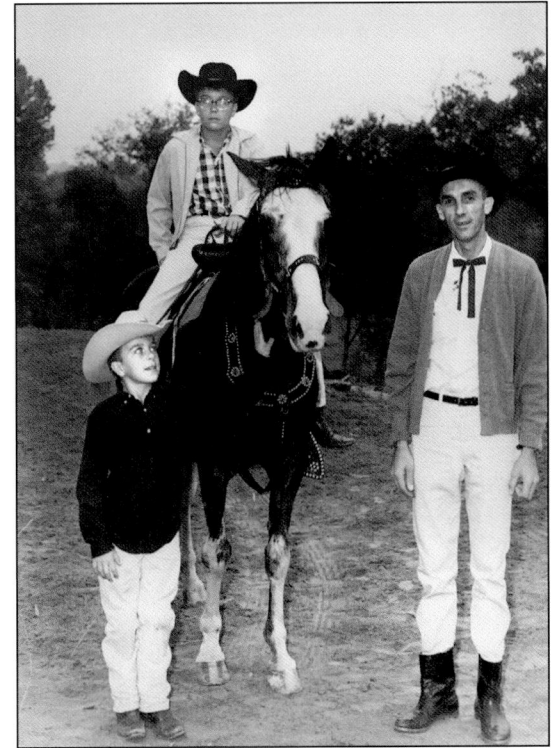

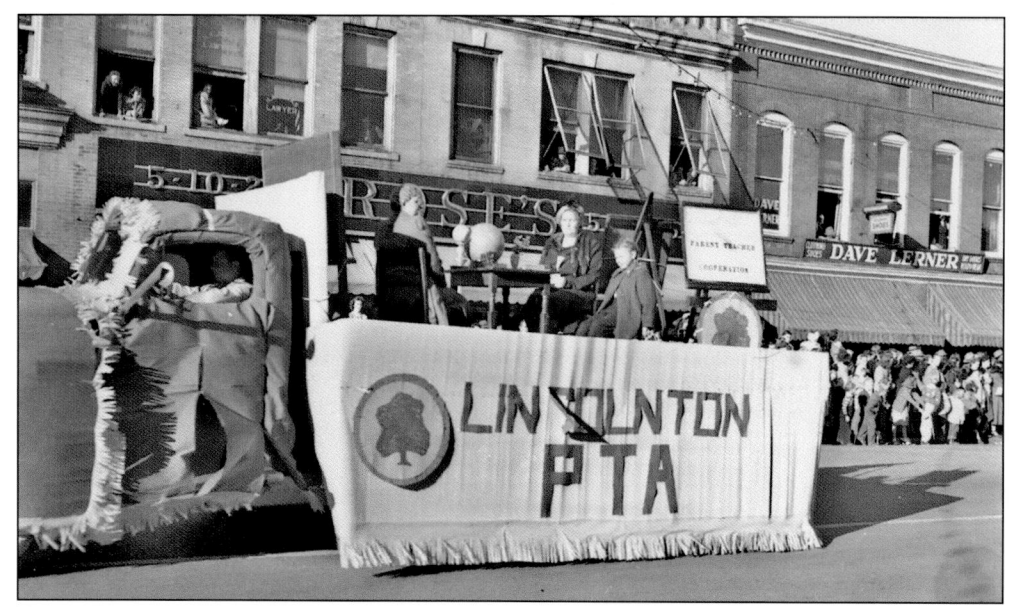

RIDE WITH EDUCATION IN MIND. In this 1940s photograph three participants on Lincolnton's Parent Teacher Association float sit behind a desk, on which rest the essential "tools of the trade" from the classroom. They get attention not only from citizens on ground level but also those who sit in the windowsills of Lincolnton's downtown businesses.

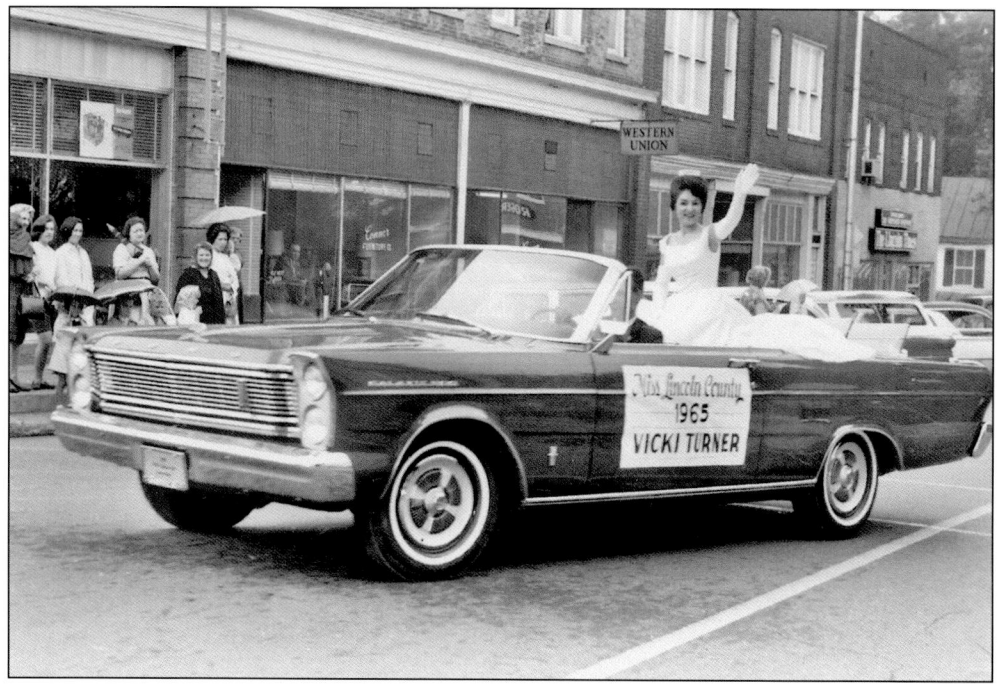

VICKI TURNER, MISS LINCOLN COUNTY 1965. Miss Lincoln County 1965, Vicki Turner, parades around the Courtsquare in Lincolnton during the large parade held on Saturday, September 19, 1964. Turner, a 1963 graduate of Lincolnton High School, performed a rendition of "I Love Thee," from *Song of Norway* for the talent portion of the Miss Lincoln County pageant. For her final number, she sang "Birth of the Blues," accompanied by Jerry Elmore.

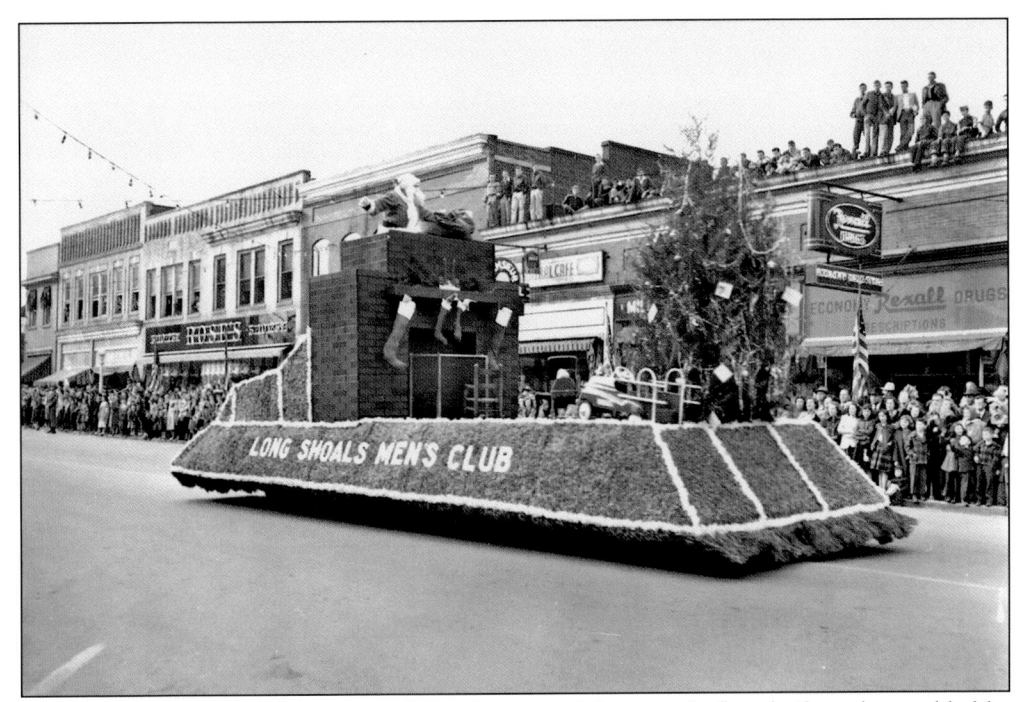

OUT HE COMES. Santa bursts out of the chimney of this parade float built and assembled by the men's club of Long Shoals. Their attention to detail leaves onlookers wondering when Santa will consume the milk and cookies left for him and when he will layout the presents for the children. (Courtesy of Paul Dellinger.)

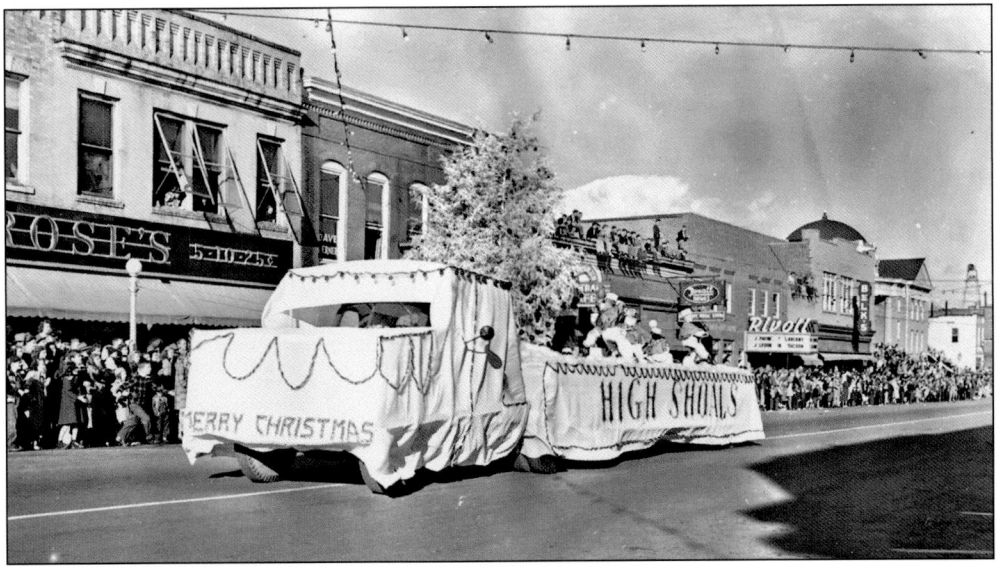

GOING ALL OUT. Families from the High Shoals community in Lincoln County have put an enormous amount of effort into decorating their parade float, depicted in this 1940s shot. Many of Lincolnton's eldest citizens recall the pride, hard work, and dedication invested in the parade float entries during this time period. They also fondly remember lining the streets with their parents, grandparents, friends, and neighbors to catch a glimpse of the glamour of the festive events.

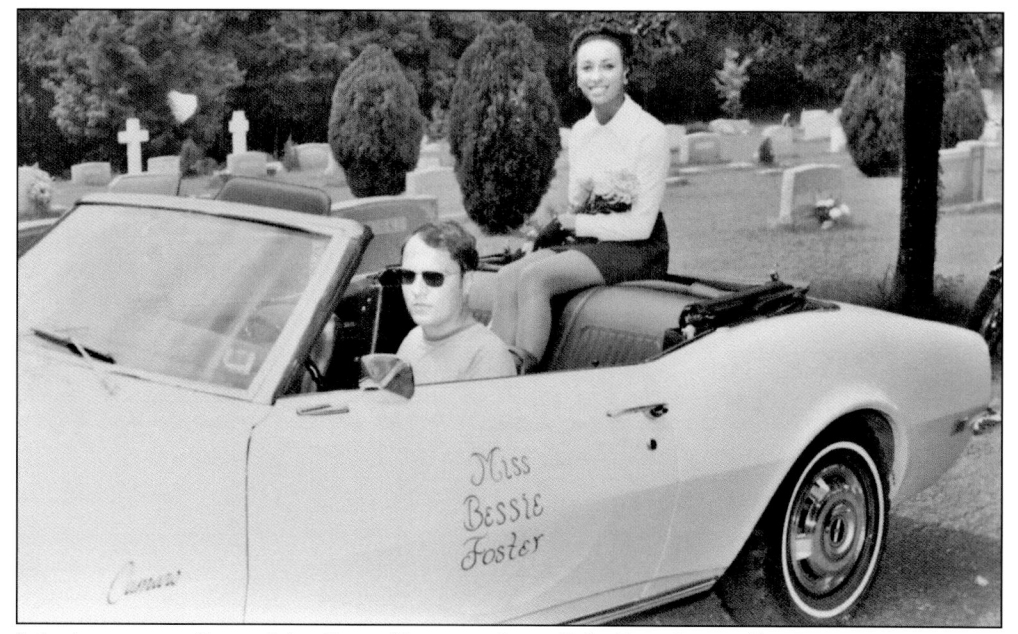

It's All in the Smile. Miss Bessie Foster smiles at Baby Ray Cornwell as her escort pauses en route to East Main Street in Lincolnton. This 1971 parade procession started at Hollybrook Cemetery and headed west towards the Courtsquare.

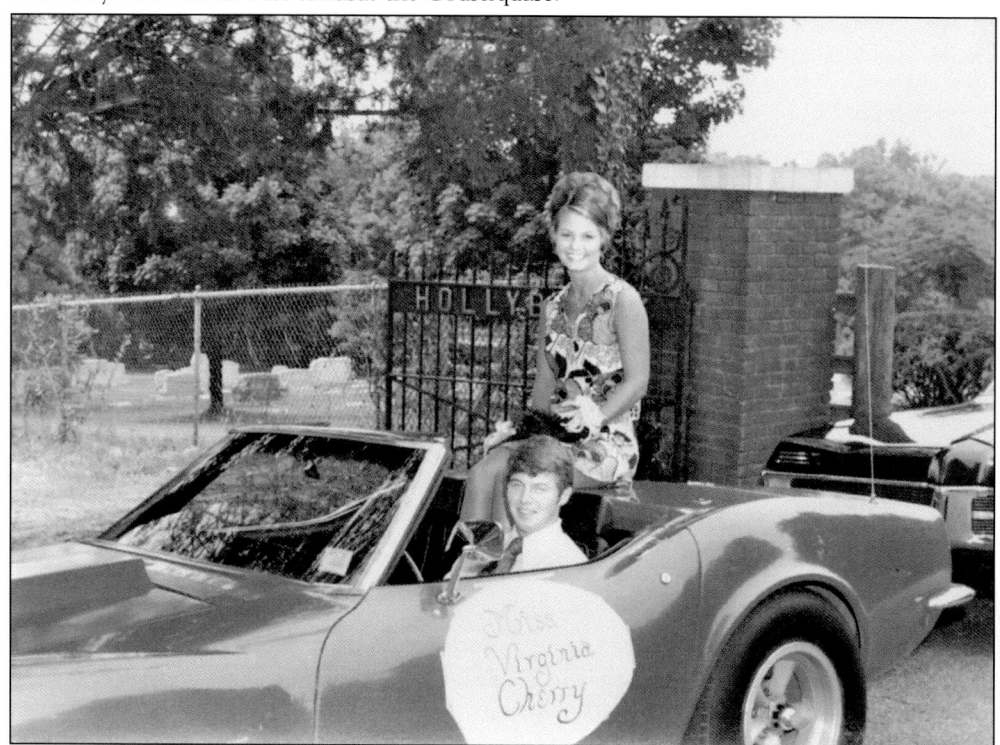

I Would Like to Thank. Miss Virginia Cherry is dressed nicely and adorned with a beautiful corsage for her showing at the 1971 parade in Lincolnton. Virginia and other beautiful girls from area high schools added a youthful feel to the annual parade and festivities.

Five
SERVICE TO GOD AND COMMUNITY

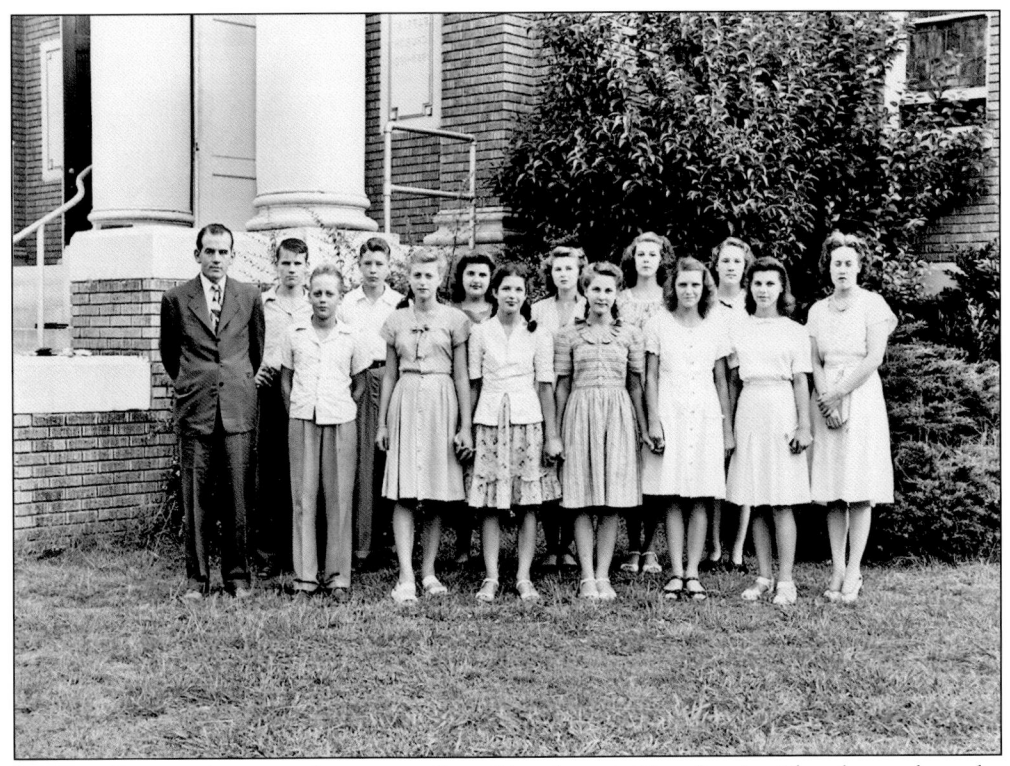

ON THE LAWN. A group of teenagers from Lincolnton's First Baptist Church stand on the church's lawn for this 1940s Baby Ray Cornwell photograph. The group, believed to be part of the church's Baptist training union, are identified, from left to right, as follows: (front row) Zeb Burris, Bill Garrison, Joan Bondurant, Peggy Connor, Colleen Buff, unidentified, Ruby Lewis, and Helen Mosteller; (back row) unidentified, Charles Holly, Sara Heavner, Loretta Kendrick, Jessie Eurey, and Lafay Bost.

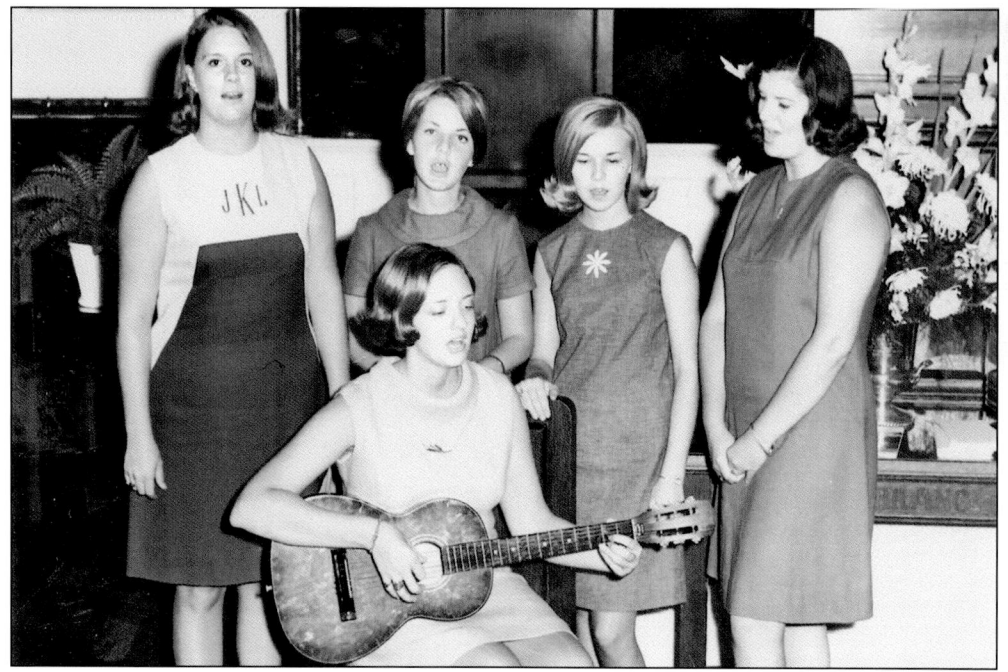

FIRST BAPTIST CHURCH SINGERS. Carolyn Barrett Thaxton plays the guitar as she and a group of ladies sing during Youth Week at Lincolnton's First Baptist Church held on July 31, 1968. The other members of the group are, from left to right, as follows: Jane Kiser Modlin, Beth Harrill Yarborough, Kay Nale, and Becky Kiser Beal.

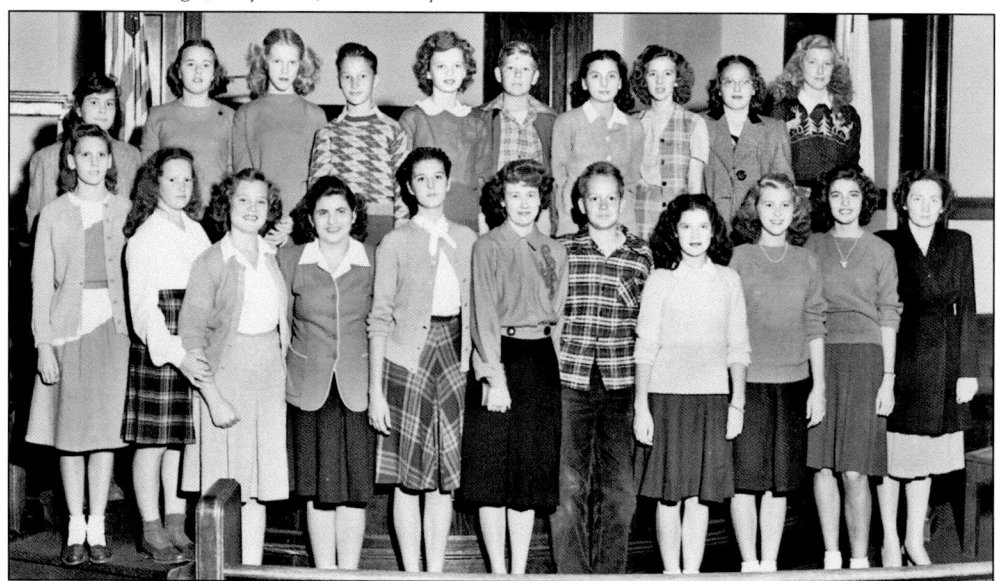

BAPTIST GIRLS AND BOYS. A group of girls and boys in the sanctuary of Lincolnton's First Baptist Church smile for Baby Ray Cornwell's camera in the 1940s. They are identified, from left to right, as follows: (front row) Mary Lewis, Shirley Buff, Ruth Delk, Sara Heavner, Jessie Eurey, Helen Mosteller, Bill Garrison, Peggy Connor, Joan Bondurant, unidentified, and Willie Lee Burris; (back row) Mildred Brooks, Eleanor Pollock, Nancy Beattie, unidentified, Wanda Reid, Vance Smith, Barbara Burris, Helen Forrester, Phyllis Honeycutt, and Nancy Stamey.

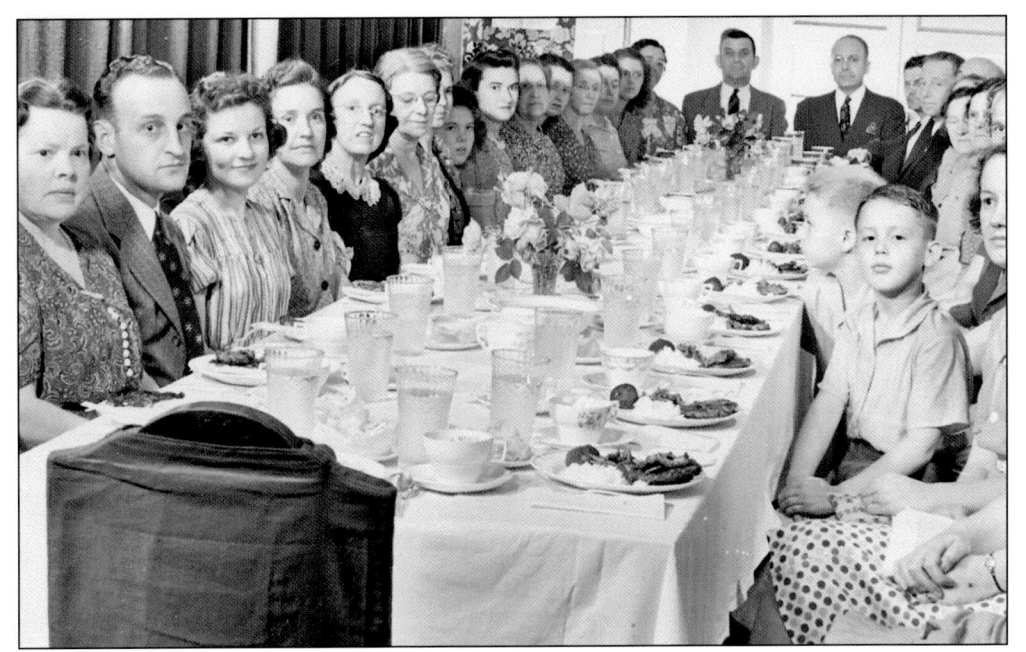

A 1941 Baptist Meal. In the basement of Lincolnton's First Baptist Church, this group takes a moment before their meal to pose for Baby Ray Cornwell. Some of the members of the group shown are as follows: Eunice Bandy, James Digh, Pansy Digh, Nell McLean Brevard, Mildred McLean Milam, Margaret Jane Childs, Pearl Proctor, J.L. Proctor, Rev. Yancy Elliott, E.B. Goodin, and Will Garrison.

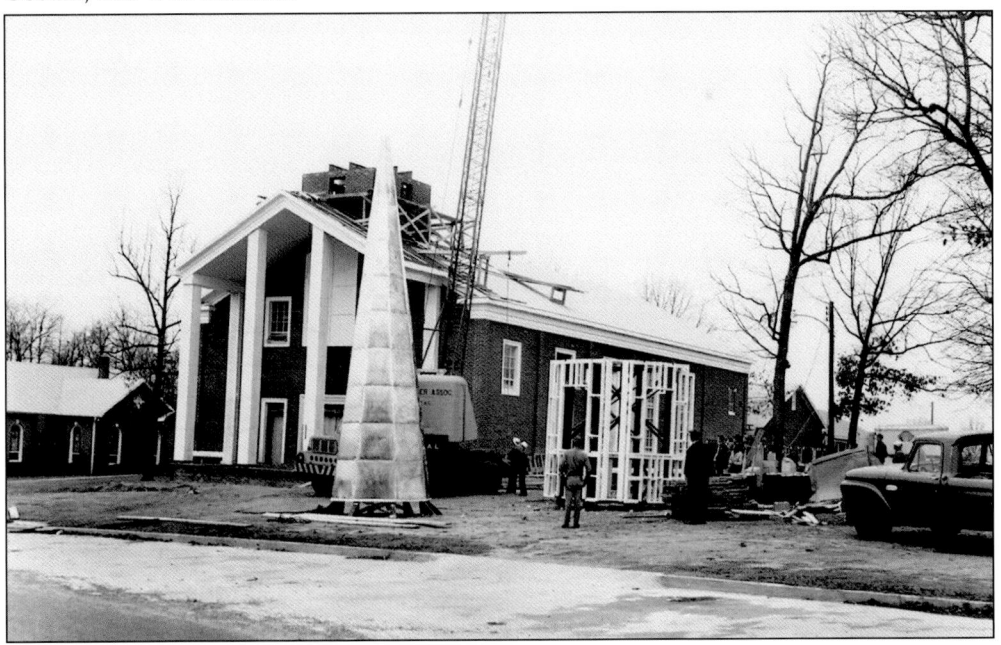

Southside Church Steeple. The crew from the Yount-Setzer Association in Charlotte, North Carolina, prepares itself to place the new copper-covered steeple atop Southside Baptist Church on Wednesday, January 6, 1965. The steeple, reported to weigh over 4,000 pounds, became part of a new church building that cost $90,000 to build.

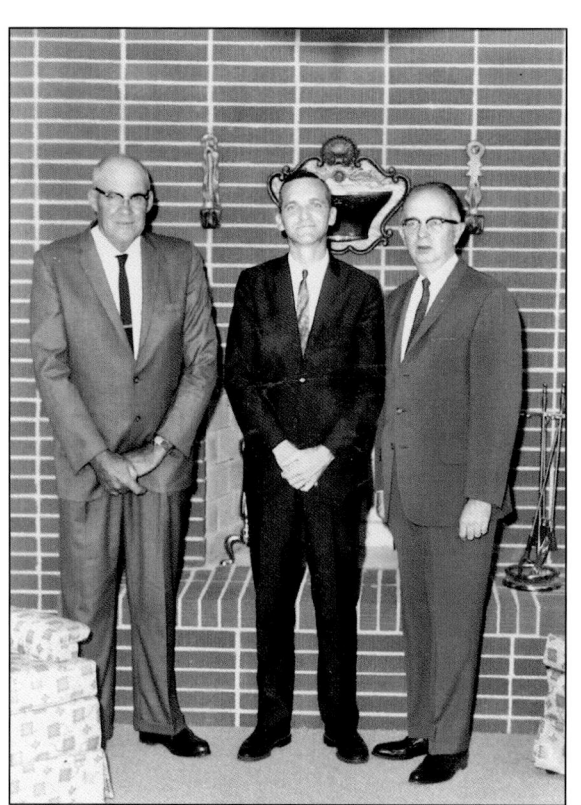

West Lincoln United Methodist Church Parsonage Dedication. On Sunday, June 23, 1968, Dr. Charles D. White, Gastonia District superintendent and secretary of the United Methodist Church, dedicated the church parsonage at West Lincoln United Methodist Church. Baby Ray Cornwell drove out to the western part of Lincoln County to capture the special event. Pictured in the photograph are E. Sain of Laurel Hill United Methodist Church; Rev. Norman Beck, pastor of the West Lincoln Charge; and Dr. White.

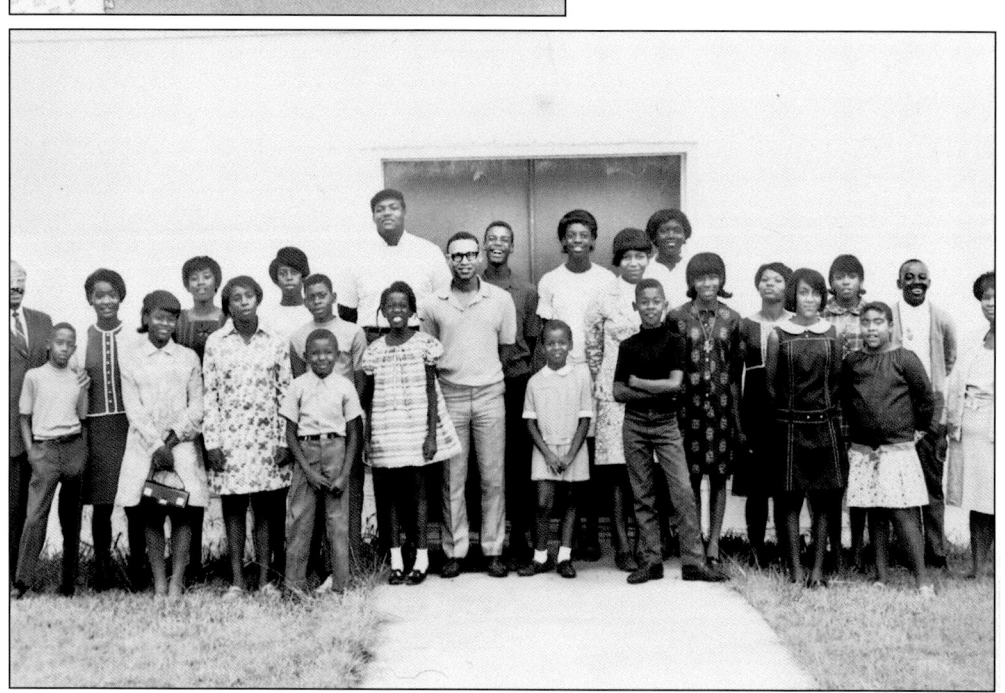

Second Baptist Church, September 1, 1968. Members of Second Baptist Church and Providence Baptist Church pose for this photograph taken on September 1, 1968, at Lincolnton's Second Baptist Church.

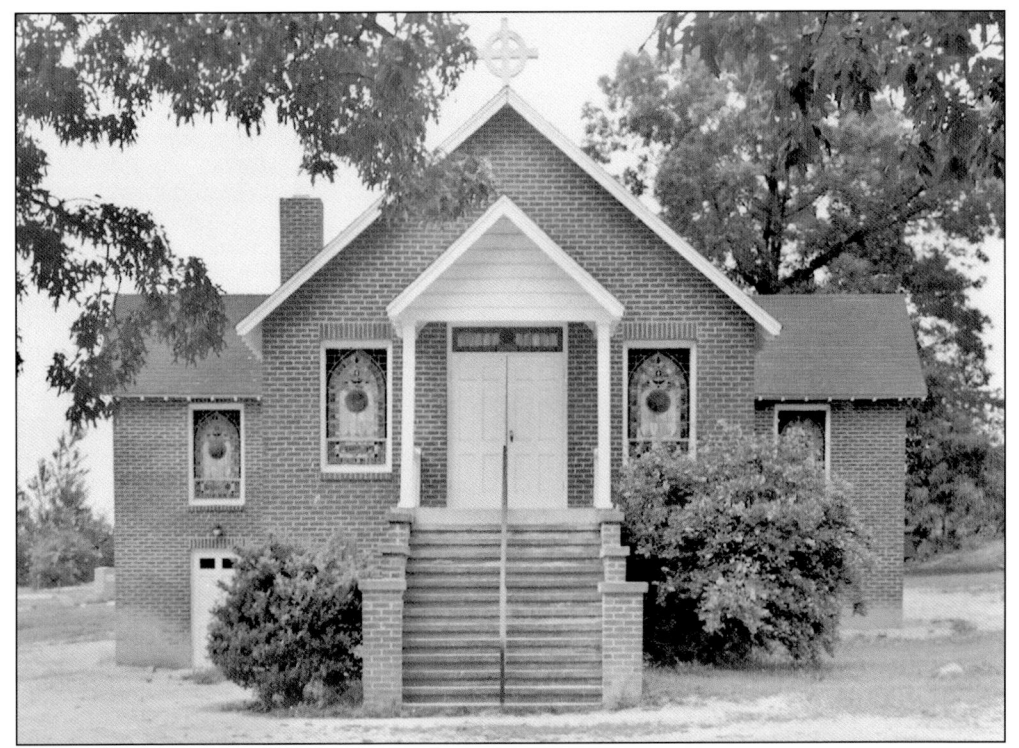

CHURCH OF OUR SAVIOUR AT WOODSIDE, LINCOLNTON. Serving the community since 1882, the Church of Our Saviour at Woodside began under the leadership of Dr. John M. Richardson; his wife, Alice Ramseur Richardson; his sister-in-law, Miss Ida Ramseur; and three daughters, Malvina, Lila, and Julia. Dr. Richardson and family organized the church as a mission school for the African Americans who worked at Woodside Plantation and the surrounding community.

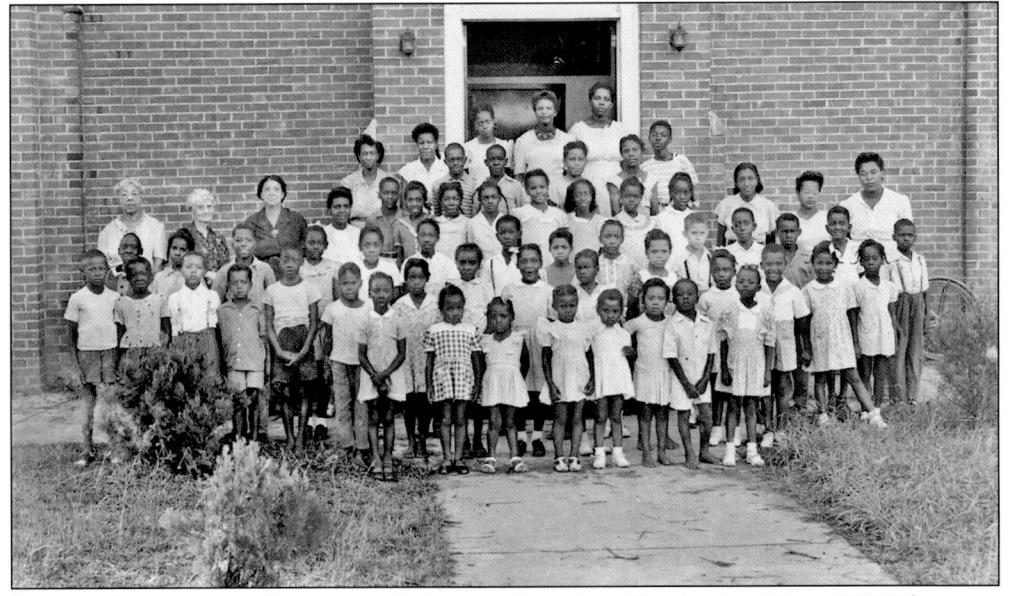

SUNDAY SESSION. Baby Ray Cornwell photographed this bible class in 1949 or 1950. The group is from an A.M.E. Zion church in Lincolnton, but they held their bible class at Moore's Chapel.

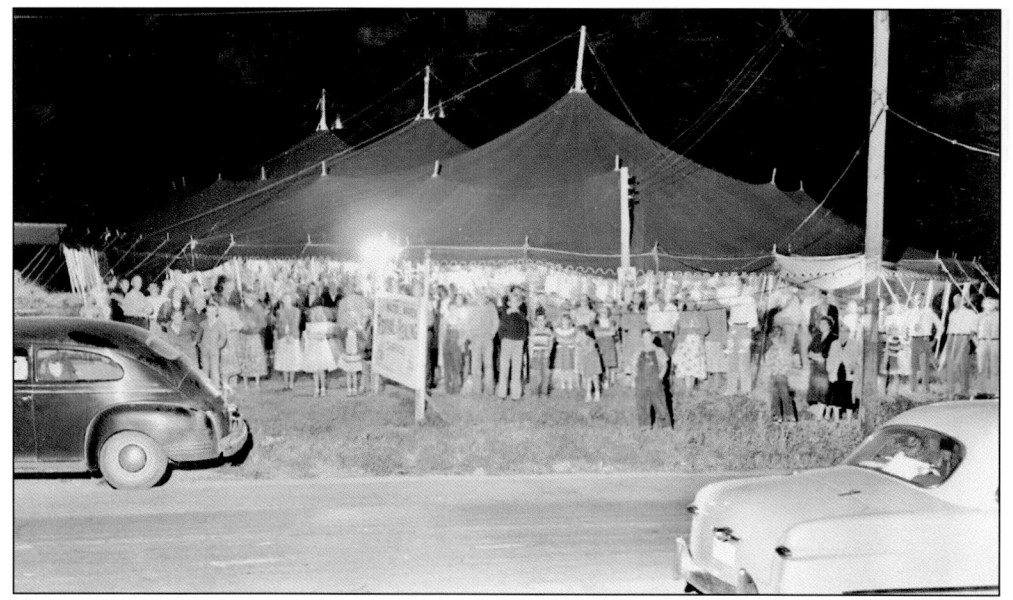

STANDING ROOM ONLY. The seams of the tent are about to burst as the crowd pours out into the street at this 1940s Lincolnton tent revival. The Walter Warren Tent Preaching Group promoted itself as a group of revivalists and healers. Many Lincolntonians recall a number of these events being held behind Carolina Roller and Supply on East Pine Street.

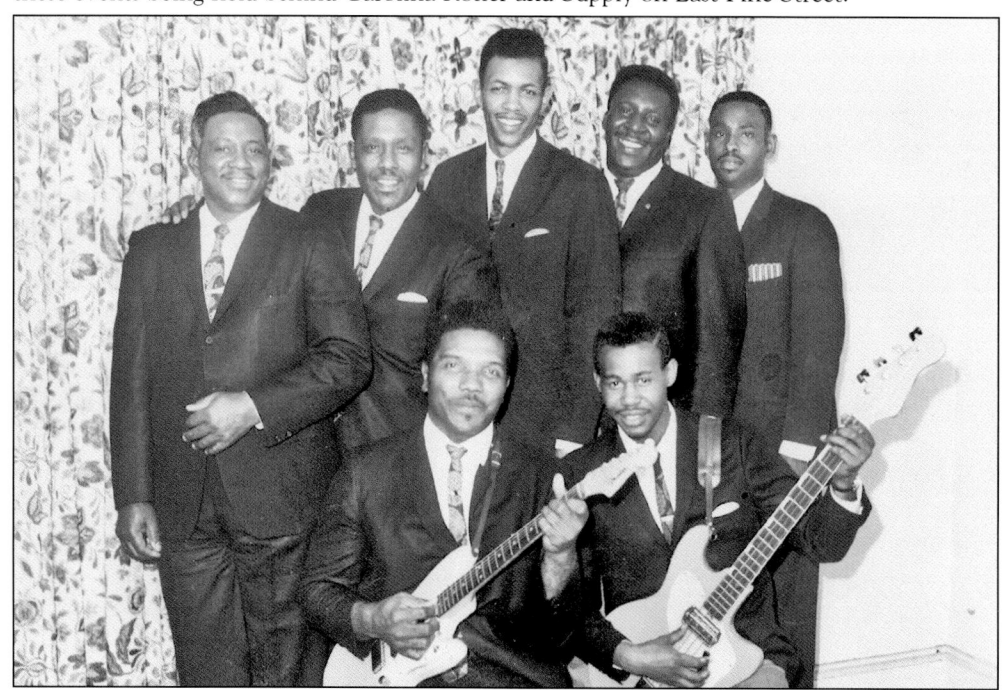

GOSPEL TRAVELERS AT WLON, NOVEMBER 16, 1958. At an early session at WLON on November 16, 1958, members of the Gospel Travelers stand ready to sing and play a few for Baby Ray Cornwell. Members of the Gospel Travelers are, from left to right, as follows: (front row) Gilliam Cord and William McDowell; (back row) Bill Washington, James Camp, William Enoch, Rayford Thompson, and Don Camp.

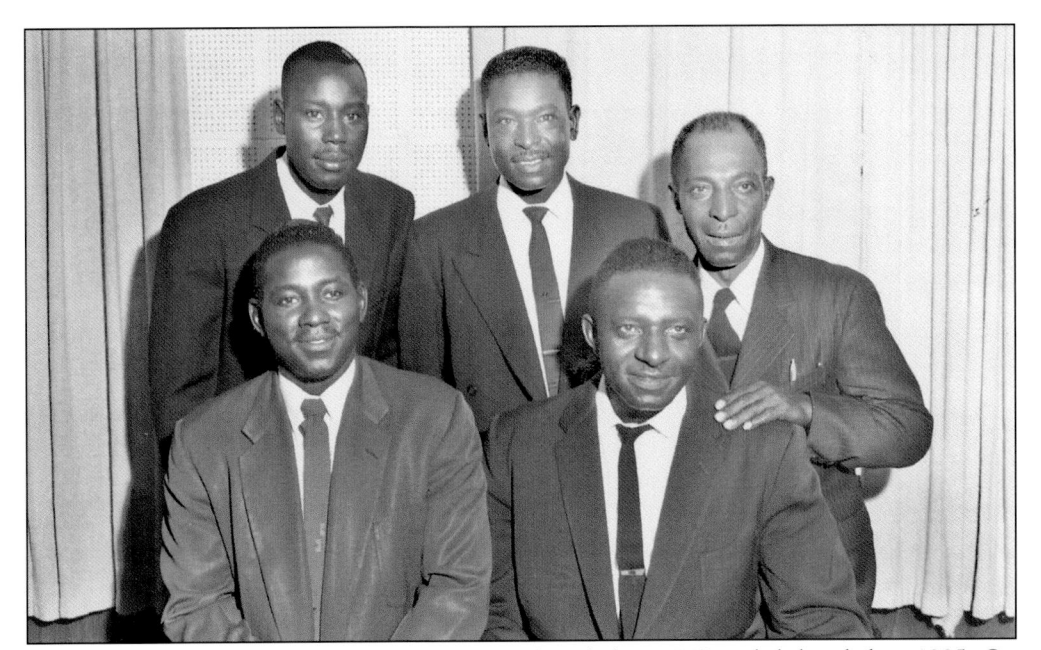

GOSPEL'S FINEST. The Gospel Travelers were founded in 1943 and disbanded in 1985. On February, 15, 1968, Baby Ray Cornwell grabs a brief moment at the WLON radio station in Lincolnton. Members of the Gospel Travelers are identified, from left to right, as follows: (front row) Bill Washington and Calvin Thompson; (back row) Ralph Roberts, Thomasine Morrell, and John Shuford.

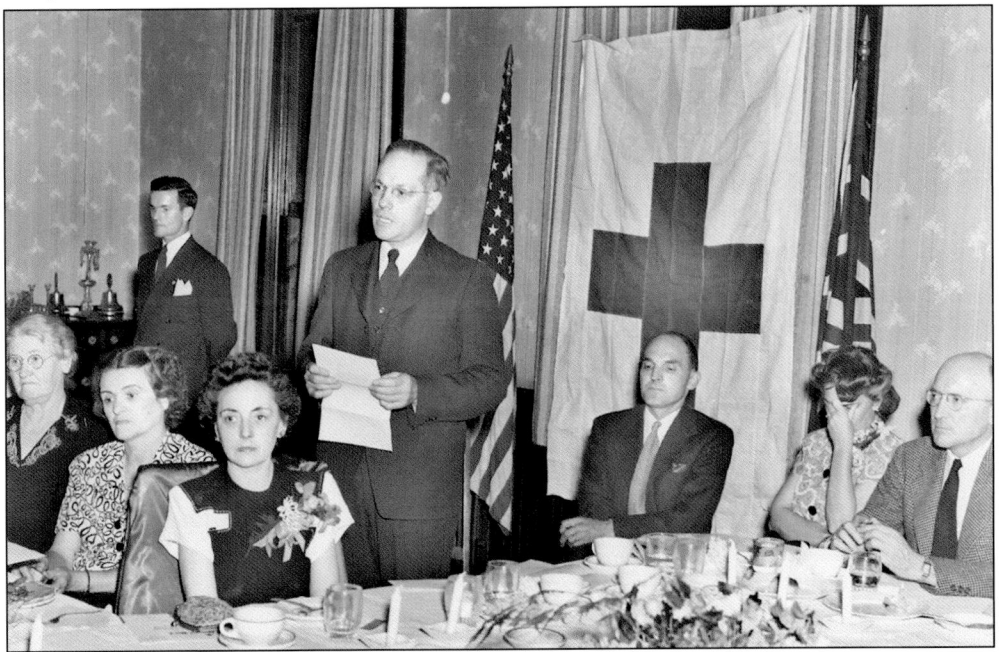

SAVING LIVES. Sometime during the 1940s, the Red Cross of Lincolnton met for a banquet and invited Baby Ray Cornwell as a guest and event photographer. In this shot, the widely recognized banner hangs behind Rhyne Little. After the bombing of Pearl Harbor, the Red Cross instigated new policies and a blood program.

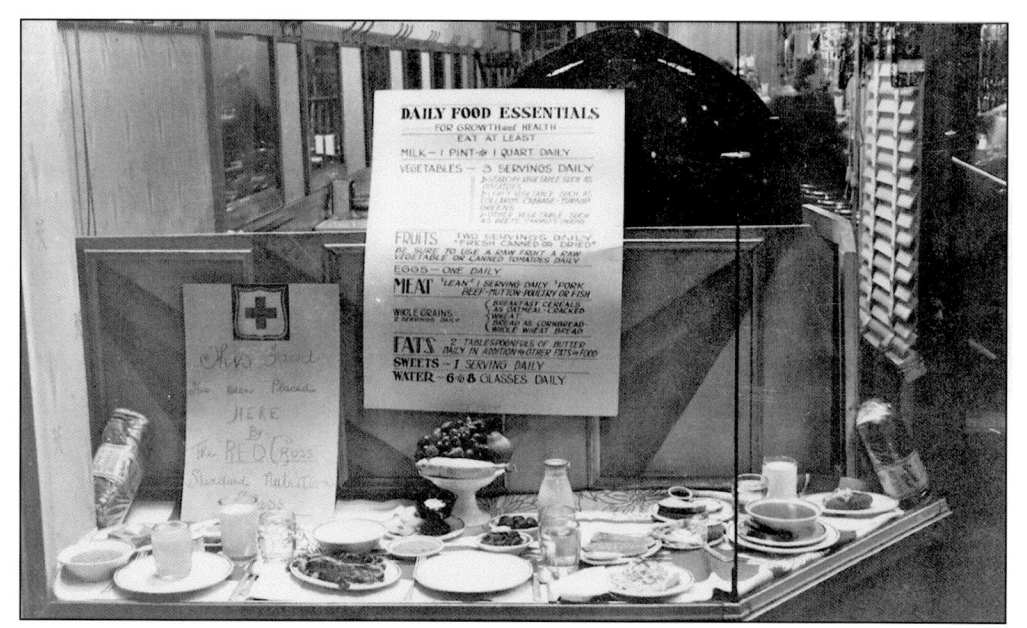

WINDOW SHOPPING. The local Red Cross planned to help the residents of Lincolnton better understand the essentials of eating healthy through this window display. Shown here are the four food groups and also examples of food from each group.

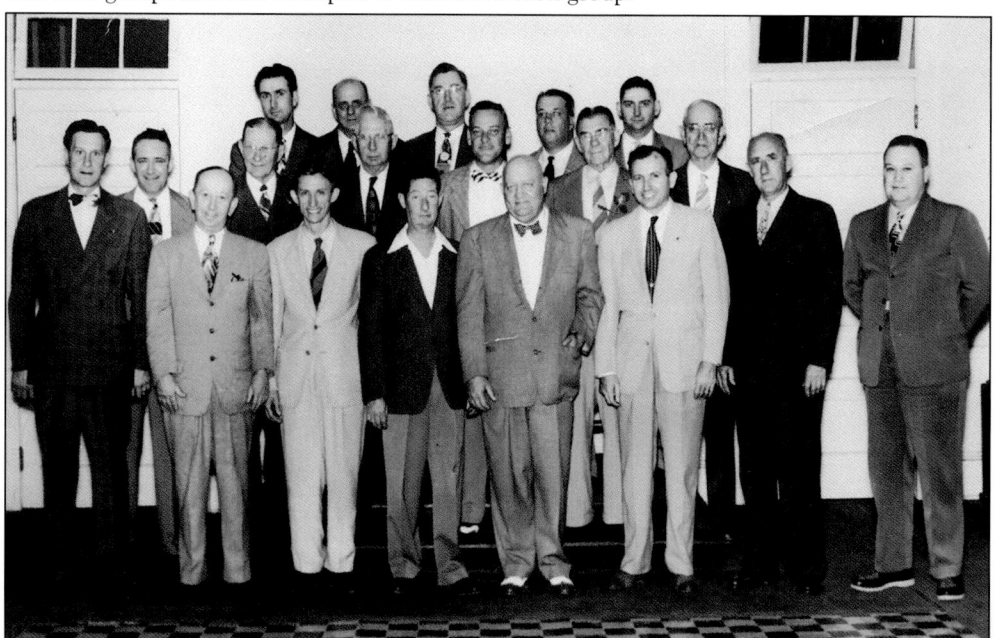

KNIGHTS OF PYTHIAS. The Fraternal Order of Knights of Pythias, an international fraternity, had an order in Lincolnton from the early 20th century until the middle part of the century. Members of Lincolnton's Knights of Pythias are identified, from left to right, as follows: (front row) unidentified, Nick Nickelson, ? Hartman, Zeb Keever, Judge Sheldon M. Roper, "Shine" Goodson, Jim Shuford, and unidentified; (middle row) three unidentified persons, Mike Whitener, and two unidentified persons; (back row) Perry Reep, Bryan L. Dellinger Sr., John Schrum, Loy Heavner, and Harold "Beef" Honeycutt. (Courtesy of Jack L. and Carolyn Dillinger.)

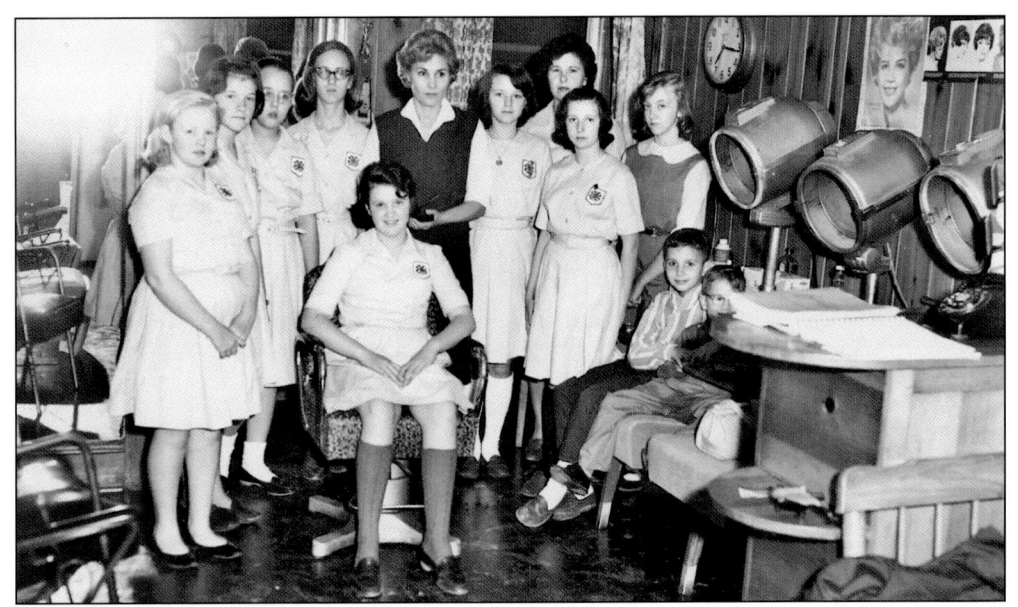

BETTER GROOMING AT CAROLYN'S BEAUTY SHOP, MARCH 30, 1965. Carolyn Gilbert's Beauty Shop welcomed the 4-H Clubs of Howard Creek and Bethpage for a "Good Grooming" project. Robbie and Greg Gilbert can be seen sitting under hair driers on the far right. The ladies are identified, from left to right, as follows: Kathy Haynes, Teresa Hoover, Karen Heavner, Susan Huss, Linda Saine, Janice Heavner, Mrs. Ruby Hoyle (leader), and Betty Guiton. Carolyn Gilbert can be seen in the middle of the group working on the hair of her daughter, Karen Gilbert. At the time Clyde Cornwell captured this image, the shop was located on Highway 27 West, five miles outside of Lincolnton.

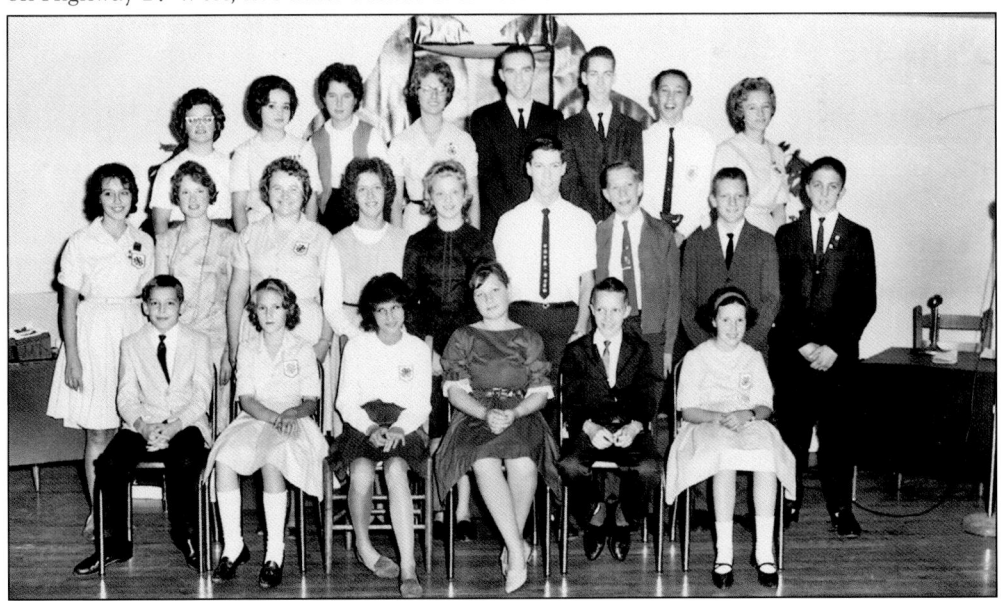

HEAD, HEART, HANDS, AND HEALTH. A 4-H group of Lincoln County poses for this 1950s photograph. The green four-leaf clover of the group hangs behind them showing the emblem of 4-H: Head, Heart, Hands, and Health. Since the 1920s, the 4-H group in Lincolnton has grown to encompass a large number of service projects and programs.

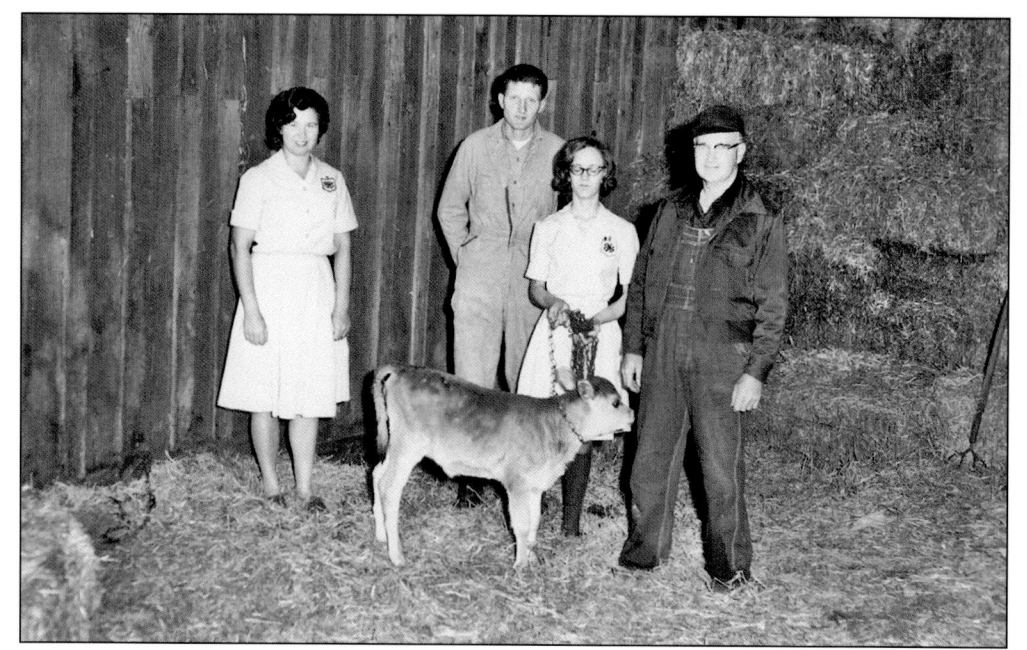

FOUR-H CALF CHAIN. Susan Huss holds the leash of her new registered Jersey heifer for this photograph taken on January 30, 1965. The other people included in the photograph are Mrs. Ray Hoyle, Dean Reep, and Everette Wise. Everette Wise donated the heifer to the Howard's Creek–Bethpage 4-H Club to help the club start a 4-H Calf Chain. Susan Huss raised, groomed, and showed the calf at the 4-H Dairy Show. She then gave the club the heifer's first born calf for another club member to raise.

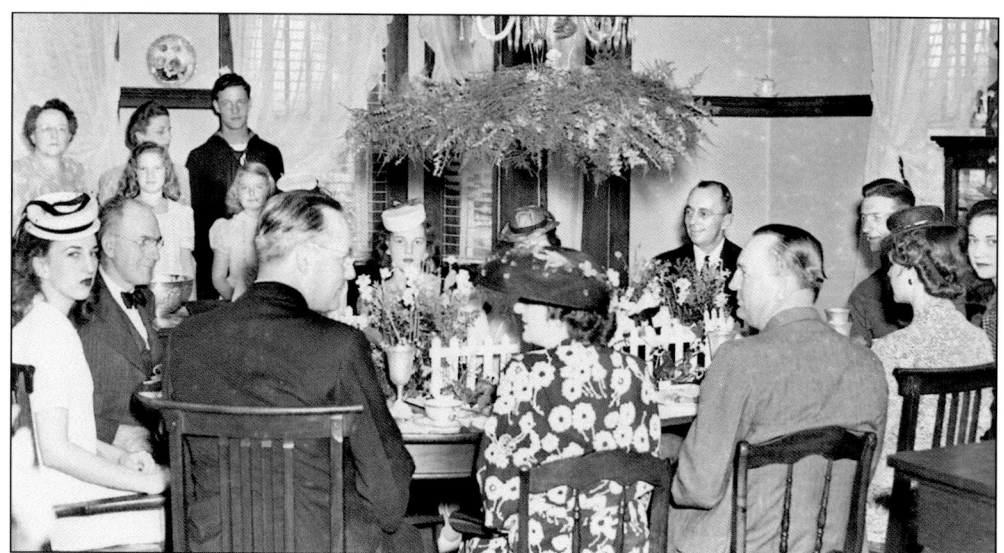

AROUND THE TABLE. Alice Kincaid (seated on the far left) partakes in the Aycock dinner at Mr. and Mrs. B.C. Lineberger's home on S. Aspen Street during the early 1950s. Other members of the party converse about major topics of the time period and prepare themselves for a festive dinner. The other members of the party include Eb Aycock, Mrs. B.C. Lineberger Sr., Mary Hoffman, Inez Hoffman, Bill Kincaid, Doris Ann Lineberger, Betty Kincaid, Jane Aycock, and B.C. Lineberger Jr.

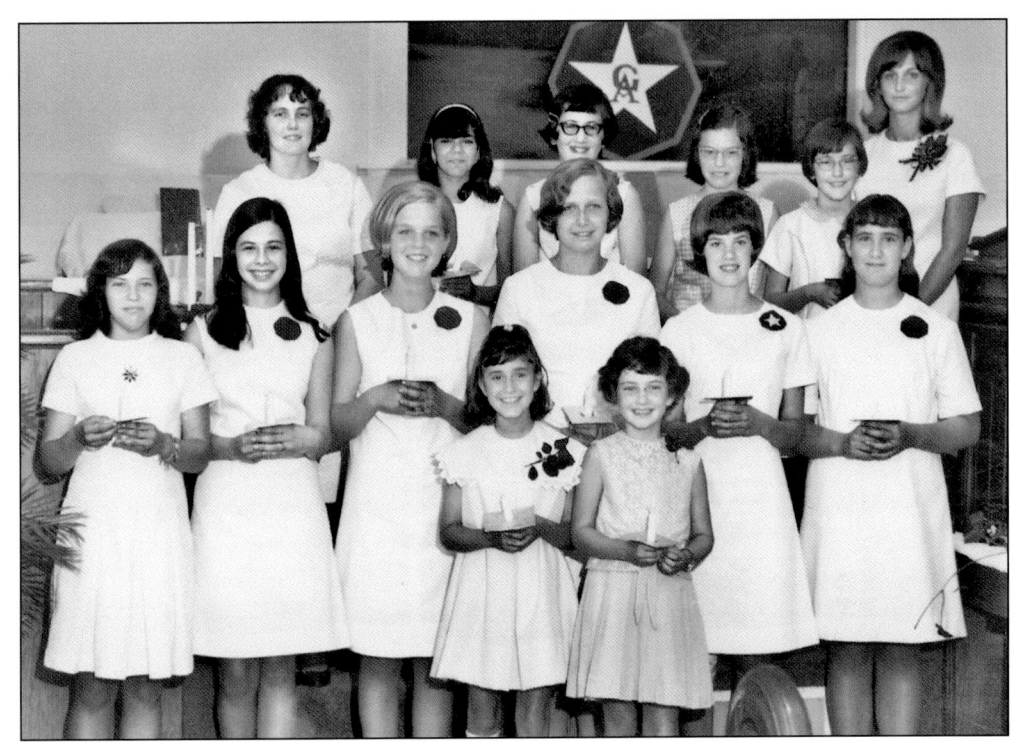

GIRL POWER. The Girls Auxiliary from one of Lincolnton's Baptist churches, is shown here in uniform and standing underneath their banner for a photograph by Baby Ray Cornwell on May 12, 1968.

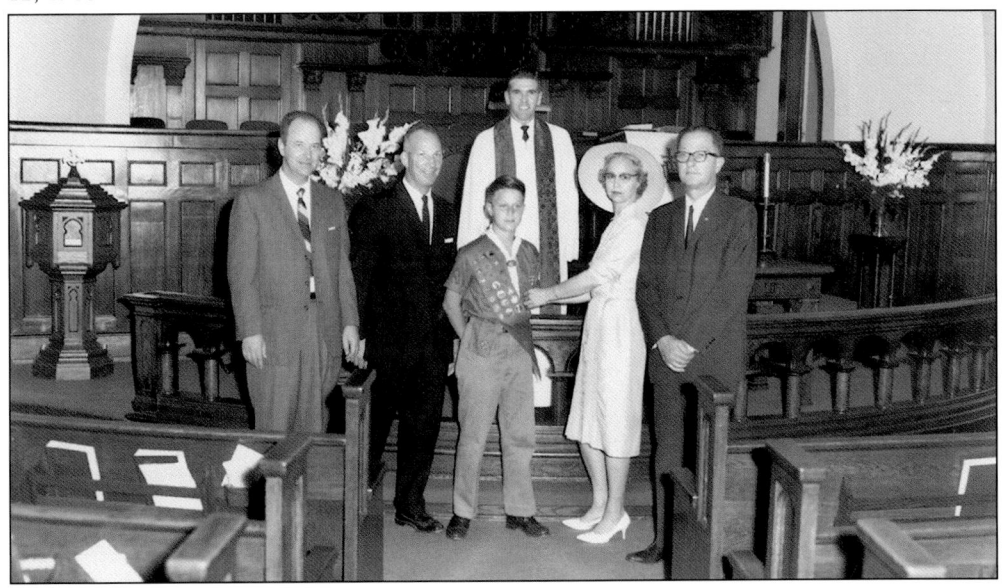

EAGLE SCOUT PRESENTATION AT FIRST UNITED METHODIST CHURCH, JUNE 21, 1964. Rev. Bernard Fitzgerald looks on from the pulpit at Lincolnton's First Methodist Church while Dorothy Crowell presents the Eagle Scout badge to her son Michael. Michael was a member of Troop No. 76 of the First Methodist Church. Other members assisting in the presentation include, from left to right, Jack Thompson, Charlie Beal, and Frank Hull Crowell, Michael's father.

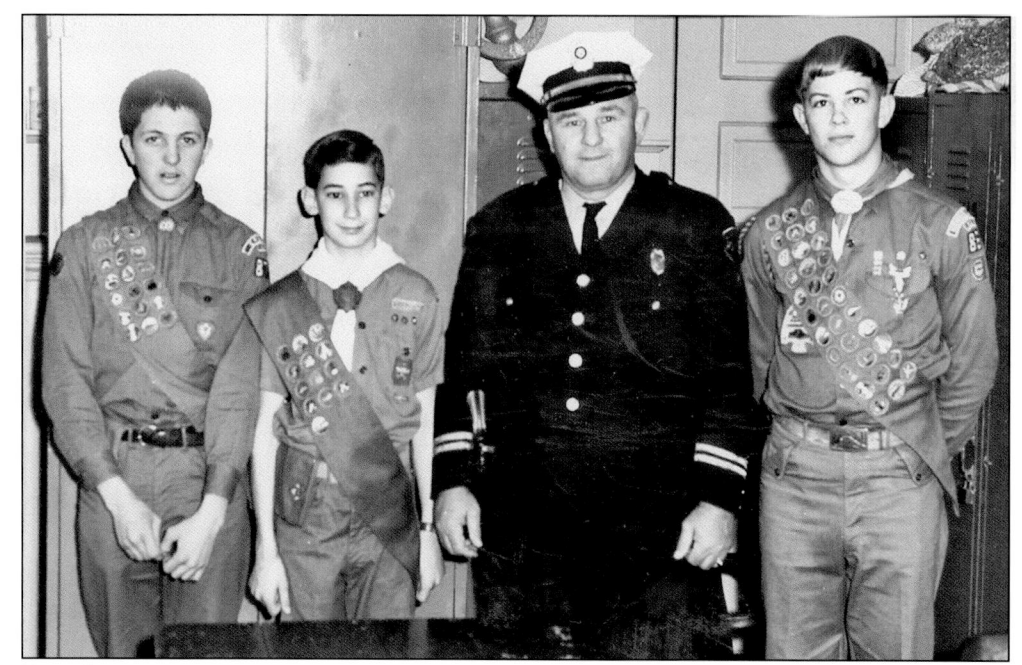

BOY SCOUT DAY, FEBRUARY 12, 1965. Boy Scouts John Rutledge, John Lockman, and Ronnie Carswell stand with Arnold Tarr, Lincolnton's chief of police, for this photograph in Lincolnton's City Hall. Ronnie Carswell served as police chief for this event, and John Lockman fulfilled the position of policeman. The scouts, shown in their scout uniforms, occupied their appointed places all day Thursday and Friday, February 11 and 12. The project taught the scouts to learn the duties of various local jobs by serving in citywide positions.

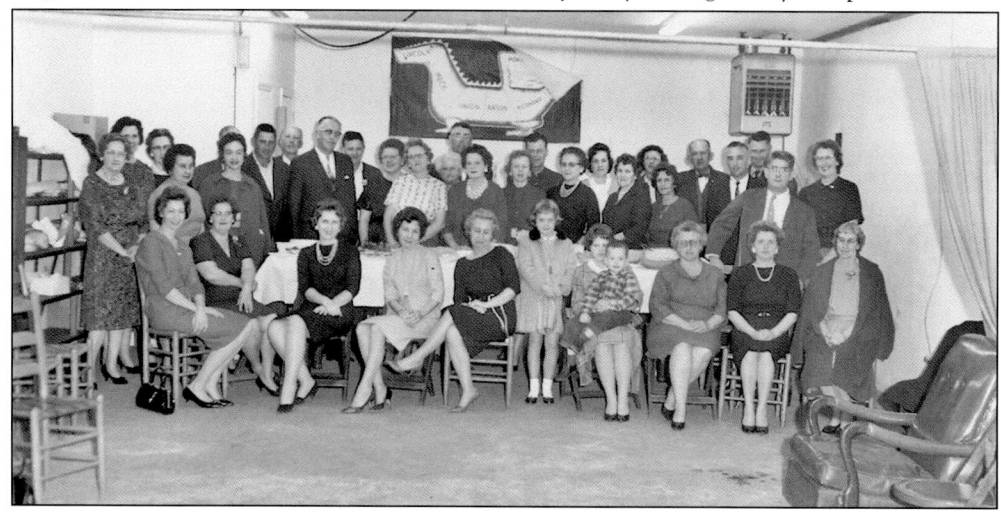

REPUBLICANS AND OFFICERS OF THE GOP WOMEN'S CLUB, NOVEMBER 20, 1963. Lincoln County Republicans and officers of the GOP Women's Club of Lincoln County met at Republican headquarters for a covered dish supper. Mrs. Ernest Sain, local club president, presided over the meeting, and Mrs. Louis G. Rogers, national committeewoman of Charlotte, was the featured speaker. The clubs officers were Edith Abernethy, second vice president; Mrs. Don Pendleton, third vice president; Linda Kistler, secretary; Mrs. F.W. (Tobe) Cash, assistant secretary; Mrs. Ralph F. Hovis, corresponding secretary; and Mrs. Leon Gatt, treasurer.

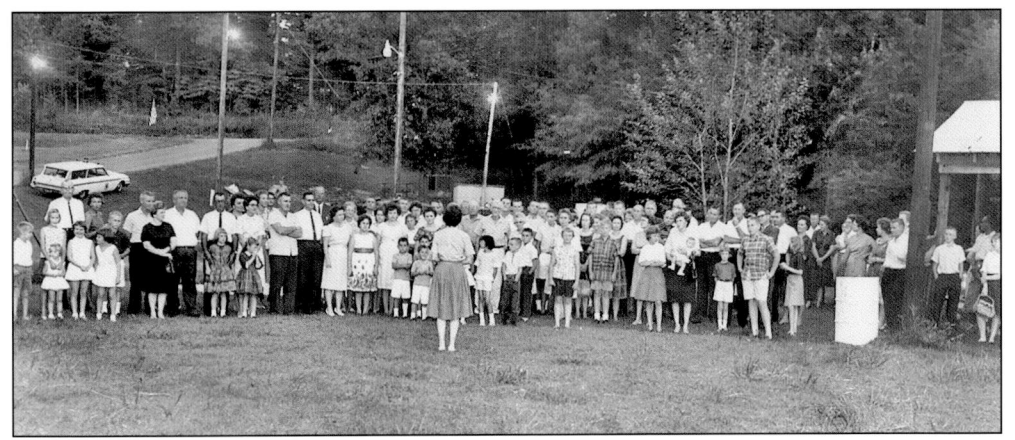

DEMOCRATIC WOMEN'S PICNIC, AUGUST 1963. In August 1963 Lincoln County's Democratic Party hosted a celebration in honor of North Carolina's 300th birthday at the city recreation park in Lincolnton. The ladies dramatized the granting of the Carolina Charter. Narrators Bill Heafner and Sandra Kennedy provided historical facts and colorful photographs and depicted each event. The group also organized a photographic display of Queen Elizabeth, Sir Walter Raleigh, Baby Virginia Dare, pirates, Scottish Highlanders, Gabriel Johnson, Charles II, and the eight Lord Proprietors. In addition, 35 teenagers who were interested in organizing a Teen Democratic Club attended the picnic.

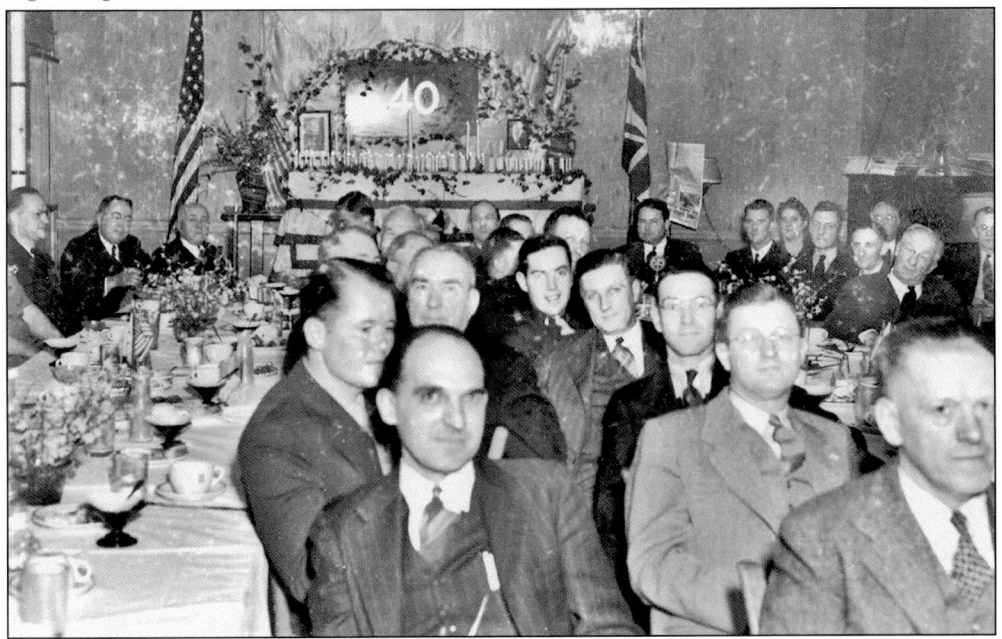

FORTY YEARS STRONG. The number 40 is highlighted on the mirror above the fireplace in what is presumed to be the North State Hotel in Lincolnton for this 1945 special occasion. The Rotary Club of Lincolnton hosted a celebratory dinner on this evening, complete with the room and tables decorated with American flags and flower arrangements. Formed on February 23, 1905, by Paul P. Harris, Rotary Clubs nationwide emphasized international understanding and cooperation during World War II and sent members to United Nations Charter Conferences. Lincolnton's Rotary Club has a long history of serving the citizens of Lincolnton and Lincoln County, and it provides scholarships to graduating seniors from the area.

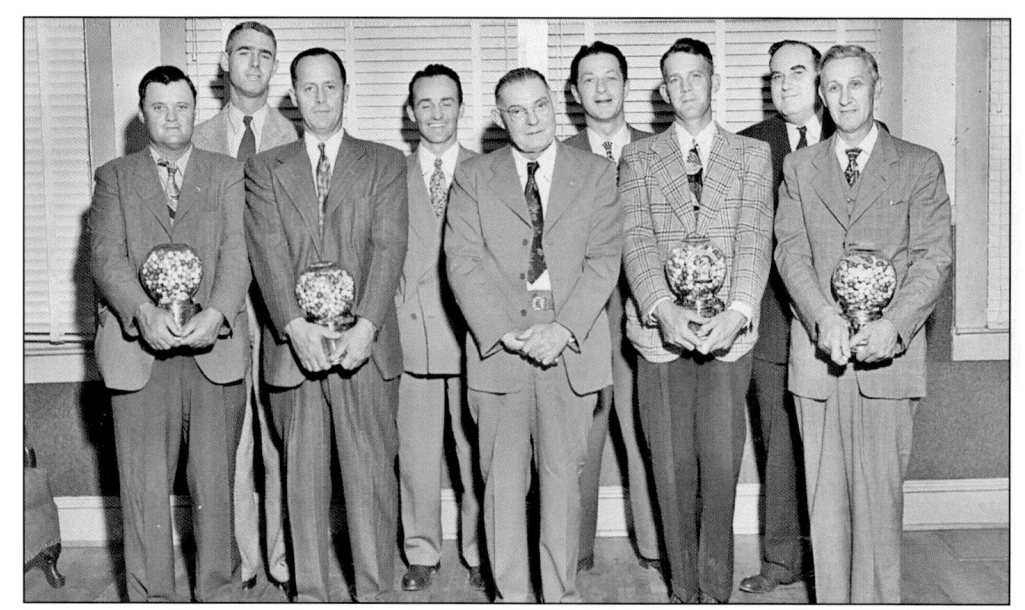

LINCOLNTON KIWANIS CLUB, 1948. Members of Lincolnton's Kiwanis Club hold chewing gum vending machines for this 1948 photograph taken at an unidentified location. The Kiwanis Club used the proceeds from gum machines to further their mission in assisting the underprivileged in the city and county. Members of the Kiwanis Club are, from left to right, as follows: (front row) Jack Llywellyn, Ken Heavner, two unidentified men, and Carl Hartman; (back row) Frank Heavner, Paul Phyne, Frank Hill Crowell, and M.T. Leatherman.

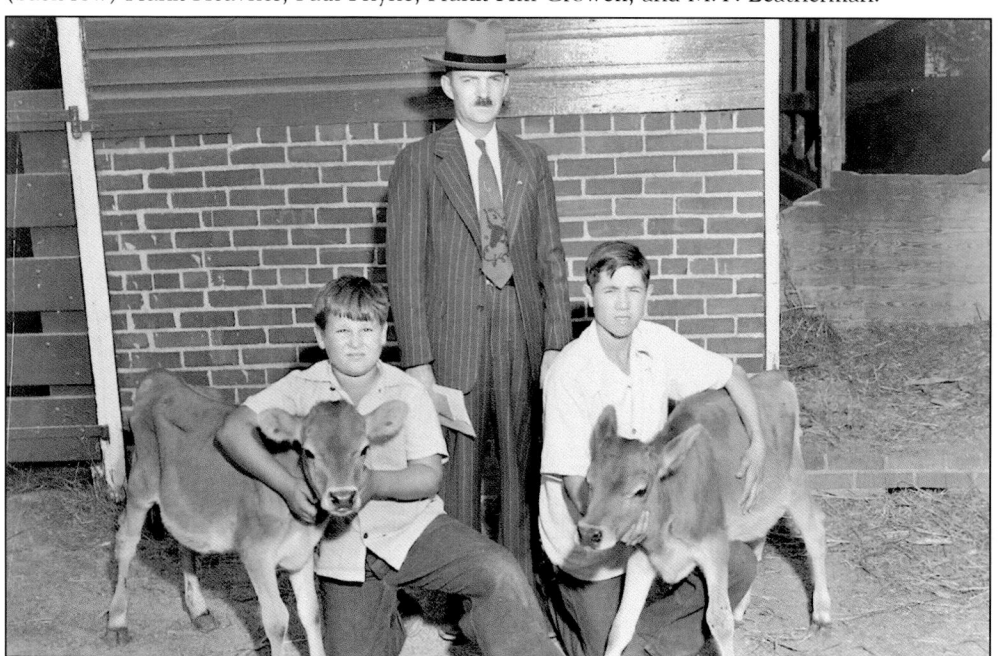

KIWANIS PRESENTS CALVES, OCTOBER 1949. Dr. C.H. Harrill, president of Lincolnton's Kiwanis Club, stands between two proud new owners of the Kiwanis sponsored calves in this October 1949 image. The Kiwanis project presented calves to James Sifford (left) of Stanley and Robert Lewis Leatherman (right) a ninth-grade student of Union High School in Vale.

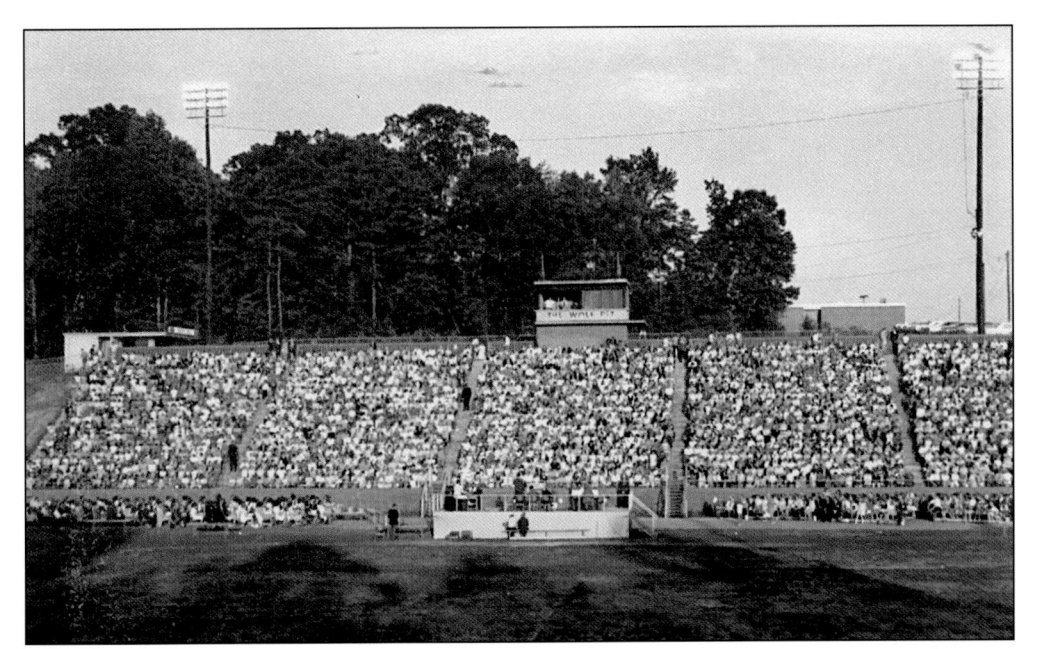

JAMES ROBINSON'S CRUSADE FOR CHRIST. Between May 17 and 21, 1971, James Robinson's Crusade converted 1,000 people from Lincolnton and surrounding areas. Robinson, of Fort Worth, Texas, packed Lincolnton High School's Battleground Stadium for the week-long crusade. Baby Ray Cornwell captured those in attendance from the perspective of looking up into the stands at "The Wolf Pit."

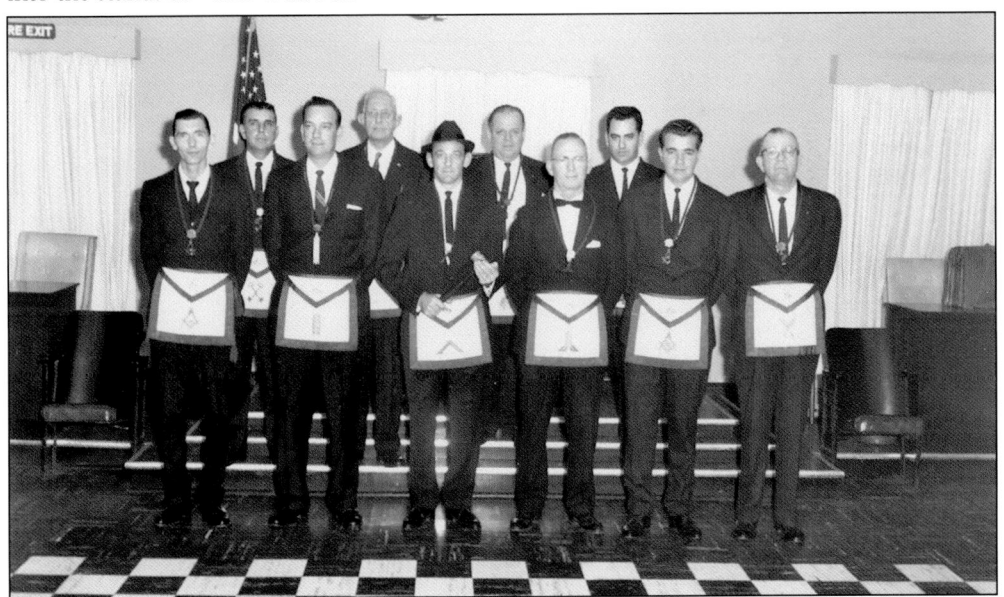

INSTALLATION OF OFFICERS, LINCOLN LODGE, NO. 137. At the first public installation ceremony of Lincoln Lodge, No. 137, the newly elected members bear the aprons and jewels of their offices for this photograph taken on January 13, 1965. The newly elected offices are identified, from left to right, as follows: Bobby Baker, Ken Mace, Glenn Beam, Milton Arrowood, Worshipful Master Risden Burris, Vic Cashion, Vance Moss, Don Houser, Sam White, and Joe Ross.

105

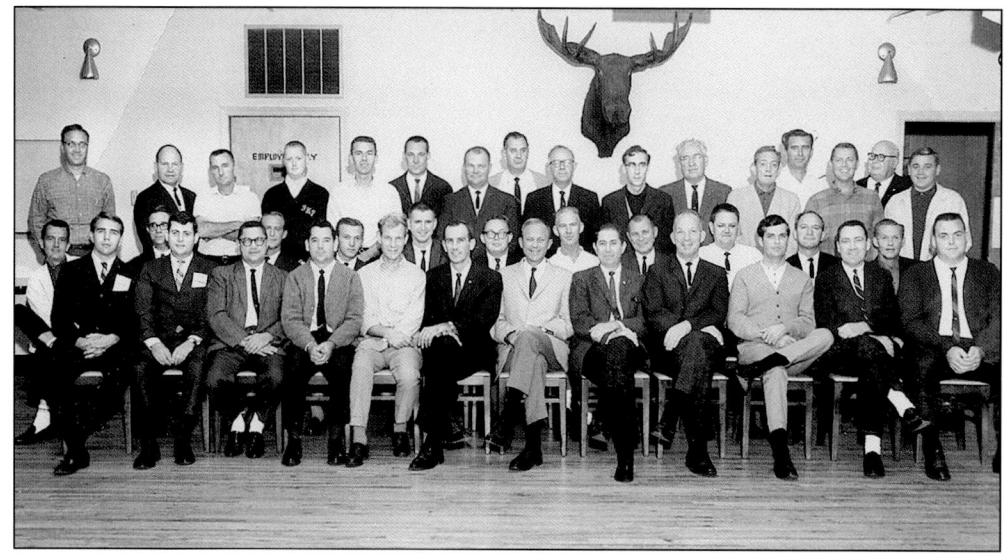

LINCOLNTON'S MOOSE LODGE. A large moose head protrudes from above the members of Lincolnton's Moose Lodge for this 1950s image. Members are identified, from left to right, as follows: (front row) Bobby Ford, unidentified, Ken ?, Bill Brown, Jimmy Mathis, two unidentified persons, David Kiser, Charlie Beal, Joey Sherrill, and David Houston; (middle row) Clyde Heavner, Ronald ?, Tommy Dellinger, Jimmy Ford, John Brumley, two unidentified persons, Carl Smith, Jimmy Cooper, Shirley Drum, and Whitey Hull; (back row) Bill (Whitey) Richard, J.C. Rudisill, Darrell Beal, Jackie Polhill, Fred Crisson, Joe Chaffin, Jr., Buster Hallman, two unidentified persons, Norman Kistler, unidentified, Ken Harkey, David Schronce, Bob Ramseur, unidentified, and Dan Auton.

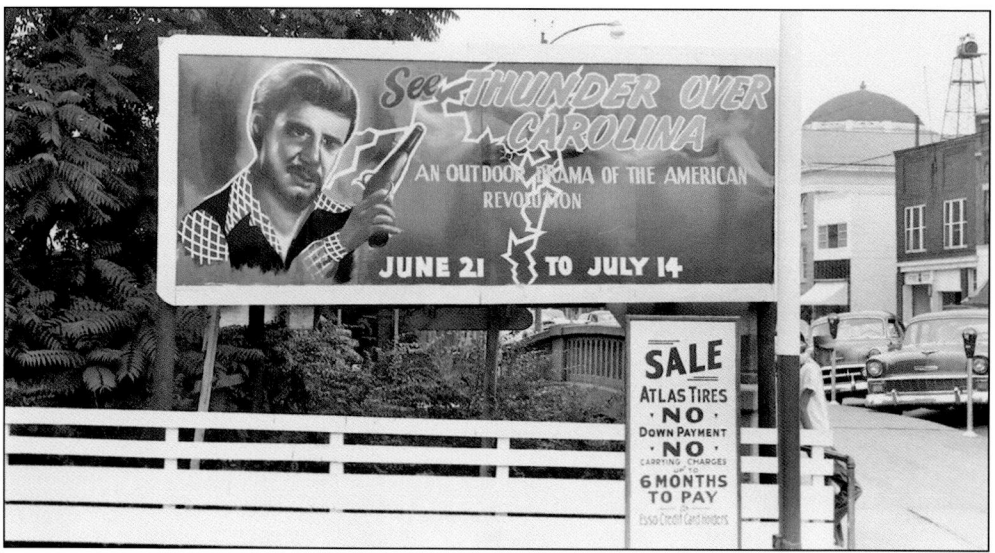

COMING SOON. On a drive towards the courthouse on East Main Street in Lincolnton, this dramatic billboard advertises the upcoming Lincoln County Historical Association production of *Thunder Over Carolina*. Touted as "An Outdoor Drama of the American Revolution," this theatrical production was held June 21 through July 14, 1956, and was organized by Mrs. Gladys Childs. Charles W. Loveland wrote the score for the reenactment of the June 20, 1780 Battle of Ramsour's Mill.

Six
SALT OF THE EARTH

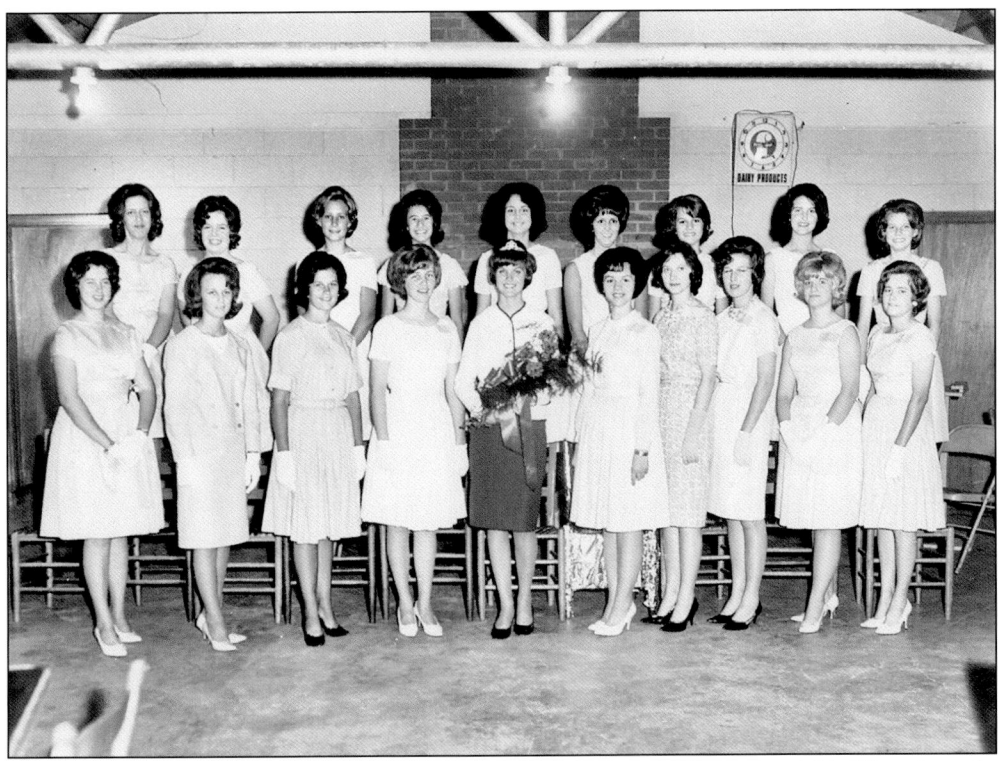

SENIOR AND JUNIOR DAIRY PRINCESS CONTEST, THURSDAY, JUNE 4, 1964. West Lincoln High School was the venue for the 1964 Lincoln County Dairy Princess Contest. Participants included the following: Nancy Wright, mistress of ceremonies; Janice Lineberger, junior dairy princess; Sue Sherrill, senior dairy princess; and Burlene Leonhardt, the 1963 dairy princess. Other ladies who entered the dairy princess contest are as follows: Freida Setzer, Cathy Reynolds, Jane Lineberger, Rita Barnes, Linda Barkley, Janet Phillips, Elaine Schronce, Patsy Schronce, Dianne Sigmon, Donna Sue Huss, Bonita Hager, Donna Yoder, Sharon Avery, Donna Adams, Judy Nixon, Dianne Propst, Pat Devine, Gail Hovis, Alice Chapman, Sue Sherrill, June Dorsey, and Barbara Barker.

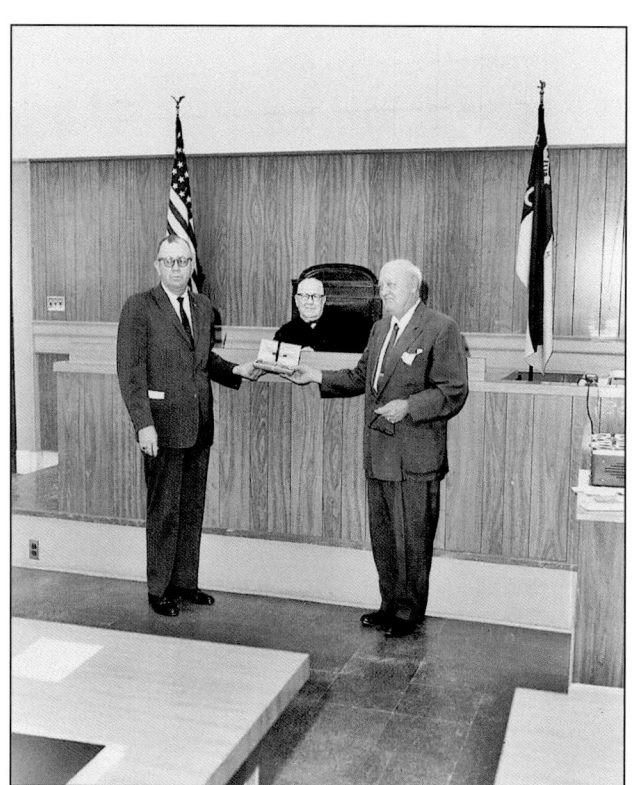

RETIREMENT OF CLERK OF SUPERIOR COURT JOE ROSS. On the morning of Tuesday, September 17, 1963, at 9:00 a.m., Judge Sheldon M. Roper called to the judge's bench retiring clerk of superior court Joe R. Ross to present him a fountain pen desk set. The presentation was to show the court's appreciation for Joe Ross's service to the bar. Presiding District Judge P.C. Froneberger watches the presentation from the bench. Judge Froneberger appointed M.L. Huggins to replace Ross as clerk of superior court. Ross was appointed postmaster of Lincolnton.

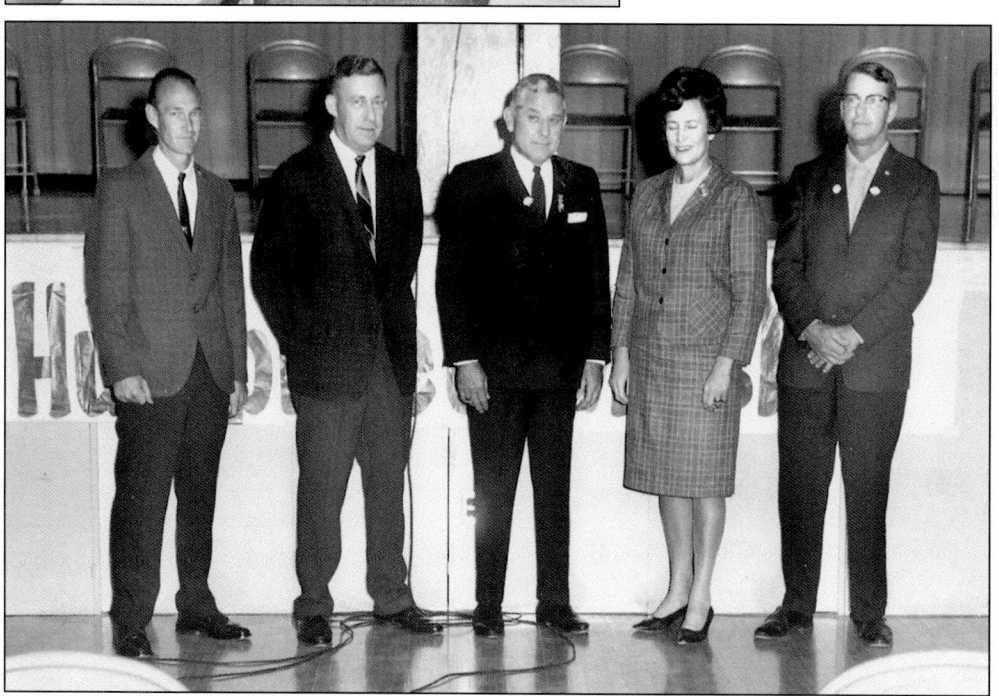

POLITICAL ARENA. After a speaking engagement for the Democratic Party in Lincolnton, these officers stand with the featured speaker during the 1960s. The officers are identified, from left to right, as Russell Dellinger, unidentified speaker, Jake Burgin, unidentified, and Guy McIntosh.

SWEARING IN SHERIFF EARLIE NORWOOD. Baby Ray Cornwell captures Joe Ross (left), clerk of superior court, while swearing in newly elected Sheriff Earlie Norwood on December 3, 1962. Sheriff Earlie Norwood succeeded Frank P. Heavner.

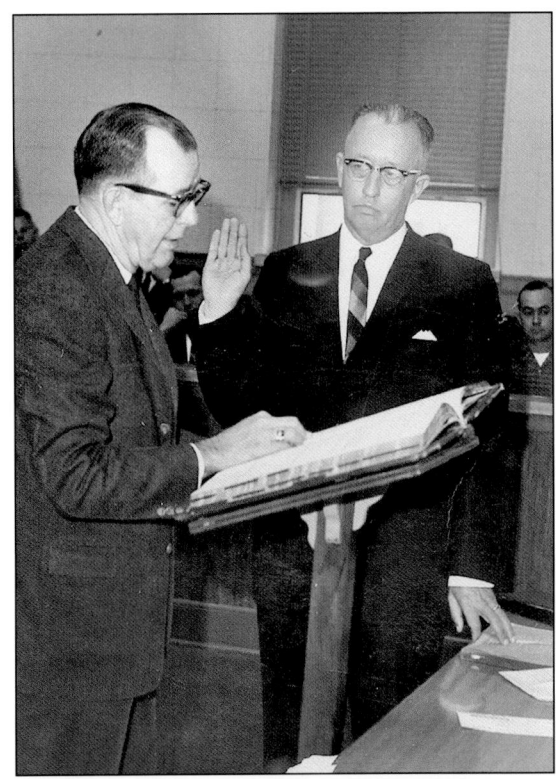

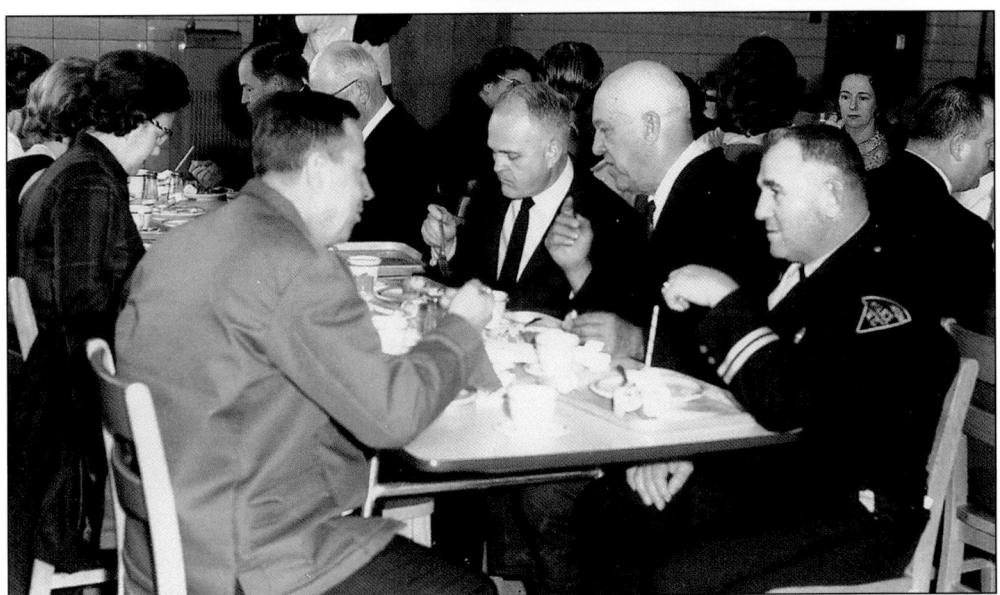

LINCOLN COUNTY SCHOOL SYSTEM CHRISTMAS LUNCHEON, FRIDAY, DECEMBER 16, 1966. City and county employees as well as friends of the local schools take part in the Lincoln County School System's annual Christmas luncheon at Battleground Elementary School. Dr. L.A. Thomas delivered the invocation before the group took part in a delectable turkey dinner. Pictured in the photograph above are as follows: Chief of Police Arnold Tarr, Charlie Randall, Dr. John Gamble, George Stoudemire, and Superintendent of City Schools S. Ray Lowder.

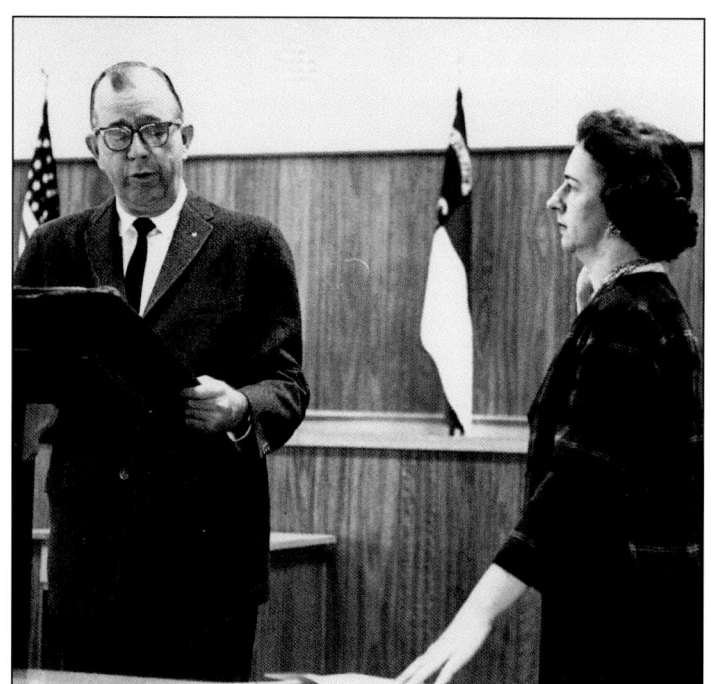

DO YOU SWEAR . . . Lincoln County Clerk of Court Joe Ross stands before Elizabeth Carpenter at the swearing-in ceremony on the morning of Monday, December 3, 1962. Elizabeth Carpenter was Lincolnton's first elected female official. (Courtesy of Betty G. Ross.)

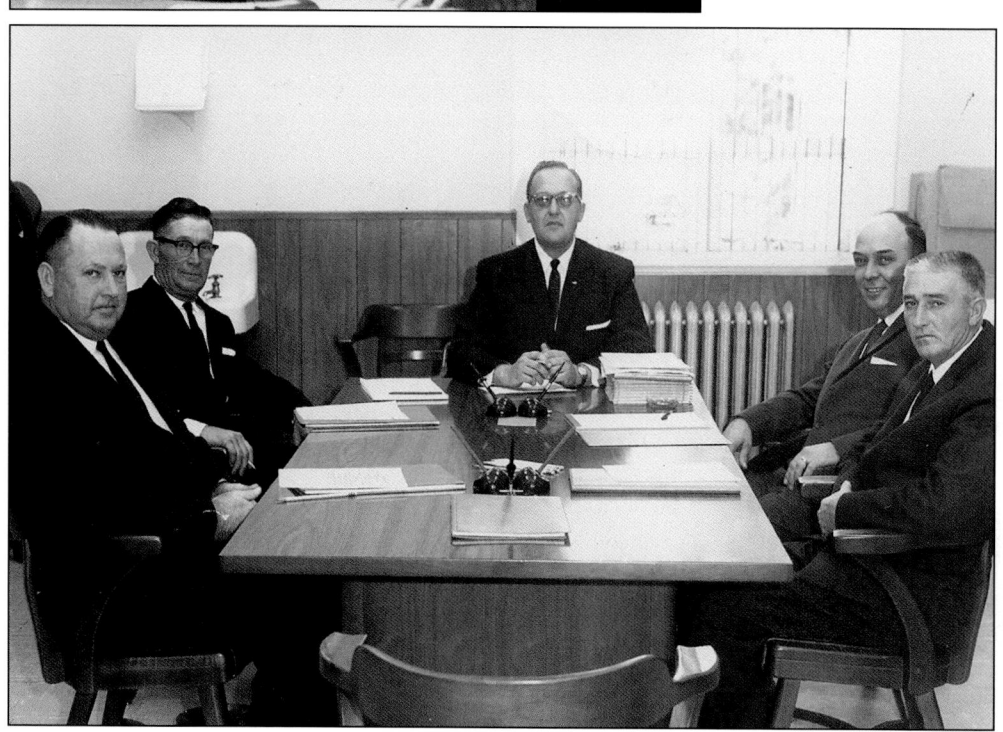

LINCOLN COUNTY BOARD OF COUNTY COMMISSIONERS, DECEMBER 3, 1962. The newly elected Lincoln County Board of Commissioners sits around a table in the Lincoln County Courthouse for this photograph featured in *The Lincoln County News*. The members of the board of commissioners are, from left to right, as follows: Don Cherry; Louie Aderholdt; Hal Hoyle Jr., chairman; Jim Warren, vice-chairman; and Ferd Houser.

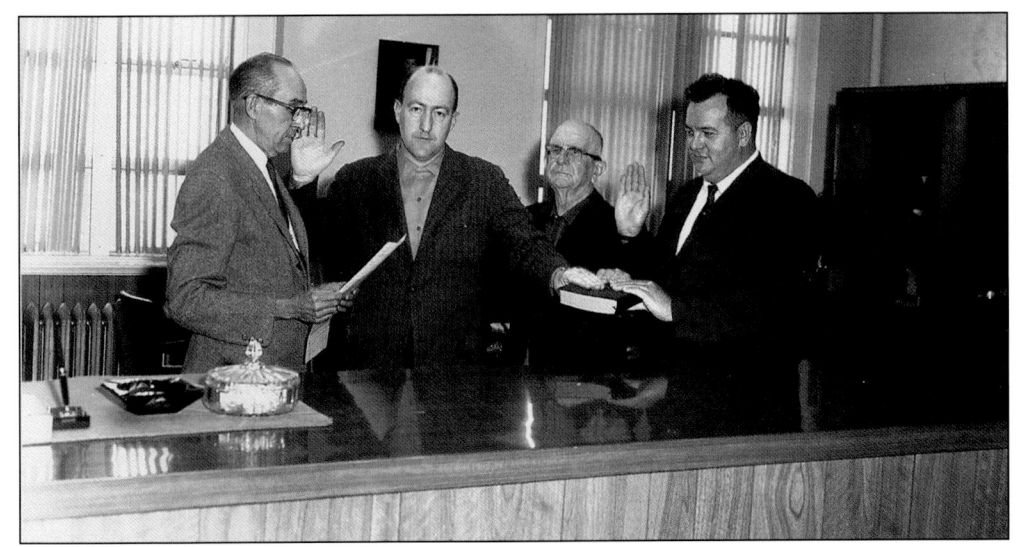

"RAISE YOUR RIGHT HAND." M.L. "Goober" Huggins reads the oath of office to Robert Lineberger and Bill Morris at a swearing-in ceremony at the Lincoln County Courthouse. "Baby Ray" Cornwell found his way into most political events for both the city and county during his career, and he supplied *The Lincoln County News* with most of its photographs during this time period before they hired staff.

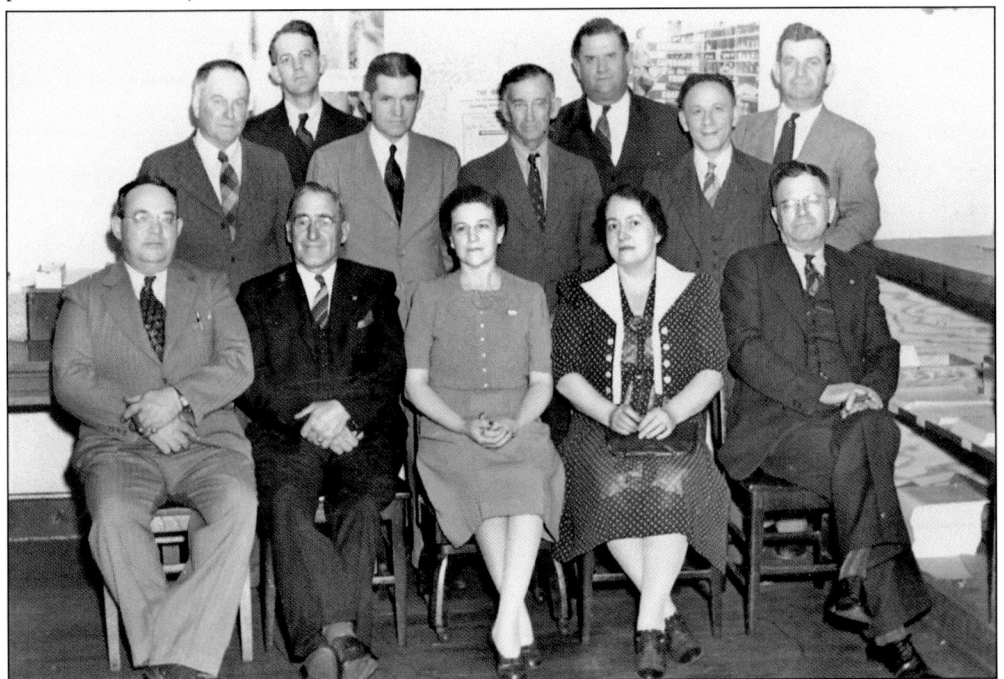

STRAINS OF WAR. The Office of Price Administration (OPA) Board of Lincolnton met in the courthouse during the 1940s and after a meeting invited Baby Ray Cornwell to capture their service for future generations. The OPA was a World War II, federally established program to prevent wartime inflation. In addition to controlling prices, these boards were also charged with the responsibility of rationing goods such as tires, automobiles, sugar, fuel, oil, coffee, meats, and sugar. The OPA was dissolved in 1947.

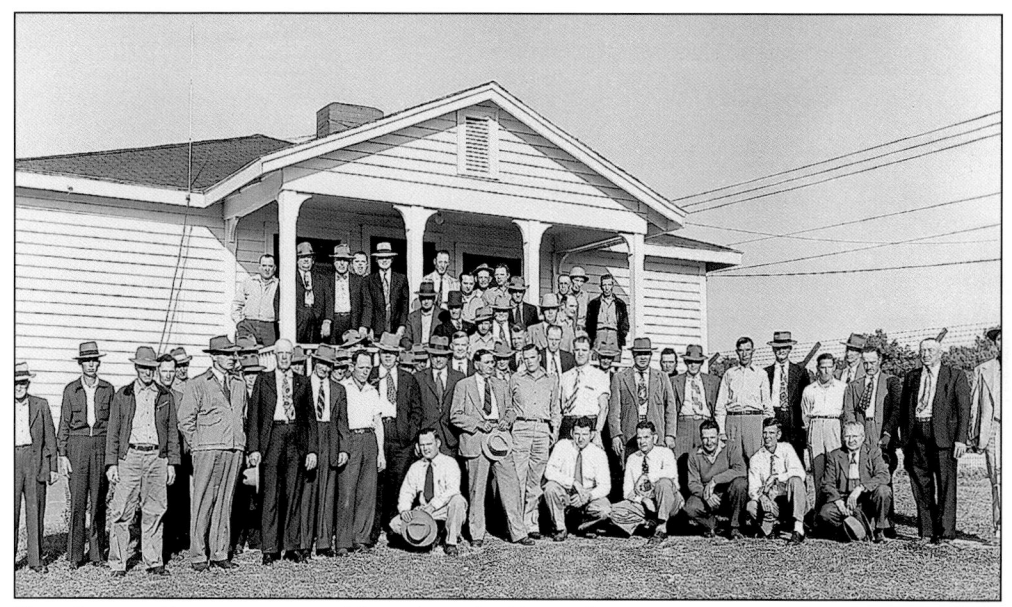

THAT'S THE SOUND OF THE MEN. Lincoln County's prison camp was known as Lincoln County Camp No. 907. The camp operated under the supervision of W.K. Dedmon of Lincolnton, who was in charge of the various prison camps in the ninth division of the North Carolina Highway and Public Works Commission. Other officials included Jake Schrum, former Lincolnton Alderman, the camp superintendent; Murill Alley of Newton, the camp steward; Charles Neal of Howard's Creek, foreman of farm work; Clyde Eaker, camp guard; and Dr. John R. Gamble Jr., the physician for the camp.

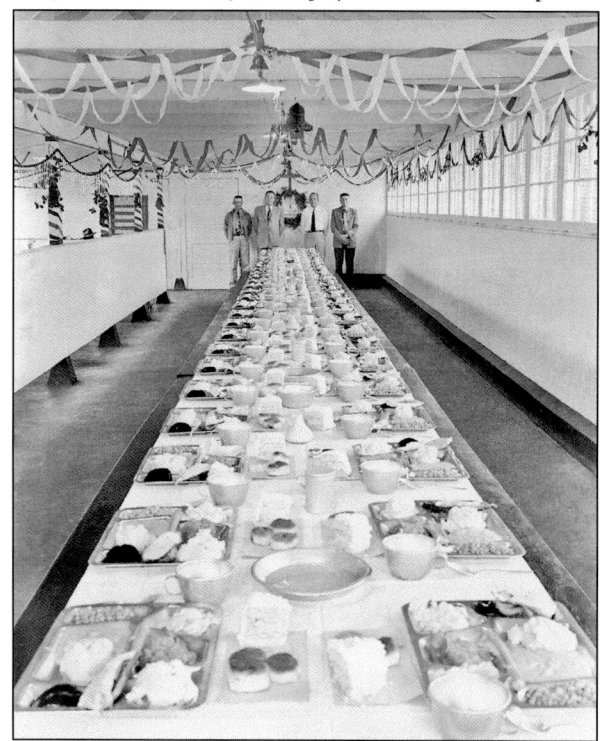

YOUR MEAL AWAITS. Festival crepe paper adorns the ceiling at the Lincoln County Prison Camp for this Christmas dinner on December 25, 1952. Four unidentified men stand at the end of the table before the inmates partake of their large holiday meal.

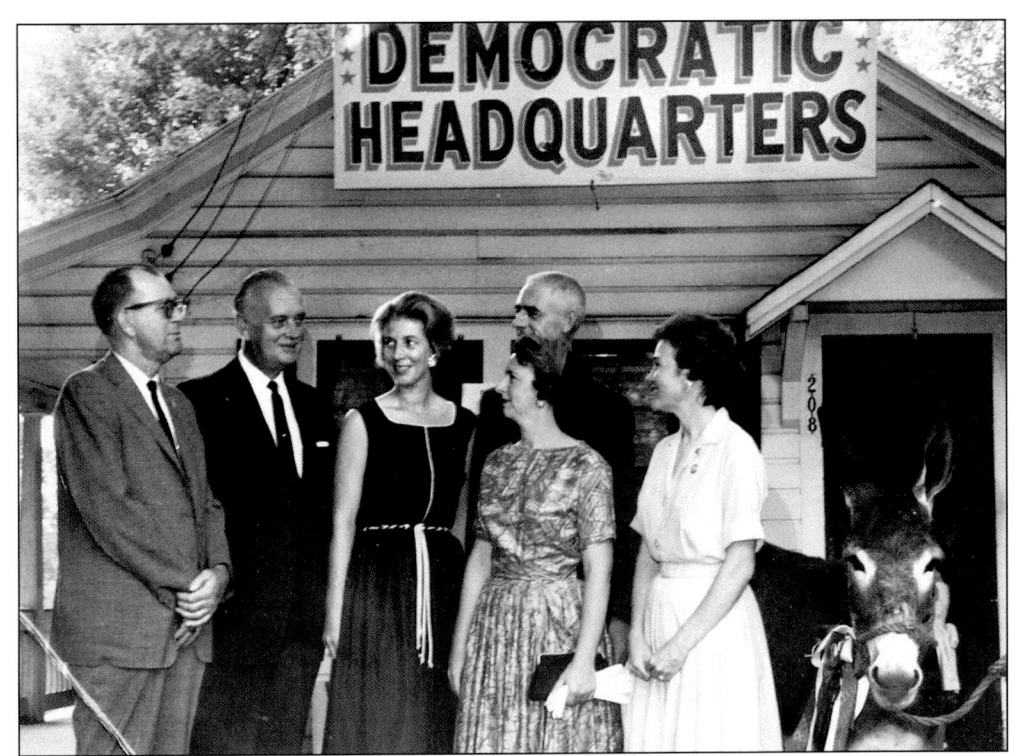

DEMOCRATIC ASSEMBLAGE. During a 1952 visit from Paul Kitchin of Anson County, Democrats assembled in front of democratic headquarters at 208 West Main Street in Lincolnton. The group is identified, from left to right, as follows: Joe Ross, chairman of the Lincoln County Democratic Party and clerk of court; Paul Kitchin; Bette Morris, vice-chairman of the Lincoln County Democratic Party; Elizabeth Carpenter, register of deeds; Frank Heavner, Lincoln County sheriff; and Charlesanna Leatherman. (Courtesy of Betty G. Ross.)

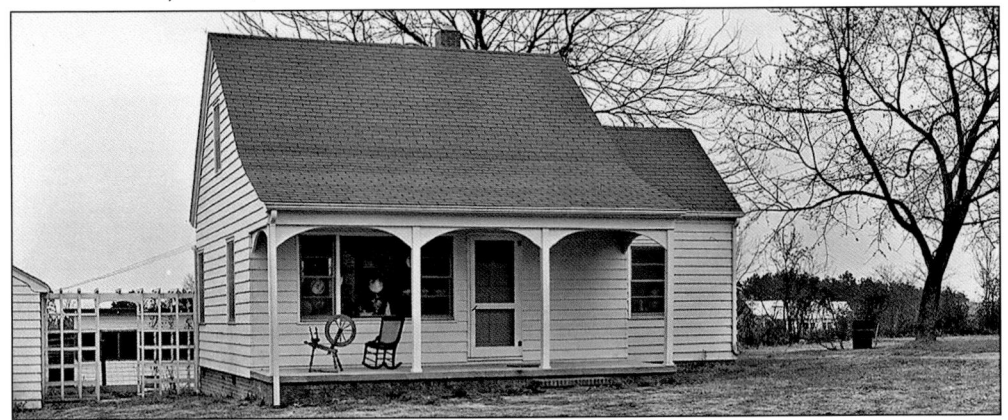

ROCKING AND SPINNING. The simplicity and utilitarianism expressed in the spinning wheel and rocking chair convey a message that is written all over this quaint house on Alexander Street in Lincolnton. Captured by Baby Ray Cornwell in January 1950, this house was built by Carl Plonk for his daughter, Polly Plonk Crisson. Plonk, a cabinetmaker and builder, advertised his antique goods in *The Lincoln County News* during the 1950s. Located at 414 North Flint Street, Plonk offered antique chests, clocks, chests of drawers, marble top tables, secretaries, bedroom suites, sofas, pictures, washstands, and mirrors.

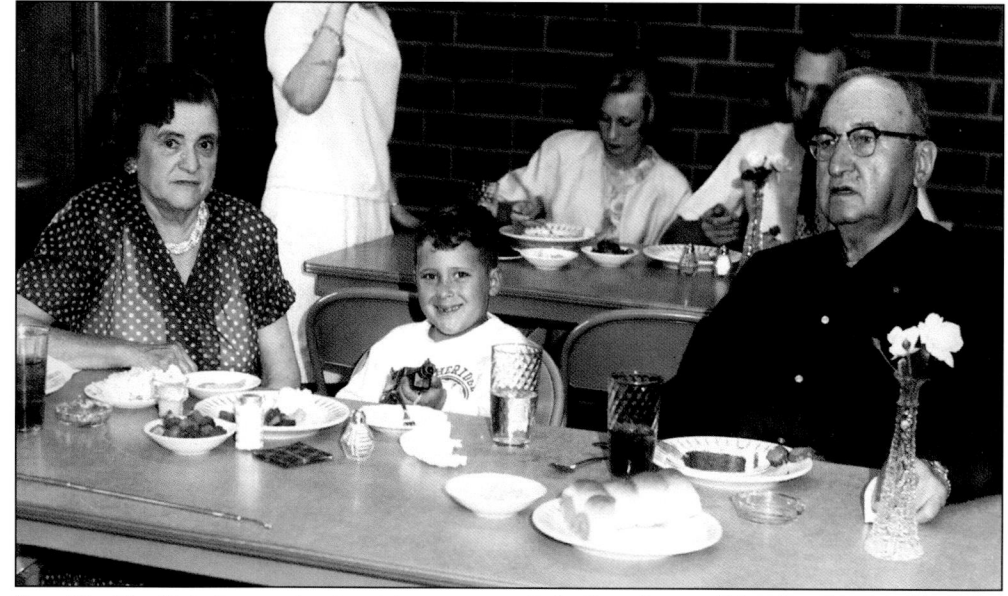

PUT 'EM UP. Cain Leonard points his weapon at Baby Ray Cornwell for this photograph at the Pumpkin Center PADA grand opening on Saturday, May 14, 1964. Seated on either side of young Cain are his grandparents, Mr. and Mrs. H.K. Leonard. H.F. Leonard was a former chief of police and alderman of Lincolnton. The Pumpkin Center PADA held the barbeque dinner at their new 2,400-square-foot building, and the proceeds went to the building fund. The new building boasted two bathrooms, storage space, and a large modern kitchen and pantry.

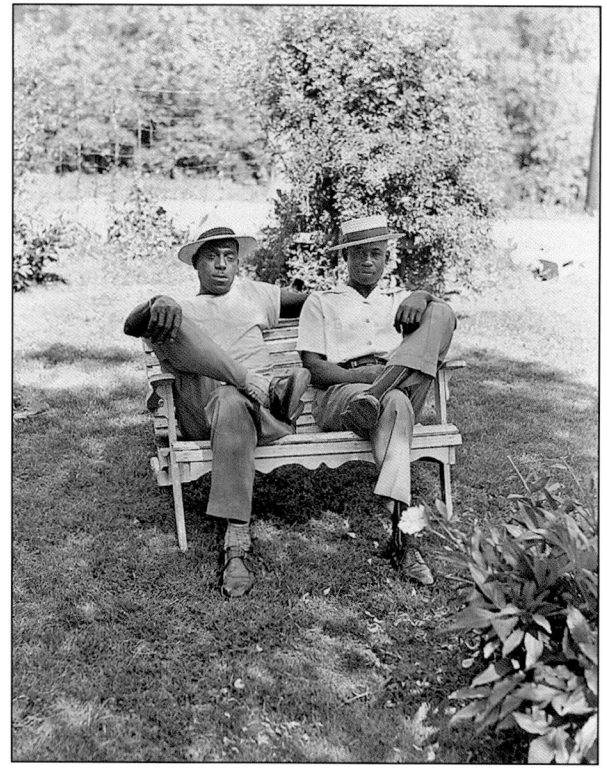

SECRET GARDEN. Two African Americans from the Cobb and Robinson families relax in a serene and cozy setting in Lincolnton for this May 1951 photograph. May flowers bloom in their midst as Baby Ray Cornwell interrupts their slumber.

SPITTING IMAGE. Shelly and Carolyn Roper took part in the 1945 May Day Celebration on the grounds of Lincolnton High School. The twins, daughters of Judge Sheldon M. Roper, take a break from the May Day festivities for a photograph by Baby Ray Cornwell. Cornwell's collection at the Lincoln County Museum of History contains many images of school superlatives, theatrical performances, student elections, bands, and May Day celebrations like this photograph.

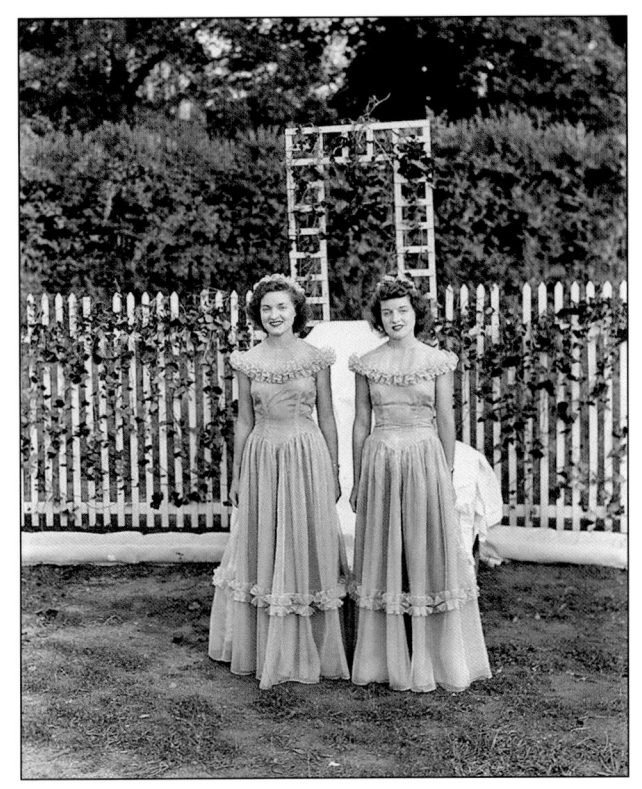

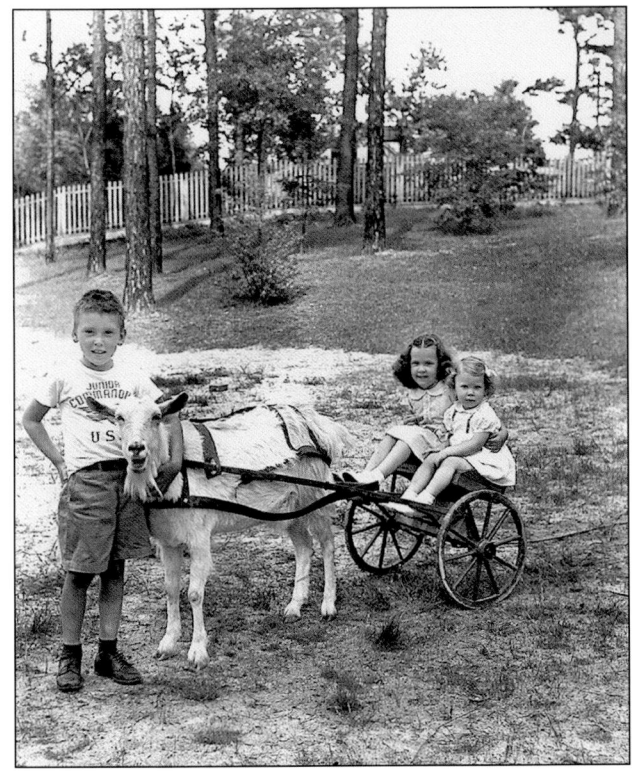

HOLD TIGHT. The "Junior Commander" brings his goat cavalcade to a stop with a smile. One girl holds the other girl with a tight grip on a small seat behind the harnesses of this homemade carriage. Cornwell just happened to be in the right place at the right time to capture this scene of everyday life for a child in Lincolnton.

115

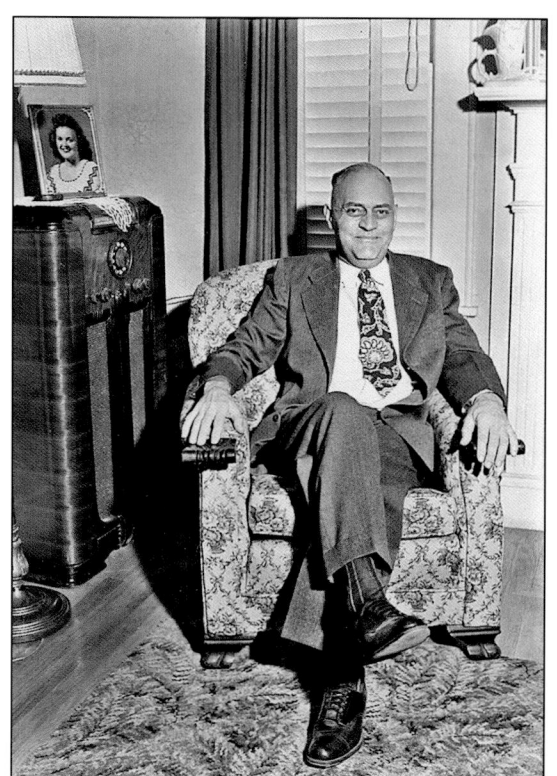

SAM DIGH, NOVEMBER 1, 1952. Sam Digh (July 4, 1902–February 11, 1953) rests in his easy chair at his home on Highway 150 West (Hilltop) in Lincolnton. A photograph of Digh's daughter, Mae Digh Ledbetter, rests atop the family radio. Sam Digh and family lived in the Carter Mill community, where Sam worked as a supervisor, before building a home on Highway 150 West in Lincolnton. At this time of this photograph, Sam was the owner of City Lunch in Lincolnton.

THE SQUAD. An intimidating assemblage of facial expressions pervades this distinguished group of men from Lincolnton during a 1940s photograph session with Baby Ray Cornwell. The group is labeled on Cornwell's negative sleeve as the "Carter Men." Their military uniforms and suits denote importance and confidence in every manner. A few of the men have been identified as Bill Carter, Clyde Carter, and H.R. Carter.

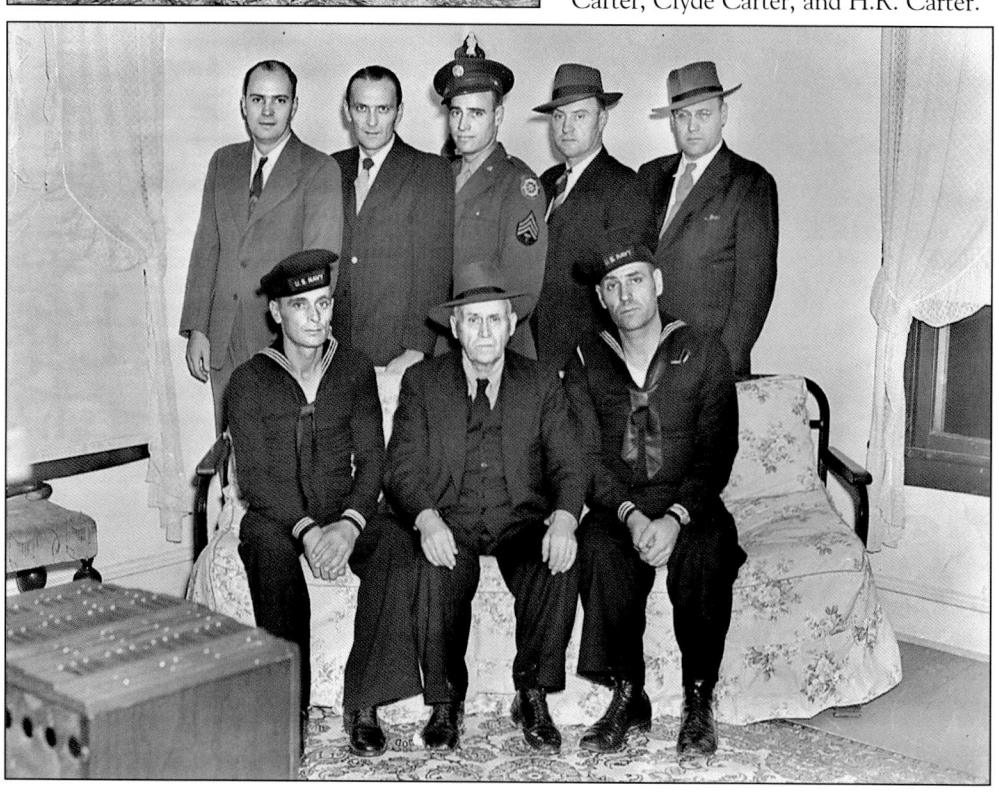

116

Two Sailors. L.C. Hovis and a friend pose for a photograph by Baby Ray Cornwell during the 1940s in Lincolnton.

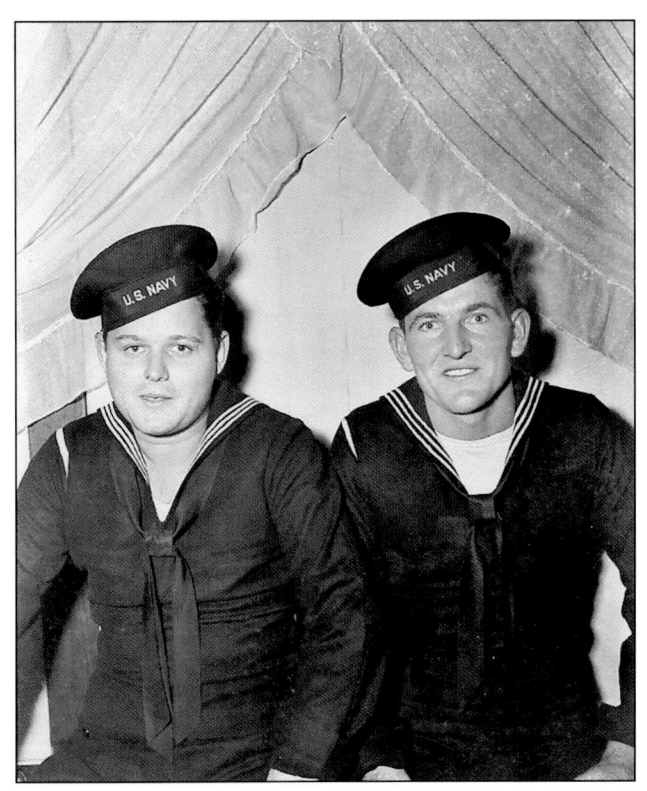

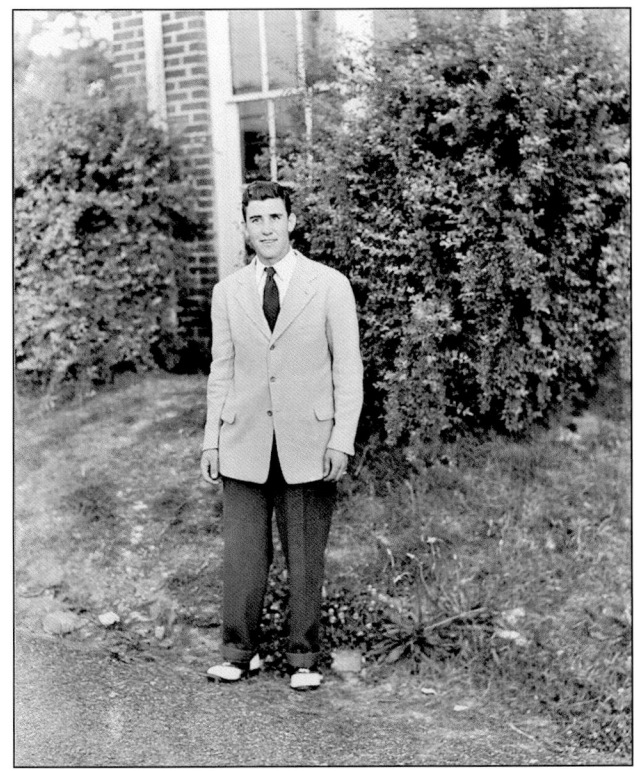

Ralph Connor Day. Born on April 16, 1923 in Stanley, Ralph Conner came to Lincolnton at age six. His parents were Bee Calvin Connor and Maggie Mae McGinnis. He left Lincolnton High School as a junior in 1943 to serve in World War II. Ralph trained in Macon, Georgia, and served in the European theatre. He was stationed with the 6th Armored Infantry and the 1st Armored Division, and he was wounded on March 12, 1944, in Anzio, Italy. After service, Ralph returned to Lincolnton to complete high school.

117

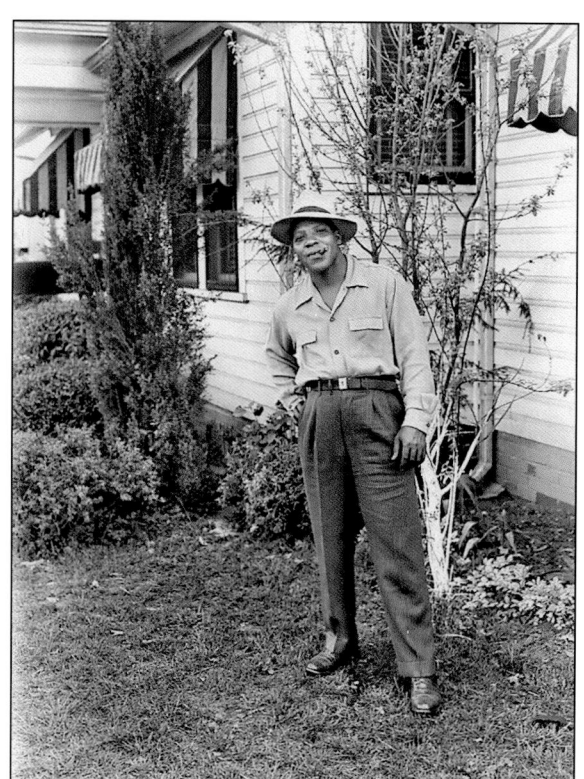

SMOKIN'. Thurman Killian, also known as Boy Killian, hangs loose with an aura of confidence and flair. Killian's pin-striped pants and hat are signs of the time for this Lincolnton plumber.

MUCH LOVE. This soldier, identified by Baby Ray Cornwell as Corbet Soldier, rests at Drum's Funeral Home in Lincolnton in September 1948. His service to the United States during World War II did not go unnoticed as flowers and floral arrangements adorn the room. The American flag is draped over his coffin in honor and memory of his undying love and commitment to his nation.

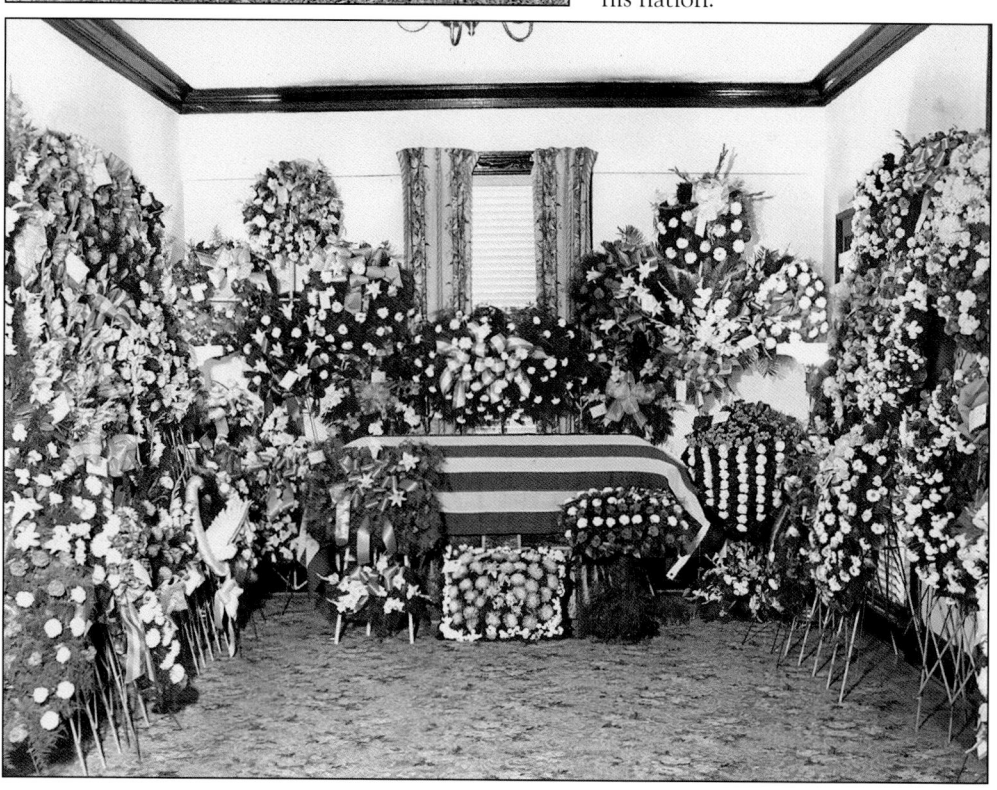

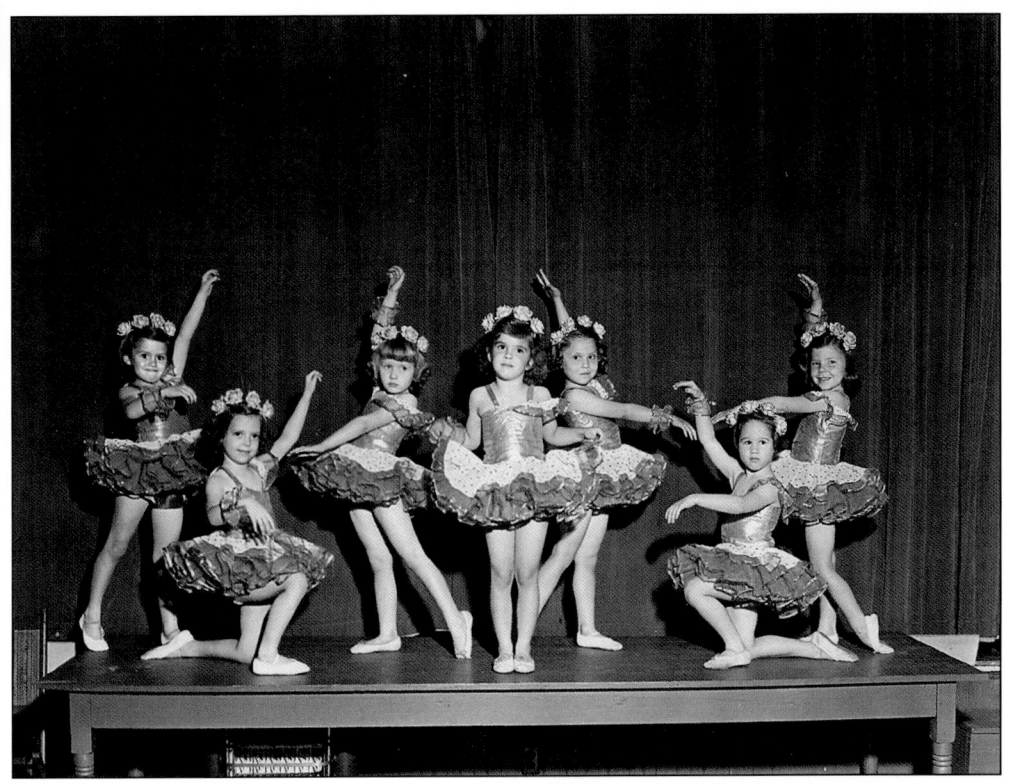

OVER THE TOP. On April 24, 1952, a large country table supports seven young dancers from Betty's School of Dance as they strike a pose in their ballet shoes and outfits. It is possible that Baby Ray Cornwell set up this shot so that he could get his subjects at eye level.

DR. ISAAC RUFFIN SELF. Sitting in his office proudly wearing his Shriner's fez, Dr. I.R. Self poses for this photograph. Dr. Self was featured in the local newspaper as the newly elected president of the local Shriner's club on March 10, 1947. A graduate of the University of Maryland School of Dentistry, Dr. Self practiced dentistry in Lincolnton for over 43 years, beginning in 1905. Dr. Self married Leila Isabel Tobey, daughter of Capt. and Mrs. Fred A. Tobey of Lincolnton, and the Selfs had two sons and three daughters. Their two sons, Dr. I. Ruffin Self Jr. and Dr. Fred L. Self, practiced dentistry in Lincolnton with their father.

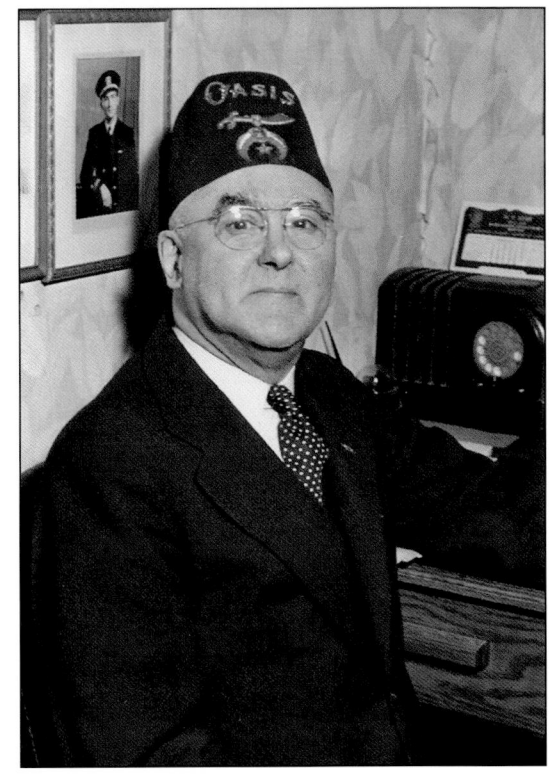

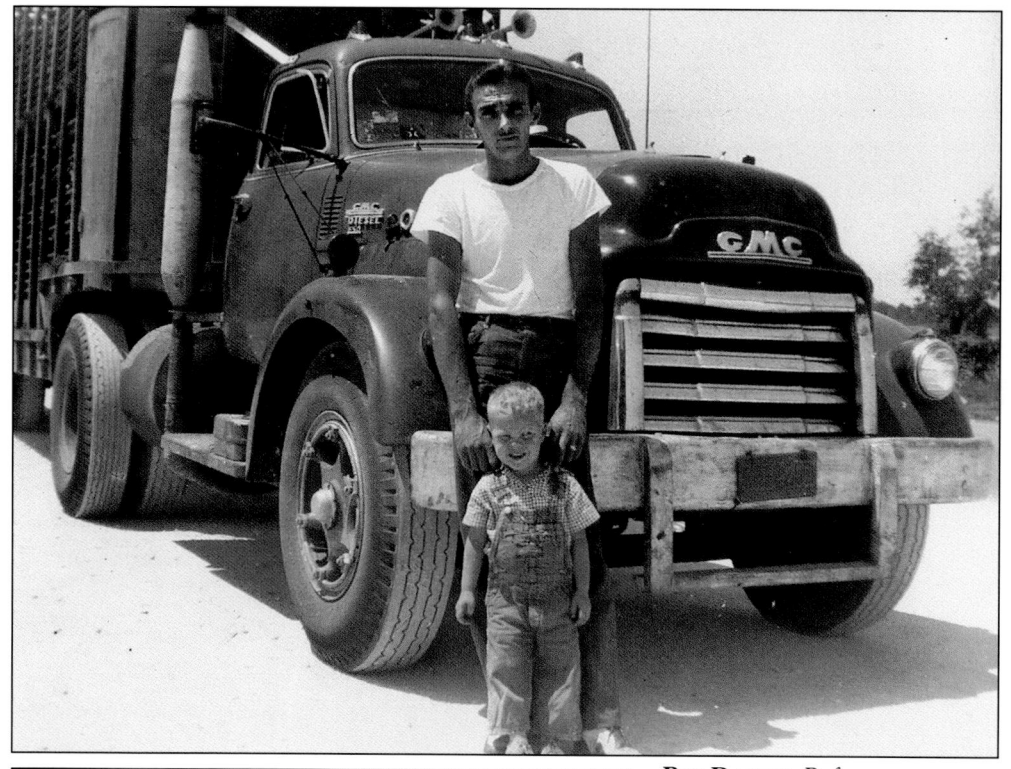

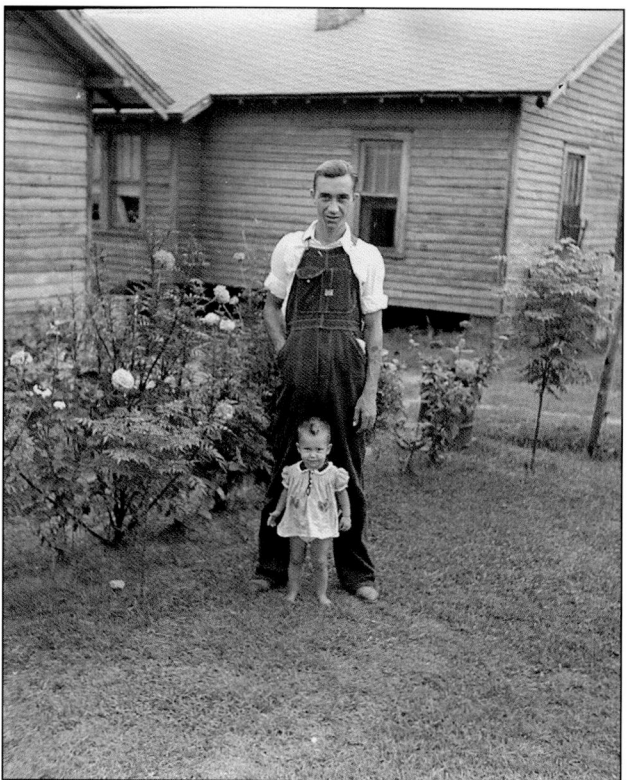

BIG DADDY. Before or en route to a delivery, this man includes his young son in this late 1940s image captured by Baby Ray.

IN HER FATHER'S FOOTSTEPS. A father's pride and honor can be seen in the face of this unidentified man as he stands behind his daughter near their home in one of Lincolnton's mill villages. Cornwell is remembered by many Lincolntonians as finding his way to every location in the county at the right moment, even when he was not commissioned to take photographs.

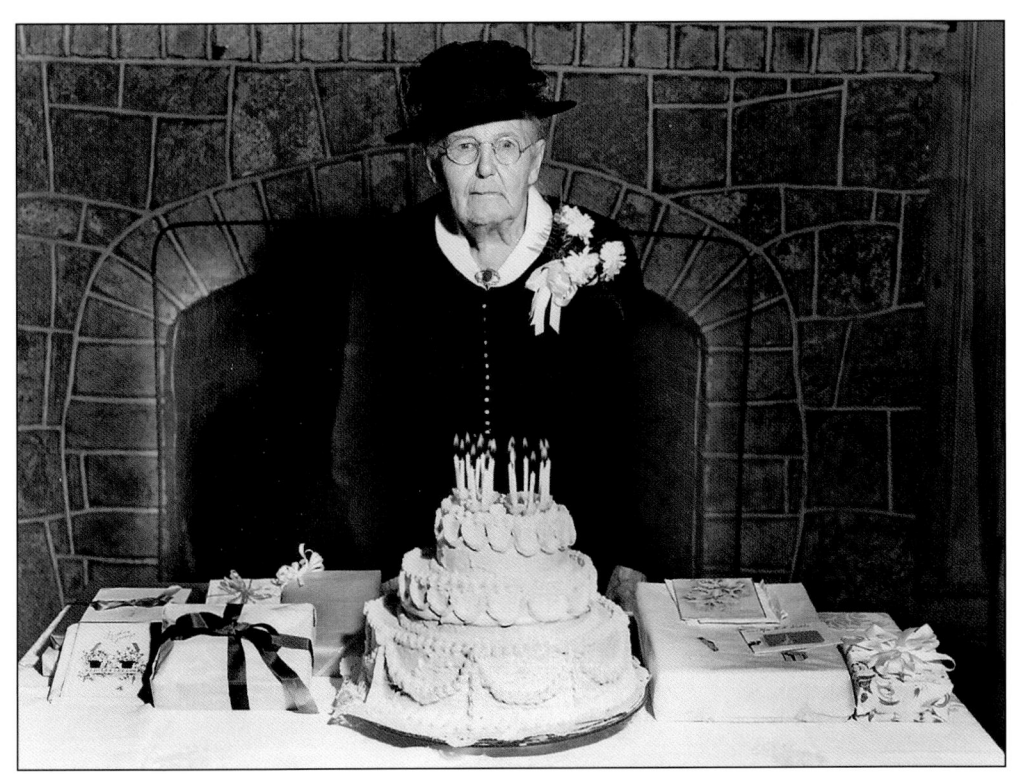

ANOTHER GRAND YEAR. Mrs. Mary Leila Willis (November 11, 1856–July 6, 1949) celebrates her 92nd birthday with a large group at Daniel's Reformed Church in Lincolnton where she was a long-time member.

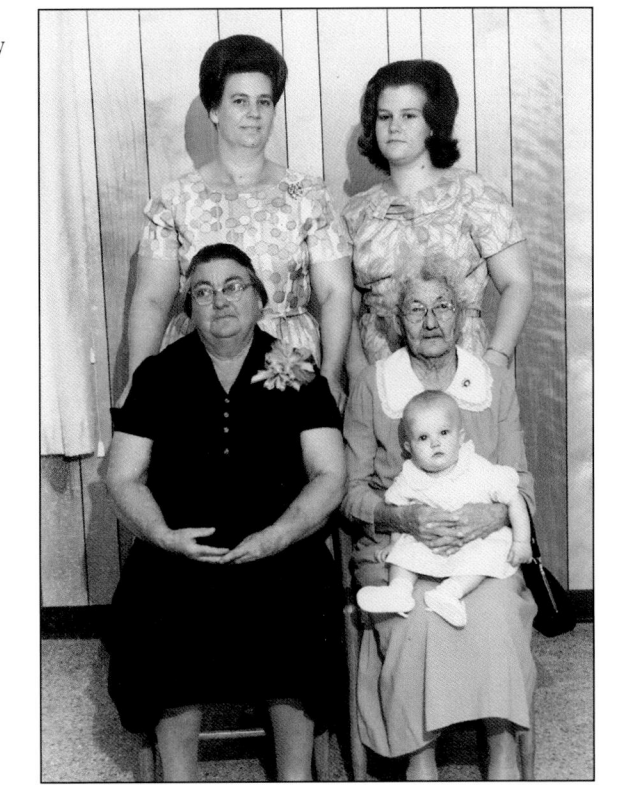

MATRIARCHAL ORDER. This photograph taken by Baby Ray Cornwell on April 16, 1967, shows the 92nd birthday of Mrs. Yarboro of Lincolnton. Highlighted in this image are the matriarchs of the Yarboro family.

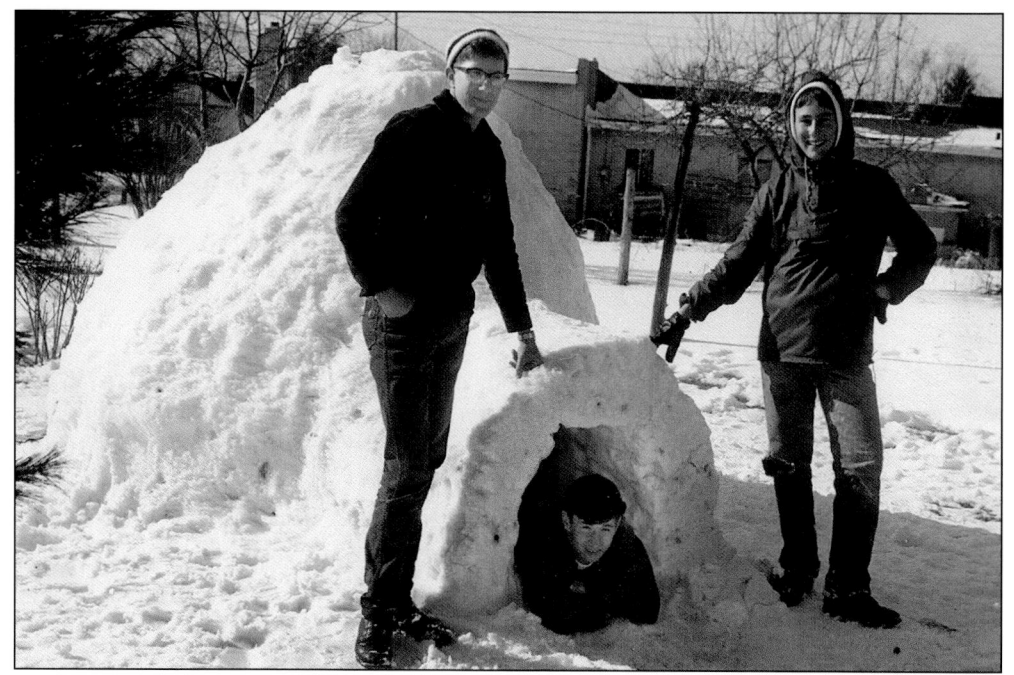

ICE COLD. According to a newspaper caption from *The Lincoln Times-News* on February 2, 1966, "these boys must have a little Eskimo in them." The three-person group took advantage of a massive deluge of snow that blanketed Lincolnton during January of 1966. Amidst the snow, ice, and freezing temperatures, the city and county began a digging-out process on Thursday, January 27. The team, from left to right, includes Dean Wilson, Butch Lawing, and Tommy Martin. All three lived in the Maiden Road neighborhood.

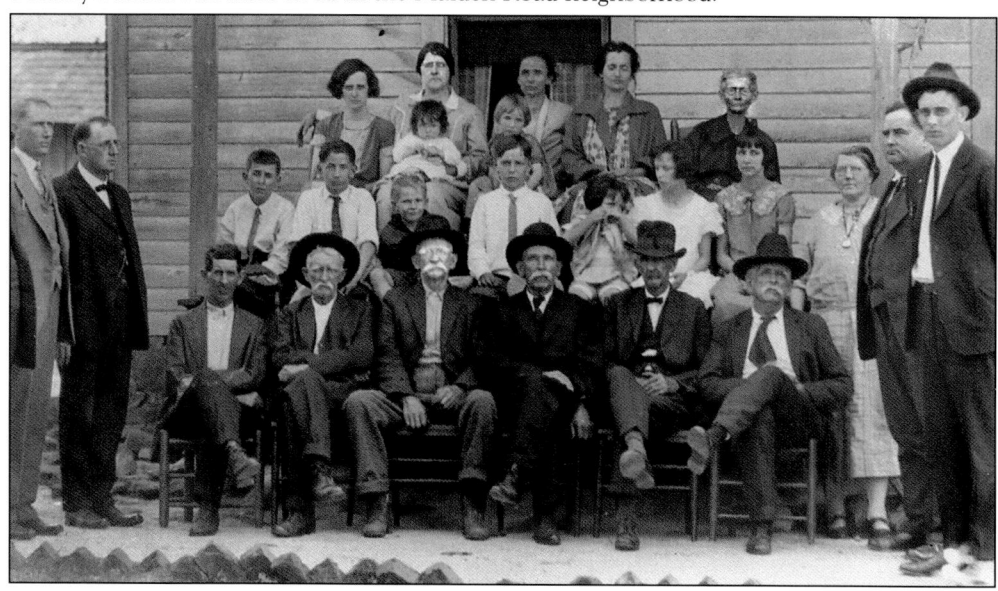

THE HOME PLACE. Members of the Armstrong family were photographed at the turn of the century and also by Baby Ray Cornwell in the 1940s. Cornwell did not take the time to record the names of the family members, the location of their home, or the date, but luckily he did write on the negative sleeve "Armstrong old photo."

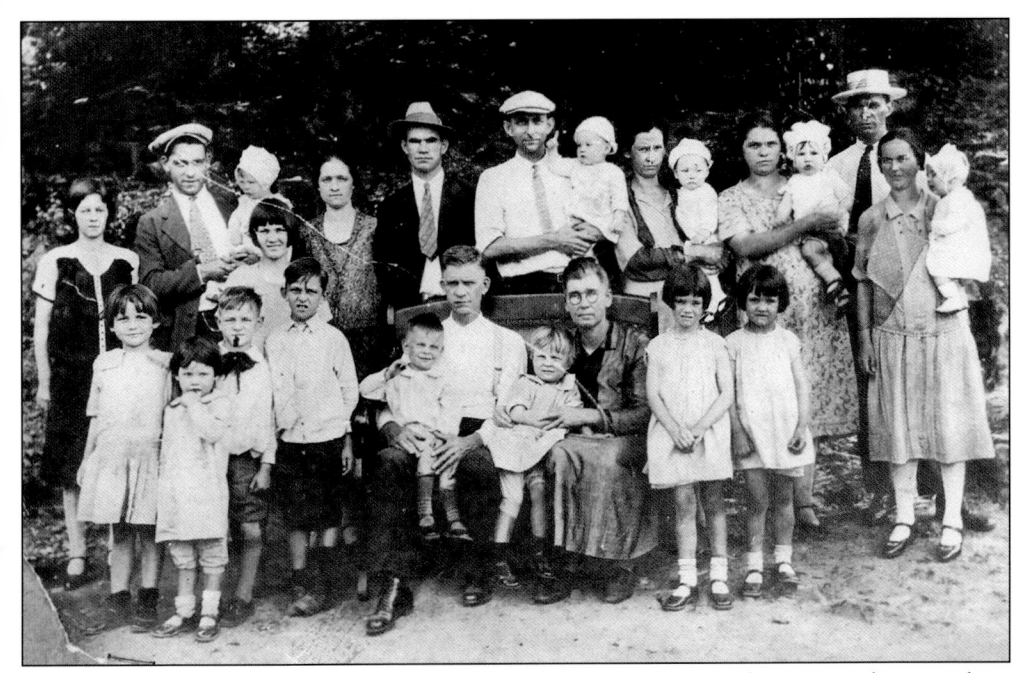

GOOD OLD DAYS. Baby Ray Cornwell not only captured the special events and images from the ordinary in Lincolnton, but he also copied old photographs for Lincolntonians. This photograph of the Drum family was supplied by Carol Drum.

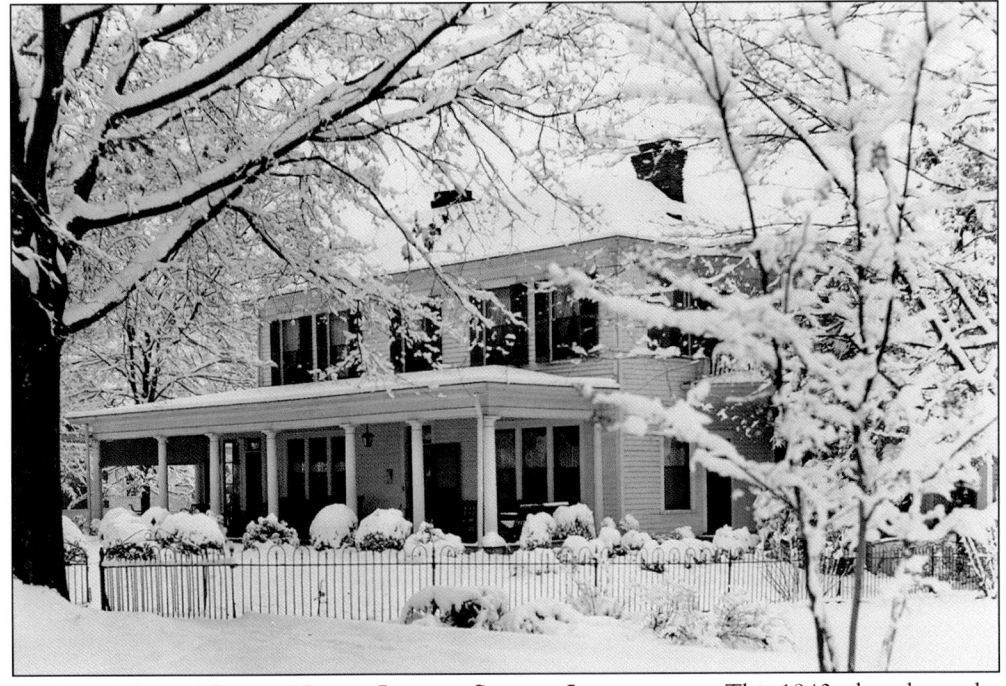

MERRITT-HOYLE HOUSE, NORTH LAUREL STREET, LINCOLNTON. This 1940s shot shows the home when the Hal Hoyle family occupied the residence. This beautiful Colonial Revival home stands as a testament to the architectural style popular during the time of its construction, c. 1900–1905.

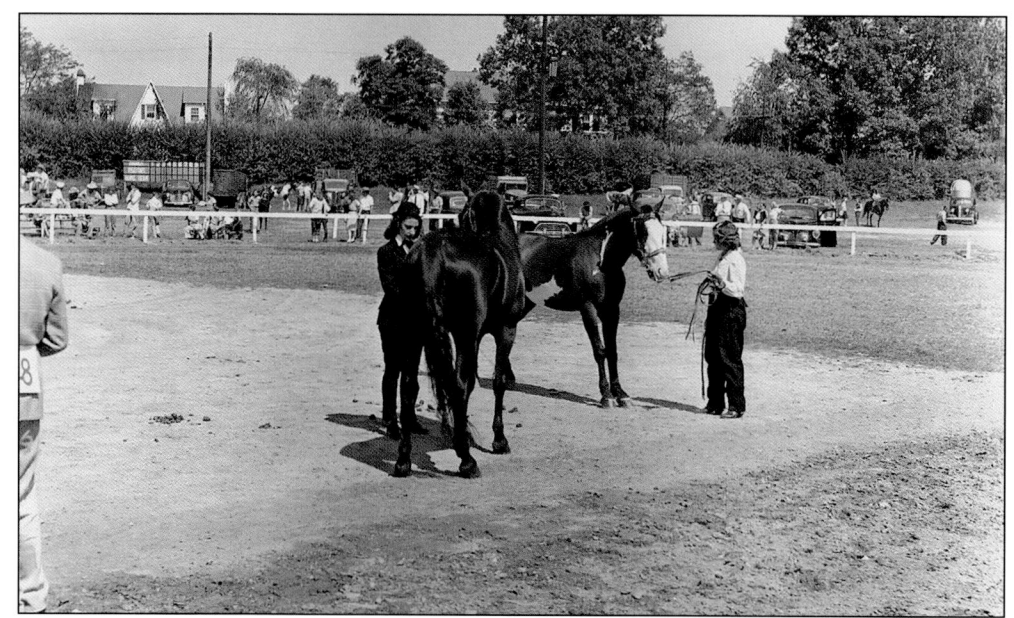

DR. STEELMAN'S HORSE SHOW. Spectators and participants park their cars and meander around the Lincolnton High School field for one of Dr. S.H. Steelman's 1940s horse shows held in Lincolnton. Dr. Steelman moved to Lincolnton from Maiden to practice dentistry sometime after June 1932. He was born on February 9, 1894, in Davie County, North Carolina, the son of T.A. and Dora Harding Steelman. In addition to his horse shows, Dr. Steelman was very active in the local VFW, Goodfellows Club, Kiwanis Club, Woodmen of the World, Knights of Pythias, Lincoln Lodge No. 137, and Lincoln County Shrine Club.

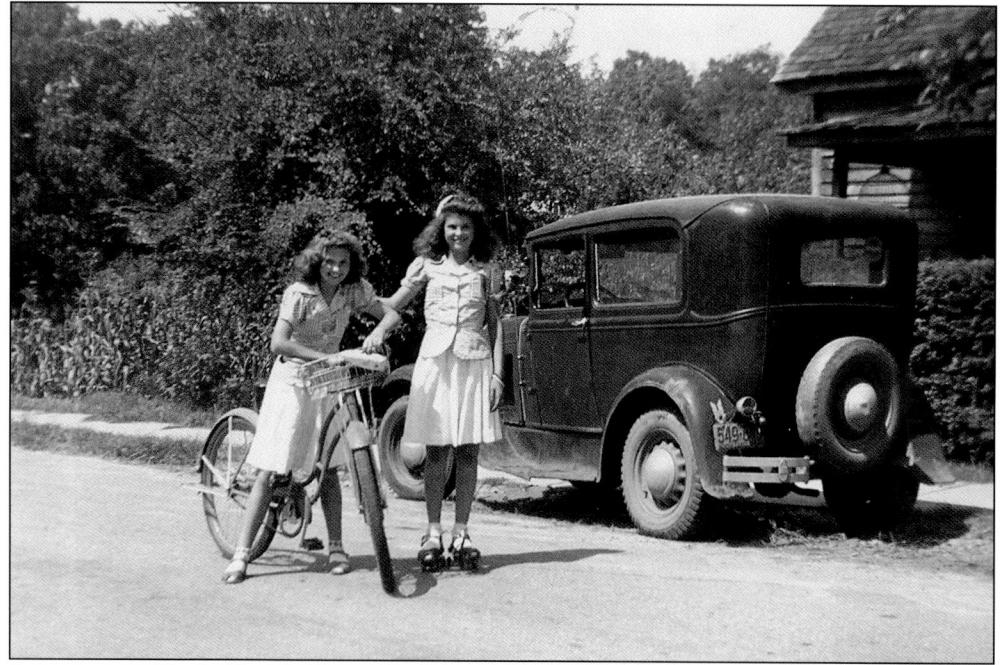

SIBLINGS. Estelle Cornwell Ross and a friend take a break from their bike ride as Estelle's brother, Baby Ray Cornwell, takes their photograph.

DON BELFIELD, PRECISION SKYDIVER. Don Belfield pauses for a photograph before entering the small plane piloted by Floyd Painter of Maiden. Belfield, a native of Chicago, was an employee of Tillman Boat and Motor Company in Lincolnton. For this exhibition, he planned a landing between Heafner Tire Company and Tillman Boat Company. Lincolnton's Electric Department had their ladder truck on hand in case Belfield landed in the power lines. The county Life Saving Crew was also available in case of an unforeseen emergency. According to *The Lincoln County News*, all of these precautionary measures were in vain as strong winds blew Belfield "out into the county."

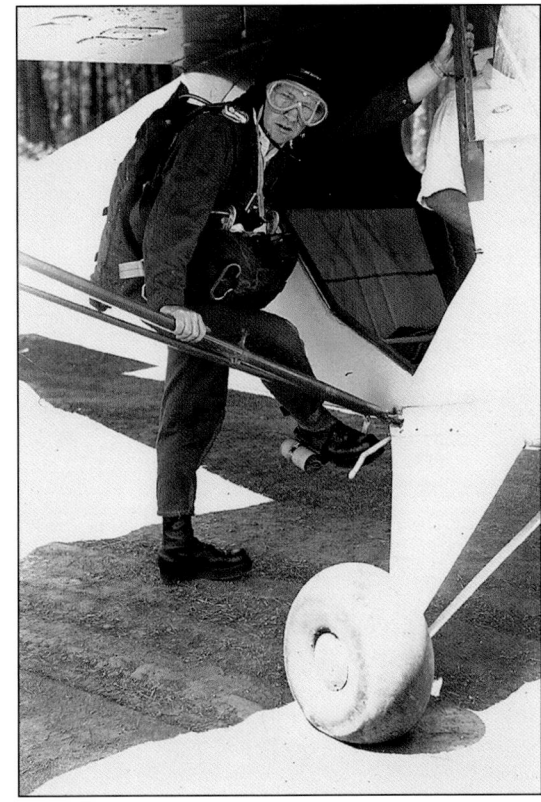

TIMBER! Amazement is the unspoken word for this large tree that fell near a home in Lincolnton on September 26, 1962.

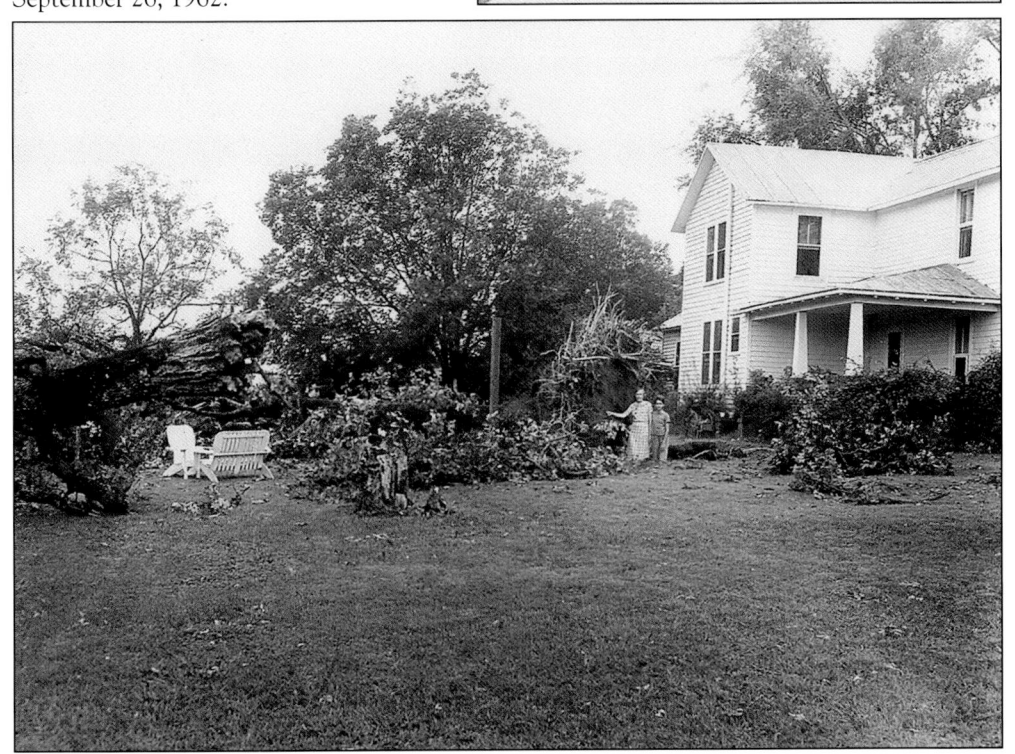

INDEX

Abernethy, 34, 53, 61, 102
Adams, 13, 37, 107
Aderholdt, 110
Allen, 20
Alley, 112
Anderson, 13, 62, 65
Armstrong, 122
Arrowood, 105
Ashe, 62
Axum, 86
Auten, 41
Auton, 106
Avery, 107
Babb, 36, 38, 41
Baity, 43
Baker, 20, 41, 67, 105
Bandy, 93
Barineau, 45
Barker, 107
Barkley, 44, 60, 107
Barnes, 6, 107
Beal, 29, 42, 44, 92, 101, 106
Beam, 42, 44, 50, 52, 54, 55, 105
Beattie, 40–42, 92
Beaver, 50
Beck, 94
Belch, 26
Belfield, 125
Benfield, 36
Biggerstaff, 43, 58
Billings, 44
Blackwell, 50
Blanton, 9
Block, 80

Bolinger, 54
Bondurant, 65, 91, 92
Borden, 86
Bost, 35, 37, 49, 91
Boyd, 50
Boyles, 26, 66, 77
Brackett, 62
Bradley, 80
Bradshaw, 50
Brevard, 93
Brooks, 38, 92
Brown, 29, 106
Brumley, 106
Buckley, 39
Buff, 60, 91, 92
Bulwinkle, 58
Burgin, 37, 108
Burris, 29, 65, 69, 72, 91, 92, 105
Byers, 26, 41
Bynum, 40, 65
Cagle, 17, 42, 60
Caldwell, 50
Camp, 97
Canipe, 31, 53
Cannon, 50
Carpenter, 10, 40, 60, 73, 110, 113
Carswell, 102
Carter, 35, 49, 50, 61, 116
Cash, 102
Cashion, 105
Causey, 53
Chaffin, 53, 82, 106
Chamberlain, 9

Chapman, 43, 50, 107
Cherry, 68, 90, 100
Childs, 12, 58, 93, 106
Chronister, 65
Clark, 55
Claytor, 29, 54
Cline, 46
Cobb, 52
Cochrane, 28, 40
Coffey, 35
Cohen, 36, 40
Combs, 20
Connor, 51, 91, 92, 117
Cooper, 106
Corbet, 118
Cord, 97
Cornwell, 27, 35, 38, 40–42, 51
Costner, 25, 26, 29
Craig, 19, 87
Crawley, 20
Crisson, 106, 113
Cronland, 50
Crouse, 20
Crowell, 26, 29, 37, 61, 62, 78, 79, 101, 104
Dameron, 50
Davis, 11, 30, 52, 66
Dedmon, 44, 112
Delk, 92
Dellinger, 26, 29, 33, 39, 42, 51, 56, 98, 106, 108
Devine, 43, 44, 107
Digh, 93, 116
Ditmars, 11

Dodgin, 50
Dorsey, 107
Drum, 26, 37, 50, 56, 106, 123
Eaker, 52, 112
Elliott, 11, 37, 93
Ellis, 35, 42, 65
Elmore, 28, 32, 41, 43, 68, 88
Enoch, 97
Eurey, 16, 50, 91, 92
Evans, 83
Everett, 54
Ewing, 50
Fair, 46
Ferguson, 42
Finger, 41, 50
Fitzgerald, 101
Ford, 30, 71, 106
Forrester, 92
Fortenberry, 49
Foster, 90
Fox, 18
Freeman, 50
Friday, 50, 85
Froneberger, 44, 108
Fuller, 42
Gabriel, 19, 36, 38, 40, 41, 43, 49
Gagnon, 80
Gamble, 55, 109, 112
Garrison, 38, 91, 92, 93
Gantt, 44
Gatt, 102
Gibson, 50
Gilbert, 26, 99
Glover, 53
Goode, 26, 40, 65
Goodin, 65, 72, 93
Goodson, 20, 48, 98
Gorbin, 44
Graham, 45, 66
Gregory, 50
Guiton, 99
Hager, 107
Hallman, 35, 43, 44, 60, 106
Hamell, 66
Harkey, 31, 106
Harnack, 33
Harrill, 40, 50, 52, 104
Harris, 103
Hartman, 20, 98, 104
Harvey, 20
Harwell, 40

Hawkins, 50
Hayes, 80
Haynes, 19, 99
Heafner, 37, 103
Heavner, 26, 35, 40–42, 50, 59, 76, 91, 92, 98, 99, 104, 106, 113
Hedgspeth, 50
Hedspeth, 40
Helms, 44, 49, 60
Helton, 48
Henderson, 30
Henkel, 50
Herndon, 52
Hill, 52
Hinson, 50
Hodge, 50
Hoffman, 26, 33, 38, 79
Holloway, 85, 86
Holly, 91
Holmes, 11
Honeycutt, 66, 92, 98
Hoover, 25, 45, 99
House, 39
Houser, 24, 26, 34, 49, 50, 60, 105, 110
Houston, 106
Hovis, 26, 35, 44, 70, 102, 107, 117
Howard, 20, 55, 70
Howell, 44
Hoyle, 19, 23, 34, 40, 55, 60, 61, 68, 74, 99, 100, 123
Hudson, 68
Huggins, 16, 19, 38, 108, 111
Huitt, 50
Hull, 99, 106
Huss, 54, 100, 107
Ingle, 29, 39, 40
Jackson, 65
James, 44, 63, 87
Jarrett, 55
Jetton, 44
Johnson, 6, 15, 29, 39, 42, 51, 54
Johnston, 50
Jonas, 87
Jones, 33, 50
Jordan, 17, 26, 50
Keener, 49, 50, 60
Keever, 73, 98
Kendrick, 91

Kennedy, 103
Kessler, 26
Killian, 52, 60, 118
Kincaid, 26, 79, 100
Kiser, 35, 40, 42, 102, 106
Kistler, 106
Kitchin, 113
Knight, 43
Knox, 20
Knuckles, 60
Lackey, 60
Lander, 14
Laney, 42
Lanier, 66
Lawing, 4, 23, 122
Leatherman, 37, 104, 113
Ledbetter, 116
Lentz, 55
Leonard, 30, 50, 58, 71, 72, 114
Leonhardt, 107
Lerner, 19, 37
Lester, 51
Lewis, 52, 91, 92
Lindsey, 87
Lineberger, 16, 33, 35, 44, 54, 56, 63, 100, 107, 111
Link, 31, 86
Lippard, 19, 50
Little, 49
Lockman, 35, 42, 102
Lohr, 26
Long, 53
Loritts, 13
Love, 39
Loveland, 106
Lowder, 19, 40, 55, 109
Lowe, 30
Llywellyn, 104
Lucas, 48
Mace, 105
Magness, 22
Mann, 59
Martin, 49, 122
Mathis, 106
Mauney, 39, 66
Mays, 48
McCullough, 39
McCurry, 42
McDowell, 97
McGill, 49
McGinnis, 117

McIntosh, 108
McKenzie, 55
McKinney, 40
McKinnon, 50
McLean, 60
McNeill, 79
Medlin, 52
Metts, 10
Milam, 93
Milburn, 44
Miller, 26, 45, 65, 79
Modlin, 87, 92
Moore, 14, 17, 33
Morrell, 96
Morris, 29, 111, 113
Morrison, 65
Moser, 126
Mosteller, 50, 91, 92
Mullen, 18, 48
Myrick, 57
Nale, 92
Nantz, 42
Neal, 112
Neely, 13
Nickelson, 98
Nixon, 6, 11, 15, 22, 50, 69, 107
Odoms, 85
Outlaw, 66
Owen, 50
Padgett, 50
Page, 25
Painter, 53, 125
Parker, 65
Payseur, 37
Paysour, 50, 79
Peek, 50
Peeler, 31
Pendleton, 50, 102
Perry, 26
Petrie, 78
Phillips, 107
Pickens, 26
Plaxico, 50
Plonk, 113
Polhill, 29, 30, 106
Pollock, 92
Pope, 52
Pressley, 50
Price, 85
Proctor, 56, 93
Propst, 50, 107

Quickel, 66
Quinton, 19
Raby, 17
Ramsaur, 11
Ramseur, 11, 30, 33, 50, 61, 70, 74, 95, 106
Ramsey, 20
Randall, 109
Rash, 50
Reel, 77
Reep, 98, 100
Reid, 50, 92
Reinhardt, 13, 29, 43, 52, 85, 86
Reynolds, 35, 40, 42, 50, 71, 107
Rhodes, 42, 60
Rhyne, 19, 45, 46, 50, 52, 66, 104
Richard, 106
Richardson, 95
Riley, 17
Roach, 41
Roberts, 54, 96
Robinson, 19, 30, 32, 39, 41, 50, 105
Rogers, 102
Roper, 47, 98, 108, 115
Roseman, 42
Ross, 36, 41, 43, 45, 60, 105, 108, 110, 113, 124
Rudisill, 40, 49, 60, 62, 65, 106
Rutledge, 102
Saettner, 82
Sain, 94, 102
Saine, 32, 50, 99
Saunders, 75, 79
Schronce, 26, 34, 50, 106, 107
Schrum, 40, 43, 60, 66, 98
Scruggs, 85
Seagle, 37, 43, 51, 66
Self, 50, 119
Sellers, 60
Setzer, 107
Shaw, 55
Sherrill, 48, 50, 106, 107
Shidal, 29, 66
Shives, 19, 40, 41, 68
Shuford, 19, 37, 42, 45, 50, 52, 57, 60, 85, 96, 98
Sifford, 104
Sigmon, 107

Sisk, 53, 69
Slaughter, 59
Smith, 20, 33, 39, 42, 50, 92, 106
Snipes, 50
Sousley, 80
Sowell, 15
Stamey, 17, 37, 40, 92
Steelman, 26, 124
Stoudemire, 109
Strank, 80
Stroupe, 43, 47, 51
Sumner, 45
Suttle, 51
Swan, 30
Tarr, 49, 102, 109
Templeton, 11
Thaxton, 92
Thomas, 50, 109
Thompson, 11, 29, 96, 97, 101
Thornburg, 24
Tobey, 119
Troianio, 41
Turner, 4, 27, 33, 48, 88
Tutherow, 11
Walls, 19
Warlick, 30, 51, 59, 60, 78
Warren, 100
Washington, 96, 97
Waters, 17
Watts, 50
Waynick, 50
Weaver, 40
Whisonant, 42
White, 50, 94, 105
Whitener, 26, 98
Wilkinson, 50, 60
Williams, 76
Willis, 29, 121
Wilson, 122
Wise, 37, 38, 47, 56, 69, 100
Wright, 107
Wyckoff, 22, 60
Yarboro, 121
Yarborough, 92
Yoder, 29, 42, 43, 60, 107